X18

BIGGLES

Biggles typ...
Royal Flying Corps and the early R.A.F.
We cannot forget Biggles the teenage
flyer with 266 Squadron; Biggles and his
chums Ginger and Algernon 'Algy'
Lacey in their battered seaplane; Biggles
battling with the Hun – and the evil
Erich von Stalhein – in the Second
World War, and his service in the Special
Air Police after it. In this book John
Pearson shows the man behind the hero
– his early years, his private life, and the
tensions and ambitions that made him
the remarkable character that he was.

*John Pearson has worked as a journalist
on various newspapers including* The Econo-
mist, The Times *and* The Sunday Times.
*He has written a biography of James Bond,
as well as books on the Kray brothers, the Sit-
wells, Donald Campbell, Timbuctoo, the
Roman Colosseum and the sex life of Edward
VII.*

'I can only sing the praises of this de-
lightful book, which I read at a sitting
and was left breathless with admiration.'
Books and Bookmen

BIGGLES

The Authorized Biography

JOHN PEARSON

Hamlyn Paperbacks

For Mat Nisberg

BIGGLES – THE AUTHORIZED
BIOGRAPHY
ISBN 0 600 20062 0

First published in Great Britain in 1978
by Sidgwick and Jackson Ltd
Hamlyn Paperbacks edition 1980
Copyright © 1978 by John Pearson and the
Estate of W. E. Johns

Hamlyn Paperbacks are published by
The Hamlyn Publishing Group Ltd,
Astronaut House,
Feltham, Middlesex, England
(Paperback Division: Hamlyn Paperbacks,
Banda House, Cambridge Grove,
Hammersmith, London W6 0LE)

Reproduced, printed and bound in Great Britain
by Cox & Wyman Ltd, Reading

Contents

Introduction

———◆———

At first we knew him simply as the new tenant of Ferndene Cottage, an unlovely little red-brick house standing four-square behind its overgrown privet hedge on the far side of the London Road from where we live.

The cottage had stood empty for some time, so we were naturally inquisitive about the new arrival, but it was some time before we learned the identity of the red-faced, rather portly little man with the leather-patched tweed jacket who would emerge from Ferndene Cottage at 8.30 punctually each morning, taking his pug-dog for a walk. In Camberley we have a lot of pug-dogs and a lot of retired army people. They seem to go together, so we assumed our newest neighbour with his jaunty walk and weather-beaten countenance must be one of them.

It was the vicar, our walking social register, who finally put us right.

'And how are you getting on with our celebrated new neighbour?' he asked my wife.

She must have looked surprised, for he went on, Wing-Commander Bigglesworth. Your husband must have read of his adventures when he was a boy – you know, Biggles, the great schoolboy hero of the R.A.F. I'm quite determined to persuade him to open the village fête. He should be quite a draw.'

But Biggles did not open the vicar's fête – nor anything else in Camberley that year. Instead, he seemed distinctly anxious to keep himself to himself, and while we were all quite proud to have a genuine celebrity in our midst, we soon accepted him as a recluse, our interest waned, and that was that. And then, one wet November evening, I was walking home and passed him near the church. He was carrying a twelve-bore shotgun and had half a dozen pigeons slung across his shoulder.

'Good shooting, Wing-Commander!' I called out. At first he seemed surprised to be addressed like this, but he stopped and instantly eased up when I said something about how hard I always found it to shoot wood-pigeon.

'Simple enough, when you've got the knack,' he said. 'I only do it to keep my eye in, don't you know?' There was a slightly awkward pause and he added, 'I suppose your wife couldn't make use of them, could she? My housekeeper can't be bothered with them, and they generally end up in the dustbin.'

I thanked him, but on the condition that he came and helped us eat them. He seemed quite pleased at the idea and two nights later he arrived for dinner. And so began a friendship that endured until his death, some three years later.

The truth, as I soon discovered, was that around this time he had grown bored with his retirement and was really rather lonely. He had retired to the country on his doctor's orders, but it didn't really suit him. He owned an elderly MG, in which he would drive to London once or twice a week. As well as shooting, he would fish a little. 'Used to do it as a boy,' he told us. 'Now that I can't play golf it keeps me out of mischief I suppose.'

I couldn't think what mischief he was likely to get up to – certainly not with his old housekeeper, Mrs Roberts. She was a frail-looking, gap-toothed, rather ghostly lady. When my wife got to know her she would often grumble on about the Wing-Commander's habits – his untidiness, his fussiness about his food, his cigarettes and his uncertain temper. But with us he was always kindness itself and soon became a regular visitor.

Although he often brought us pigeon – and partridges and pheasants, now that the season had begun – what he really liked to eat was steak, and what my wife called 'nursery food' – fish-cakes and shepherd's pie and sausages and mash. His favourite food of all was toad-in-the-hole, particularly the crispy bits around the edges of the dish. Apart from a couple of pink gins before dinner, he would drink very little. What he apparently enjoyed most of all in life now was talking, particularly with the children present. At first I never knew quite how many of his tales were true and how much was pure fantasy, but he was certainly a splendid raconteur when in the mood, and after dinner he would sit for hours, smoking his disgusting pipe and reminiscing about his life. Whenever this occurred it was impossible to get the children off to bed.

All this was rather strange, for to the world at large, Biggles – as I have to call him – remained secretiye to a degree about his life. I remember seeing him one morning chasing two news reporters down the garden path of Ferndene Cottage with his twelve-bore. All they had wanted was an interview to mark the fiftieth anniversary of the founding of his legendary old squadron, No. 266 of the Royal Flying Corps, but for Biggles it had been unforgivable of them to have tried to beard him in retirement in this way.

'Gutter journalists,' he called them, when he told us all about them later, 'prying into people's private lives. They'd all be horsewhipped if I had my way with them.' But he said this with a twinkle in his eye, and certainly exhibited no inhibitions about telling us the details of his private life – quite the contrary.

He enjoyed these evening reminiscences by the fire; they offered him at least some relief from the boredom of his life in Camberley. His present state of health depressed him, for like many very active men who had always taken perfect health for granted, Biggles found it hard to cope with ill health when it came. His back used to trouble him a lot and he was slightly diabetic. His eyes bothered him as well.

'Doing my best to fight off the Grim Reaper!' was the invariable reply if one asked how he was – but once he was embarked upon his stories of the past he seemed to forget all his present troubles. He even managed to look different, for as he talked he was re-living scenes from a life he had obviously enjoyed. His hazel eyes used to gleam and he had an air of such gusto and absorption in his tale, that it was just as if a younger, more adventurous self had taken over.

As far as we could judge, Biggles held little back. He frequently referred to his outlandish family, his childhood in India, his schooldays and his earliest experiences in the air. My children were avid readers of the Biggles books, and would interrogate him mercilessly, making him go over particular adventures, asking for extra details and making him repeat the circumstances of some favourite incident. And so, from these winter sessions round the fire, I learned the outlines of the story of his life. Much was familiar already from the writings of Captain W. E. Johns, and this I have tended to compress or refer to in passing in the narrative that follows. But there was much that seemed totally unknown and it is this completely new material that I have concentrated on in my attempt to write the biography of this most remarkable and kindly man of action.

Where Biggles' own version of events differed from those of Captain Johns, I have naturally deferred to Biggles. I found that Johns had used his 'author's licence' somewhat freely to adapt the adventures of his hero to suit his young readership, and had at times skilfully changed the circumstances to fit his tales. In the interests of good storytelling, Biggles approved of this at the time.

1

An Indian Boyhood

'I'm a Victorian and proud of it,' Biggles used to say, 'born in May 1899,' – and in a number of important ways Biggles remained a genuine Victorian all his life. He was what one might call 'old-fashioned', in his somewhat strait-laced attitude to life, the emphasis he always placed on 'manners' with the young, and his views on morality. Also, his whole life as an adventurer and pioneer air pilot had more in common with the careers of the tough empire-builders of the old Queen-Empress than with the 'softies', as he called them, among the young men of today, who incurred his wrath.

His family traditions also helped make him what he was. The name Bigglesworth, as he took great pains to explain when asked about it, started as an attempt to anglicise the Flemish, *Beiggelschwarz,* for one of Biggles' far-off paternal ancestors had been a Dutchman of this name who settled in Aberdeen at the beginning of the eighteenth century, set up as a naval factor and married a local girl. She was a MacGregor – Biggles was always rather proud of that – so that from the start the Bigglesworths were an unusual mixture of wild Highlanders and dour Flemings from the flattest countryside in Europe. The mixed strain soon produced a number of unusual characters, wild self-denying men with a savage knack of embarking on lost causes. 'The nineteenth-century Bigglesworths,' Biggles once remarked, 'were generally considered slightly mad.' One of his great-

great-uncles was a missionary in India who lost his faith and ended as a fakir on a bed of nails in Rajasthan. Another was an explorer who set out to find the source of the Nile in a canoe. A third was last seen in Brazil, searching for a golden city. 'The Bigglesworths,' he said, with something like a note of sadness in his voice, 'tended to be losers.'

One of the few who wasn't, and the only Bigglesworth to reach the history books, was Biggles' celebrated uncle, Brigadier General 'Bonzo' Bigglesworth, who battled as a subaltern at Majuba Hill, helped save the day at Omdurman, deposited an arm at Mafeking, and left the army in disgust when the Boer War ended. He bought a small estate in Norfolk – a run-down country house with a few acres of indifferent farmland and the shooting rights across a stretch of woodland – and there he stayed until his death in 1925. 'The ideal *un*improving landlord', as Biggles called him.

As a boy, home from India, Biggles often stayed with him, and he spoke affectionately of the old one-armed fire-eater he remembered. 'Treated me like a son and I was a good deal fonder of him than my real father,' he confessed. And, by all accounts, Biggles and the General had a lot in common.

The old man was an enthusiastic and alarming motorist whose red de Dion was for many years the terror of the Norfolk lanes. He also had the perpetual schoolboy's love of gadgetry, and his best-known inventions were an explosive kite for siege warfare, an inflatable saddle, which he fondly hoped would revolutionise amphibious operations in the field, and 'the Bigglesworth Terrestrial Torpedo'.

This alarming weapon, powered by a small Steadman petrol engine, could carry several hundredweight of high explosive for over half a mile at a speed of twenty miles an hour. One of Biggles' early memories of holidays in Norfolk was of a field test in which the torpedo went off course, all but demolishing the stable block. The General was apparently delighted at this proof of its effectiveness and never ceased to blame 'those flaming blockheads in Whitehall' for not adopting it when the Great War broke out. 'Could have shortened it by several years,' he claimed. Biggles used to laugh about this, and his uncle's antics, but I always thought he probably inherited something of the

General's attitude to 'bureaucrats and damn-fool politicians' from those early days.

By all accounts, Biggles' father, John Henry Bigglesworth, was utterly unlike his elder brother and Biggles rarely talked about him, except with bitterness. A sober, quiet, studious man, he settled early for a life as an administrator with the Indian Civil Service, rather than compete with his famous brother's reputation by entering the cavalry. He was romantically good-looking, if a trifle dull, and six months after his arrival Calcutta witnessed the one exciting gesture of his life, when he eloped with the daughter of the Governor of Bengal, nineteen-year-old Catherine Lacey.

'Hideous mistake' was Biggles' verdict on the marriage on the one occasion when he brought himself to mention it to us. Grandpapa Lord Lacey was an exacting martinet, remembered – if at all, these days – for the speed with which he put down the Jumna Riots of 1884, and he attempted much the same tactics with his wayward daughter. Here he was less successful. For Catherine Lacey proved of sterner stuff than the malleable Bengalis, claimed that she was pregnant, and insisted on her right to wed the now appalled John Henry Bigglesworth. Lord Lacey never saw his daughter again, and the offending newly-weds were speedily despatched to Garhwal, a dreary district, south of West Bengal. Eight months later, in January 1894, their first child, Biggles' elder brother, Charles, was born.

John Henry Bigglesworth's career never recovered from the blunder of his marriage. He seems to have attempted to make the best of things in the approved, long-suffering Scottish manner, and was to be a conscientious Assistant Commissioner, governing an area half the size of Wales. But with that influential unforgiving father-in-law in Bengal, he had no chance of getting any further. The Indians he ruled respected him. His wife, alas, did not. Her elopement had been an escape from the boredom of Calcutta. How much more boring was her life now as the wife of a meticulously-minded government official stuck in a bungalow in Garhwal.

I soon realised, from chance remarks that Biggles dropped, that there must have been something that went terribly wrong early in his childhood. (Indeed, attentive readers of the Biggles' books might have guessed as much.) But it was some time before I found out exactly what had happened.

Biggles was always reticent about his parents, but it was not hard to get the outlines of what was clearly a most wretched marriage – that imperious, impossible mother with her 'vapours' and her sulks and rages, the disappointed father who increasingly took refuge in his work, and young James Bigglesworth bearing the brunt of much domestic misery.

Clearly, he adored his mother, but as so often is the case with adoring second sons, she preferred his elder brother, Charles. For Charles, just five years older, was everything that James was not – big-boned, athletic, and a hearty, cheerful boy whose easy manner and good looks earned him friends everywhere. In painful contrast, James was undersized and shy. (Biggles showed us a few photographs surviving from this period of a white-faced, skinny little boy with straggly fair hair and melancholy eyes.) Then when his brother Charles was away in England at his boarding school, this vulnerable small boy was hit by the tragedy that changed his life. The Bigglesworths became involved in scandal.

His mother had just reached those dangerous female cross-roads of the early thirties when she met her fate – in the rolling eyes and eager haunches of Captain the Honourable 'Banger' Thomas of the 45th Rawalpindi Horse. The Captain was undoubtedly a bounder and probably a cad. All that Biggles could remember of him was his waxed moustache, his gleaming riding-boots, and the stench of the Trichinopoly cigars he always smoked. (All his life, Biggles seems to have believed that a liking for cigars was a tell-tale symptom of a man who could not be trusted with a woman.) But for all his faults – or possibly because of them – the Captain had no difficulty captivating the sprightly Mrs Bigglesworth.

One can picture all too easily the hackneyed stages of this tropical romance – hot nights on the verandah with the cloying scent of frangipani in the air and languid evenings at the Polo Club with nothing but the mournful rhythm of the punkah to distract the lovers. Then, the whispered gossip in the bored society around the Club, the gathering suspicions of the neglected husband, the jealousies, denials, desperate affirmations, all of which culminated in that moment of high melodrama when, for the second time in Catherine Lacey's life, she bolted.

Biggles was eleven, and his brother Charles, in England, was about to enter Sandhurst. Everybody's sympathy went out to the abandoned husband, and no one seems to have given much attention to the small boy who was suddenly without the mother he adored. But when all possible allowances are made for John Henry Bigglesworth's hurt feelings, the fact remains that he behaved quite dreadfully towards his son. Even in old age, Biggles could not quite forgive him. 'He told me she had died, and never spoke of her again.'

This was a crucial point in Biggles' life, and he would bear the scars of it forever. His grief was pitiable, and for several months was so extreme that he fell seriously ill. (This was the source of that mysterious illness Captain Johns refers to in his brief, carefully censored references to this period. Not unnaturally Biggles never wished the facts to be revealed while he was alive.) The boy's life was actually despaired of for some while, and when he did recover, he remained extremely delicate, always prone to malarial fevers, stomach upsets and prostrating headaches.

He finally grew out of them, of course, and the natural toughness of the Bigglesworth stock ultimately kept him free of illness till his seventies. But in the long run, the most serious effect of his mother's disappearance was on his emotional development. He once admitted – in one of his rare, unguarded moments – that he was obsessed by the memory of his mother. He was intelligent enough to sense that there was far more to her 'death' than the adults told him, but never dared to ask his father for the truth. He said he always felt she was alive and used to dream of finding her and being reunited with her in some far-off place. But he was also naturally tormented by the certainty that she had abandoned him. He had no way of knowing what had really happened. At times he blamed himself, but nothing could alter his belief that this one woman he had really loved had callously betrayed him. Throughout his life Biggles would always be a wary man where women were concerned.

It was his mother's disappearance that also helped to turn young Biggles to adventure early on in life – if only to escape the boredom and the loneliness of life at home. Had his mother been there, this could not have happened, but with his father finding his relief in overwork – and possibly in drink, according to one hint Biggles dropped – he was left more or less to his own devices, and before long was escaping into the rich, exciting world beyond the narrow confines of the Club, the schoolroom, and the houses of his father's European friends. He soon found his way around the maze of little streets that made up the Indian quarter of the town, and grew to love its noise and smells and teeming sense of life, so different from the dull security of home. Then he explored the countryside, with its dusty villages and ancient tracks that led to the forests and the hills. Here, for the first time, in the middle of this great sub-continent, he sensed the vastness of the world, and used to envy the kite-birds sailing so effortlessly in the pale blue skies above him. He would go off for days alone, searching for he knew not what, and finally return exhausted to his father's bungalow. His father rarely noticed his absence.

Since his brother left, Biggles had no European friends of his own age. After the disappearance of his mother, he must have felt that all the Europeans were inquisitive or pitying, so he avoided them and kept his secrets to himself. The few friends he had, he found among the local Indian boys; his favourite was a boy called Sula Dowla, son of an assistant overseer at a nearby tea estate. He was a bright boy, who spoke perfect English and who was flattered when the son of Biggles Sahib became his friend.

For Biggles, this was an important friendship, for Sula Dowla led a gang of other small Indian boys, a raggle-taggle lot, who used to haunt the bazaars, stealing what they could, and waging war on gangs from other districts. Biggles became an honorary member. He spoke Hindi perfectly, was up to any mischief going and, though undersized, could out-wrestle and outrun every member of the gang. He also soon began to organise them. He explained to Sula Dowla that as the son of Biggles Sahib, he could not countenance their criminal activities. Sula Dowla pulled a rueful face and said that his members did it merely for fun. Biggles replied that it would simply lead to trouble and was stupid. It would be far more fun to organise the gang on a proper basis, impose strict discipline on all its members, and plan their forays on the other gangs on sound military principles.

This was Biggles' first experience of warfare, and from the start he showed a sort of genius for it. He was a daring leader who carefully rehearsed his followers before each campaign. One of their earliest successes was a night-time raid on the headquarters of their deadliest enemies, the much stronger 'Buffalo Gang', who had set up camp in a deserted warehouse on the outskirts of the town. Biggles planned the whole attack meticulously, spending several days on what he called 'intelligence', sending out members of his gang to watch the warehouse, trailing the leading 'Buffaloes' around the town, and finding out which nights the warehouse was inhabited. He and Sula Dowla also spent much time on 'tactics', planning the line of their attack, choosing their weapons, and also planning how to meet the enemy when they retaliated – as they surely would.

Biggles would long remember that first 'battle' of his life – assembling his 'troops', giving each of them his final orders, and then the excitement of the surprise attack. Biggles knew that they had little chance of beating the 'Buffaloes' by sheer brute force – they were too big and numerous for that. Instead, he was relying on a secret weapon to bring terror to the enemy. A few days earlier he had asked his father for some fireworks and *papier-mâché* masks for Guy Fawkes day. (Although they were in India, Biggles' father was always keen to celebrate the festivals that he had known in England.) His father had agreed, but Biggles had an idea for a special Guy Fawkes celebration of his own. He gave each member of the gang a Guy Fawkes mask, whilst he and Sula Dowla took charge of the loudest of the fireworks. Then they all crept towards the warehouse.

For a while they lay in wait, and then at Biggles' signal every boy began a fearful wailing. The racket was enough to wake the dead, and while it was at its height, Biggles and Sula Dowla lit the fireworks and lobbed them through the warehouse windows. Then, as the first of them exploded, Biggles and Sula Dowla led the charge, waving their wooden swords and screaming like banshees. But it was probably the Guy Fawkes masks that did the trick. The sight of them was too much for the 'Buffaloes' and they fled, leaving their camp to Biggles and his small victorious gang.

This was the beginning of a whole series of successful 'wars' which Biggles and Sula waged; but although Biggles seems to have enjoyed the planning and organising of what he called the gang's 'intelligence section', there were times when he grew bored with the little town and tired of his friends. When these moods took him he would long to be away and would dream of travelling – across the hills and the far-off Himalayas to the north and on to China, or westwards to Bombay and then across the seas to Africa. The only books he read were books of travel and the only adult who remotely understood him was one of his father's few real friends, the legendary white hunter, Captain Lovell of the Indian Army.

Lovell, by all accounts, was an extraordinary character, a short, fat, dumpy little man with a glaring eye and a bristling red moustache. In youth he had been known as a great *shikari,* with countless tigers to his credit and a reputation for extrordinary toughness. (At Kaziranga, in Assam, he was once badly mauled by a tiger, left in a swamp for dead, and reappeared some three days later, dragging the tiger's skin behind him. 'I got the brute' was all he said before collapsing.)

This was a story that appealed to Biggles, and although the Captain was now past his prime and living on his pension in Mirapore, near Garhwal, he became the first of Biggles' boyhood heroes. Biggles used to call him 'Skipper', and the old hunter, who apparently liked nothing more than talking about himself, seems to have done a lot to teach him his earliest philosophy of life. Biggles once asked him if he had ever known fear.

'Course I have, boy,' the old hunter answered. 'Only a damn fool doesn't feel afraid when faced with death. But it's the man who *is* afraid, yet faces up to it, who deserves a royal salute. That's the true test of courage, James my lad. Such men are gold, pure gold.'

Biggles remembered that. He was also impressed by Captain Lovell's admiration for what he termed 'gameness' in a man.

'Doesn't much matter, James my boy, whether you win or lose as long as you're really game until the end. Gameness is what distinguishes the men from the boys, when the chips are down.'

And it was Captain Lovell who instilled in Biggles his own special version of 'the White Man's Burden'.

'Whenever I was really up against it, I would tell myself, "Skipper, old boy, you're British. And a Britisher is worth two Huns, five Frenchmen and a dozen darkies. So pull yourself together!" '

With sentiments like these to spur him on, Biggles became increasingly demanding of himself. By the time he was seven he had learned to shoot – potting at crows with a small shotgun of his father's which all but blew his head off when he fired. Now on his expeditions through the local countryside he was rarely without his rifle, and whilst he theoretically believed that hunting for sport was 'barbarous' (this was his father's view), he found enough occasions when wild animals were threatening life and limb to give him an excuse for action.

On one occasion he despatched a rabid pariah-dog which had been threatening the children in a nearby village. Another time he was on hand to deal with a leopard that had been stealing livestock and was threatening an old villager who had tried fruitlessly to scare it off. And on one memorable occasion the boy's longing for excitement and adventure nearly finished his career for good.

This was the time when the district where he lived was suffering the rare attentions of a man-eating tiger. There had been vague reports about the beast – goats had disappeared, a native woman had been killed some miles away at Delapur, and Captain Lovell had been in his element trying to track it down. Typically, Biggles' father gave scant attention to these stories. Certainly he did nothing to warn his son about the danger and Biggles had continued his carefree wanderings with Sula Dowla.

Some people naturally attract danger. Biggles did so all his life, and even as a boy the tendency was there. He always said that he had no intention of searching for the tiger – nothing was further from his thoughts. But some mysterious intuition made him take his rifle with him that morning as he strolled to Sula Dowla's house beyond the tea plantation. And something made him take a short cut home across a stretch of scrubland known as 'the Plains'. It was on the Plains, emerging from a patch of scrub, that Biggles and the tiger came face to face.

Frequently in later life Biggles would be faced by almost certain death, and every time some instinct of survival seems to have brought him through. It did so now. For the first time he was experiencing that strange clear-headedness in the face of danger which is the hallmark of the man of action. He could smell the rank stench of the animal, see the dull gleam in its yellow eyes and sense its vicious power. But, to his surprise, he was not afraid. Quite calmly, he considered what to do and found himself repeating some advice old Captain Lovell had once given him. 'If you surprise a dangerous animal, never run. It's fatal and you wouldn't have a hope. Stand absolutely still, stare the beast out, and do your best to show him that you're not afraid.'

He did this now and for what seemed an age Biggles and the tiger stayed stock still, facing one another. Gradually it seemed that the advice would work. The tiger moved its head away, as if anxious to escape Biggles' gaze. Its tail dropped and it was on the point of slinking off when Biggles made a terrible mistake. He sneezed. The tiger turned to face him in a flash, growled, crouched back on its haunches and prepared to spring.

There was no question now of simply staring at the beast. The time for action had arrived, and very slowly Biggles raised his rifle to his shoulder, sighting the animal between the eyes. It moved forward, limping slightly, stopped as if still undecided, crouched again, then, uttering a low growl, darted forward. Biggles fired – to no avail. The beast came on. He fired again, still uselessly it seemed, and the tiger was almost on him when he fired straight at its open mouth.

He never knew quite what happened next, for as he closed his eyes and waited for the blow to fall, the tiger uttered one last fearful growl, swerved past him and went bounding off into the shelter of the undergrowth. Then came an anti-climax. Biggles ran home to tell his father of the tiger and of his miraculous escape. But John Henry Bigglesworth seemed unimpressed. Not even a tiger in his own back yard could bring a flicker of excitement to that cold impassive man.

'Wounded it eh, did you boy? That's bad. Wounded tiger is the very devil. I'll send out word so that the people keep well clear of the Plains, and we'll attend to Mr Tiger in the morning.'

Biggles waited, hoping for praise or possibly some brief paternal sympathy. Even in Garhwal it wasn't every day a boy of thirteen had an encounter with a tiger and escaped to tell the tale. But all his father said was, 'Go and drink a glass of water, boy. You look as if you need it.'

It was a remark that Biggles never would forget. And when, next day, he duly watched his father and the Captain shoot the tiger at the climax of a full-scale tiger hunt across the Plains, all that Biggles felt was bitterness and dreadful disappointment. His father fired the fatal shot, but when the Captain shouted, 'Oh, good shot, Bigglesworth! Great work!' Biggles felt cheated. It was

his tiger, not his father's. But he had learned enough about that
distant man to keep his feelings to himself.

He also kept his feelings to himself a few weeks later when his
father, with his habitual absence of emotion, calmly informed
him that he had a week to pack up his belongings. He was off to
England to the boarding school where his brother Charles had
been.

This was a moment of profound unhappiness for Biggles.
Much as he longed to travel, he could feel nothing but despair at
the idea of exchanging the freedom of Garhwal for a boarding
school in that far-off island with its cold, fog, and icy seas. With
Charles now at Sandhurst, he would be absolutely on his own –
no Sula Dowla he could take on expeditions through the forest,
no gangs of small Indian boys to organise in battle, no Captain
Lovell to tell tall tales about his exploits as a hunter. Even the
bungalow where he had grown up appeared precious to him
now. Suddenly his whole world seemed threatened, but he had
no one to confide in, and so once again he kept his fears and
sadness to himself. When the day of his departure dawned he
shook hands with his father, bade a dignified farewell to all the
members of his gang who had assembled at the bungalow to see
him off, and managed to fight back his tears. He had told Sula
Dowla that when he had finished school he would return, but in
his heart of hearts he knew he never would. Had Captain Lovell
known just how 'game' young Biggles was being at that
moment, he would have been proud of him.

Malton Hall School near Hertbury was not the place to make a
sensitive small boy feel particularly at home. It was a mid-
nineteenth-century foundation, set up as a sort of poor man's
Wellington College, to turn out the future soldiers and colonial
administrators the Empire needed. Discipline was strict, food
more or less inedible, and bullying the order of the day. Biggles
arrived there for the autumn term of 1912, at a time when the
school was still under the direction of its elderly headmaster,
Colonel Horace 'Chevy' Chase, an unbending figure with a
steely eye and closely cropped grey hair. Chase was a martinet,
far more the keen ex-soldier than a scholar, and the school
reflected this.

Biggles had been unwell. The voyage and the English climate had brought on a serious recurrence of malaria, which meant that he had to spend some weeks convalescing with his uncle, the General, at his place in Norfolk. From the start they got on well together. The General was a kindly man beneath his fiery exterior, and he felt sorry for the motherless small boy. His sickliness disturbed him, but he was delighted when he found he was a first-rate shot. He did his best to 'build him up' – with massive meals of half-cooked beef which Biggles hated – and Biggles' recovery did credit to the General's care. (In fact, the most important element in the boy's recovery was simply the old General's kindness and concern. Unlike his cold fish of a brother, 'Bonzo' Bigglesworth was an emotional, warm-hearted man, and Biggles instantly responded to him.) When Biggles left for Malton Hall, his uncle gave him half a sovereign and some good advice.

'If anyone tries to bully you, my boy, punch them on the nose. It always works, however big they are, provided you punch hard enough.'

To start with, Biggles loathed his school. During his first interview with the Headmaster he was exhorted to stand up straight and not to mumble, and told he was expected to live up to the example of his brother, who had been head boy and had apparently brought glory to the school through his success in the Sandhurst examinations. Colonel Chase pronounced it 'Sandust' and at first Biggles didn't understand him. When he did, he tactlessly replied that he had no intention of entering the army.

'What do you want to do then, boy?' the Head inquired.

'Travel, sir,' said Biggles with alacrity. At which the Head said, 'Humph! We'll have to see about that,' and ended up by warning the small boy not to come snivelling to him with his troubles. Biggles decided there and then that he would rather die than do so, and with a sinking heart went off to face his fate.

Biggles soon found that he could deal with the bullying. He was wiry and tough and though undersized had learned some useful tricks in his battles with the rival gangs in India. He also had a powerful temper when he considered that his dignity was threatened; when a larger boy caller Hervey picked on him and called him a 'mangey punkah wallah' he saw red, and promptly put his uncle's good advice to practical effect. Hervey did not pick on him again.

But what did worry Biggles, more than the bullying at Malton Hall, was the sense he had of being out of things. This was his first experience of English boys *en masse* and he was made to feel a foreigner among them. They were so different from the courteous Sula Dowla and he found them arrogant, uncouth and rather boring, with their tedious school slang and their obsessional concern with football. Biggles did not like football. (After polo, it struck him as a very common game, but he had the sense to keep this to himself.) None of them spoke Hindi or had shot a tiger and there was not a single boy at Malton Hall he would have chosen to accompany him into the jungle.

On the other hand, he longed to be considered one of them, if only as an antidote to loneliness. And so he consciously began to copy them – the words they used, their attitudes to life, the whole strange tribal rigmarole of Edwardian middle-class small boys. This was the beginning of that exaggerated pre-war Englishness that Biggles never lost. That over-hearty turn of phrase, the breezy manner and the apparently unthinking code of 'what one expects an Englishman to do' were not so much the real Biggles as a protective pose that he adopted. And as so often happens with adopted poses, it stuck. But beneath the carefully conformist self that he was now adopting, Biggles remained entirely his own person, sharp, intelligent, and something of a loner.

He made it clear that he had no intention of following in the footsteps of his famous brother. He was no athlete, cricket bored him even more than football, and he utterly lacked the temperament for team games. Nor, as Colonel Chase soon realised, was Biggles reliable 'prefect material' as his brother Charles had been. He was not exactly a 'subversive element' – one of the Colonel's favourite phrases for schoolboy wickedness – but he remained emphatically an individual throughout his time at Malton Hall, and, for all his efforts to conform, a definite outsider.

According to Captain Johns, at this time Biggles appeared a 'slight, neatly-dressed, delicate-looking boy [with] thoughtful eyes, a small firm mouth, and fair hair parted at the side'. He was, he adds, 'no better and no worse than any other schoolboy of his age and era. Like any normal boy he excelled in some subjects and failed dismally in others. He was thoughtful and inclined to be serious rather than boisterous.'

Biggles confirmed this picture of himself. The subjects he 'excelled' in were history, geography and French. (He had inherited a flair for languages from his mother.) Mathematics was an absolute blind spot for him; so was science, but he possessed mechanical aptitude above the average.

He had few close friends, and those he did have tended to be outsiders like himself. His best friend at Malton Hall, a bespectacled, extremely spotty boy called Smith, was to become a distinguished scientist who was killed in the Second World War on one of the early tests of airborne radar. But at Malton Hall, Smith rather took the place of Sula Dowla as a sort of deferential crony, always on hand to give Biggles aid and moral support on his various escapades.

For, just as in India, things still had a habit of happening to Biggles, and before long he achieved a reputation as a 'character' – one of those unusual boys who tend to land in trouble and can be relied on for the unexpected. Very early on, for instance, there was the extraordinary episode of the dancing bear.

It all began one lunchtime with an announcement from the Head that a highly dangerous animal, a large brown bear, had been reported in the neighbourhood. He thought it had escaped from a menagerie, and armed men were already out pursuing it. There was no need for alarm, but the boys should all be on their guard and if they saw the animal should report it and keep well away.

Biggles was playing games that afternoon and thought nothing more about the bear until, walking back towards the school, he noticed several men with rifles. One of them shouted to him to go back and suddenly he saw the cause of their alarm. By the hedgerow, eating berries, stood a fully-grown male brown bear. Biggles had often seen such bears in India; indeed one of Sula Dowla's friends had been the son of a beggar with a dancing bear in the back-streets of Garhwal, and he always had a soft spot for the animal. Certainly the idea of a similar bear in England being treated as a ravening wild beast appeared ridiculous, particularly as the bear in question was already looking rather lost. It had a collar round its neck and a long thin chain exactly like the dancing bears that he had seen in India. And so, without a second thought, Biggles walked on towards the bear, oblivious of the shouted warnings from the men behind him.

The bear looked at Biggles and Biggles looked at the bear. For some moments neither moved, then Biggles behaved exactly as he did with the bear that he had known in Garhwal. He spoke to it in Hindi, told it not to be afraid, and offered it the sugar bun that he had been saving for his tea. The bear hesitated, grunted and then thoughtfully accepted it. As it did so, Biggles picked up its chain and carried on addressing it in Hindi. For a while the bear munched his bun, then very slowly it began to dance. Biggles encouraged it and then began to lead it back towards the school. As he did so he shouted to the men to drop their guns.

'I was just longing to see the look on old Chevy's face when I walked into his study with the bear,' he said when he recounted the tale to us. 'He was a humourless old devil and it might have cheered him up.' But unfortunately before he reached the school the owner of the bear appeared, a wandering Indian from a circus, who was overjoyed to find his animal safe and sound. He was effusive in his thanks and led the bear away before Biggles had a chance to enjoy the sight of Colonel Chase confronted with a fully-grown dancing bear.

It was from this day that the Headmaster seems to have had his doubts about Biggles, but his reputation with the other boys began to grow. There were other episodes to follow. On one occasion he and the faithful Smith started a wild-goose chase for some non-existent 'buried treasure' which had half the inhabitants of the nearby village digging up the Common. And another time, he totally disrupted the School Corps field-day by capturing the 'enemy' headquarters long before the battle started.

From time to time the question would be mooted as to exactly what he wanted for a career. Despite the united influence of both his uncle and the Head, he remained resolutely against the idea of the army. 'Not my thing at all. Too much confounded discipline, and anyhow my brother was already in the Rifle Brigade and I'd had enough of following *his* footsteps, thank you very much,' was Biggles' attitude. Instead, he thought quite seriously of studying Oriental languages at Oxford, but the war was to put a stop to that.

Curiously enough he did have one uncanny foretaste of his future while he was still at Malton Hall. He was on the playing field one afternoon, trying, as he put it, 'to avoid the dreadful tedium without exactly·dropping off to sleep', when suddenly he heard a noise he thought at first must be his uncle's old de Dion on an unexpected visit. It grew louder and then, over the elms at the end of the cricket field, appeared an aeroplane, a Bleriot two-seater. None of the boys had ever seen an aeroplane before and, inevitably, all thought of cricket was abandoned. The plane circled the field, the pilot waved, then someone shouted, 'Look, he's coming down!' And so he was. At what seemed breakneck speed the Bleriot was heading for the cricket pitch and Biggles never would forget his first sight of a perfect three-point landing.

'I don't know why, but I felt something turn over within me. I'd read about aeroplanes of course, but I'd never thought about them seriously till that moment. For some reason, when I clapped my eyes on that confounded Bleriot I knew that I was hooked. Don't ask me why, but I knew for certain that that was where my future lay.'

The pilot was an old Maltonian, a boy called Morris whose father was a rich tobacco merchant. Biggles had known him as a senior boy a few terms earlier, and Morris was obviously enjoying showing off to his erstwhile schoolmates. Even Colonel Chase appeared impressed. Morris stayed for a hero's tea in the pavilion, then donned his goggles and his flying helmet and flew off. He was killed in a flying accident not long after, but this did nothing to deter Biggles from the great ambition of his life. If Morris could fly then so could he. As for crashes – 'at that time of life one never really thinks about them,' he said. Biggles had fallen unreservedly in love with the idea of flying. It was his dream, his secret hope, the answer to that restlessness which had pursued him since his mother left. But, since it meant so much to him, he kept it strictly to himself, knowing quite well that if he talked about it openly he would be mocked by the other boys and branded as an eccentric by the Head, who thought that all careers except the army were ridiculous.

So it was that Biggles grew up with the idea of flying as an exciting yet forbidden dream. The only person he confided in was the old General, when he was back with him one summer holiday, and the General, as Biggles had expected, was distinctly sympathetic.

'Thinking of buying one of these flying machines myself. Dashed exciting, I'd have thought. Use it to fly up to London. Quicker than the train,'

Alas, upon inquiry General Bigglesworth was advised that whilst a one-armed man could manage a de Dion – just – it was impossible to pilot a new flying machine one-handed. Biggles was even more upset than his uncle at the news – for several weeks he had been picturing himself slipping back to Norfolk during holidays and somehow teaching himself to fly in secret – but the General did his best to comfort him. 'Before long you'll be piloting a plane yourself,' he said prophetically; and in the meantime, to console his nephew, he took him off to see one of the earliest displays of aircraft at the tiny flying field near Hendon where all the latest aircraft – Bleriots and Farman biplanes and a brand new Sopwith interceptor – were on show. The star of that particular afternoon was the celebrated B. C. Hucks, the first man in the world to loop the loop, a feat which at that time was rare enough to bring a murmur of excitement from the crowd.

Apart from his dreams of flying and the friendship of his extraordinary old uncle, Biggles had few consoling features in his life. He always had admired his brother, Charles, but they had never been particularly close, and on the few occasions when they saw each other now, Biggles was painfully aware of the gulf between them. This was partly due to age and partly temperament. Charles was very like their father, and the army had brought out the keen, conformist side of his heredity. As a promising young subaltern in a famous regiment, he was also rather on his dignity towards his undersized young brother, and disapproved of Biggles' lack of enthusiasm for the army and for Malton Hall. (Biggles suspected Colonel Chase of passing the word along that Biggles Minor just 'wasn't up to scratch'.) Charles was also on much closer terms than Biggles with John Henry Bigglesworth. Since he had arrived at Malton Hall, Biggles' letters to his father had soon trickled down to one or two a term, but Charles wrote regularly, and felt obliged to lecture Biggles on his duty to what he called 'the pater'. Biggles resented this, and if truth be told, would not have cared too much if he had never seen or heared from his father again. Needless to say, one subject was always totally taboo between the brothers – their mother. Biggles suspected Charles of knowing more than he let on about the whole mysterious business of her departure from Garhwal and her reported death, but on the one occasion when he tried to tap his brother on the subject, Charles replied tersely, 'that's all over and done with', and promptly changed the subject. They never talked of her again.

This did not mean that Biggles had no contact with his mother's family. Lord Lacey – unforgiving to the last – expired in Calcutta at the end of 1910. (According to one version of his death, he was overcome by a fit of apoplexy in the bath brought on by anger when a servant offered him carbolic soap.) In later life, Biggles regretted that he had never seen him. The title passed to Biggles' uncle, Henry Lacey, a man as different from his father as anyone could possibly imagine. He was a gentle, absent-minded man, a botanist by training, who lived in a big ramshackle house in Lewes. On hearing that he had inherited the title, his chief concern was that his duties at the House of Lords would interrupt his lifelong search for wild flowers. He need not have worried. Henry Viscount Lacey visited the House of Lords on two occasions – once to take his seat, and once when he had been to a wedding at St Margaret's, Westminster, and could not find a lavatory. The remainder of his life was dedicated to his monumental *Wild Flowers of Heath and Hedgerow*, which was published privately a year or two before his death in 1953.

Biggles always spoke of his botanising uncle as something of a joke. He used to be invited to the house at Lewes, but much preferred staying with the General. Motorcars and land torpedoes were more to his taste than wild flowers, and Lord Lacey was so distant and eccentric that he really had no time for Biggles. But on the other hand, Lady Lacey, Biggles' formidable Aunt Priscilla, apparently felt sorry for him and used to try to organise his life. At times she could be something of a menace. 'Bossy old harridan' was how he described her to us. 'Always trying to rope me in for good works and telling me to wash behind my ears.'

The Laceys had a son called Algernon – 'freckle-faced, spoiled little brat I always thought him in those days'. Algernon was almost two years younger than his cousin, and it would have been impossible for any boy to have escaped the domination of a mother like Aunt Pris. Biggles tended to ignore him and it was not for several years to come that Biggles realised the truth – the insignificant Algy hero-worshipped him and would do so in his own strange way for the remainder of his life.

There was another way in which the Laceys were important to Biggles at this time, for it was through them that he finally got news about his mother. His aunt had no inhibitions about telling him exactly what had happened, and it appeared his mother was now living in the South of France. Captain Thomas had deserted her long since, and she had married a French businessman, a Monsieur Duclos.

For weeks after hearing this Biggles could think of nothing else, and was all for contacting her at once, but Aunt Priscilla prudently advised him otherwise. 'You must be very understanding, James, dear boy,' she said. 'Your mother – whether she deserved it or not is neither here nor there – has been through hell, and now at last has found a new life for herself in France. Her husband, as I know only too well myself, is an extraordinarily jealous man. I've no idea how much she's told him, so we must be extremely cautious. I will be seeing her this autumn when we are in Cannes, and I will ask her what she wants to do about you. We must, of course, respect her wishes utterly.'

Biggles longed to see his mother; now that he knew she was alive he could not wait to be reunited with her. But he also knew his aunt was right, and so he waited as the weeks dragged by, and he was back at Malton Hall when he finally received a letter from his aunt. She had seen his mother and had talked to her about her sons. She had told her how eager Biggles was to see her, but his mother was inflexible. She sent her love, but felt 'the time is not appropriate for a meeting'. (In fact, as Biggles told us, she had disguised her age when marrying her second husband and had not even told him of the existence of her two grown sons.)

Biggles was nearly fifteen by now, and had sufficient self-control to hide his feelings, but he suffered horribly and, even more than when his mother left, felt himself rejected by this icy-hearted woman that he loved. It was then that something closed up inside him and he no longer really cared what happened to him. During his final years at Malton Hall he became moody and withdrawn. He had no close friends (even the faithful, spotty Smith had left him), dodged games whenever possible and hardly bothered with his work. Everything in him now was set on one ambition – flying. But he told nobody about it and it was not until the early summer of 1914 that there appeared a slender chance that all his dreams would finally come true.

2

Biggles Learns to Fly

'It's funny, looking back,' Biggles remarked one day, 'but when the 1914–18 war broke out, my greatest fear was that it would all be finished before I had a chance to join the fighting. Only goes to show how stupid one can be, but you must remember that everybody seemed to think the war would be over by Christmas, and of course my brother Charles was off to join his regiment in France. I was bored stiff at dear old Malton Hall and the war appeared my one great chance to get into an aeroplane. But there I was, just fifteen, with the summer holidays half over, and not the faintest hope, it seemed, of ever getting closer to the enemy than my uncle's house at Lewes. So I tried to volunteer. I went to the recruiting office, which was in Brighton in those days, and told them I was eighteen. There was a sergeant there, a great big fellow with a huge moustache, and when he saw me he just roared with laughter. "Back to school with you, Sonny Jim," he shouted. "When they start needing schoolboys at the Front we'll write and let you know."'

Not for the last time in his life, Biggles was experiencing the effect of his lack of size and extraordinary youthfulness. But there was nothing he could do except soldier on at Malton Hall, and offer up his private prayers that the war would continue long enough to let him play his part in it. Which all too horribly it did. The early months of optimism and euphoria passed, and soon the boys of Malton Hall began to realise the nature of the struggle as the Head read out the names of more and more quite recent old Maltonians, 'who have made the supreme sacrifice for King and Country'.

But the idea of death made no impression on young Biggles, and his ambition stayed the same as ever – flying. He used to keep a scrapbook on aeroplanes and famous fliers – men like the legendary Captain Ball who shot down the first German airship over Britain, and the fearsome German ace, von Richthofen – and as the war dragged on, and life at Malton Hall seemed more and more beside the point, Biggles was becoming quite an expert in aeronautics. He still felt hideously out of things – especially with his brother Charles becoming something of a hero now. He fought with gallantry at Mons, was awarded the M.C. and promoted captain on the field of battle.

Early in 1916, Charles, by now a major with his own battalion, was wounded badly in the leg. That Easter he was back in Norfolk, convalescing with old General Bigglesworth, and it was then that Biggles finally decided he had had enough of Malton Hall and waiting patiently for his turn to come. Another boy at school called Turner, who was two months junior to Biggles, had just been accepted into the Royal Navy as a midshipman. Biggles informed his uncle that he intended following him. The General was appalled. A Bigglesworth in the Navy! What was his silly nephew thinking of? He positively forbade it. But Biggles was determined and explained quite coolly to his uncle that he intended entering the Navy and transferring to the newly formed Royal Naval Air Service as soon as possible.

'I don't give two hoots what uniform I wear,' he said. 'All I want to do is fly.'

The General knew his nephew well enough to realise he wasn't bluffing, and when he had calmed down sufficiently to think coherently he offered him a deal.

'Listen, my boy!' the old gentleman began, 'I want to hear no more about this Naval nonsense. It's bad for my blood pressure. But if you promise not to mention it again and wait until you're seventeen, I'll see what can be done to get you commissioned into a decent regiment. You'll have to lie about your age of course, but with my backing they'll accept you. From then it will be up to you.'

And so it came about that early that summer of 1916, Biggles was summoned to Whitehall. Because of the frightful losses at the Front, young officers were needed, and thanks to a letter from his uncle, Biggles was accepted as a second lieutenant into a rifle regiment, after some two weeks' very basic training at the regimental depot outside Aldershot – and even then his luck continued. The depot was in chaos. Nobody seemed to know or care what happened to this raw young subaltern, and when he applied for an instant transfer to the Royal Flying Corps, nobody objected. Pilots were desperately needed out in France, and by the end of September it seemed that Biggles' dearest dream had suddenly come true. He had a brand-new fur-lined flying coat which reached his ankles, a flying helmet, a pair of goggles, and an official posting to the R.F.C.'s No. 17 Flying Training School at Settling in Norfolk.

'They called the place a training school for fliers,' Biggles said. 'In fact it was more by luck than judgment that anyone came through that so-called flying course alive. Most of the instructors there were pilots who had been sent back from France as "unfit for combat duties", and the aircraft that they had were even worse, clapped-out old Farman biplanes that should have been in a museum when the war broke out. They were nothing short of flying death-traps. Get one in a spin and it was impossible to pull out of it. If you tried to dive, the wings came off. The crash rate was a damned disgrace, and as for training, it was survival of the fittest – or the luckiest.'

Biggles was both. After a week or so of dual flying, his instructor – a shell-shocked veteran called Captain Nerkison – decided that the time had come for him to solo, which he did, miraculously without mishap.

'When I think back to it,' laughed Biggles, 'I get the cold shudders. I wasn't really fit to drive a farm cart, let alone a plane as tricky as a Farman. But at that age, nothing seems impossible, and apart from a very bumpy landing, I survived.'

Here one must make allowance for his modesty, for it is clear that from the start Biggles was that rarest of all beings, a natural pilot. Even the erratic Captain Nerkison must have realised as much, for with less than two hours' solo flying in his log-book,

Biggles was sent on to the second stage of training – to the grandly titled No. 4 School of Fighting at Frensham on the coast of Lincolnshire.

The training here was still quite elementary – 'in at the deep end – sink or swim' – as Biggles put it, but he was taught the rudiments of combat flying, and for the first time had a chance to fly some of the newest aircraft which were coming into service with the R.F.C., planes like the legendary Sopwith Pup with its powerful rotary engine, and the two-seater F.E.2. He was taught basic navigation, lectured on 'flying tactics', and given his chance of target practice, against several ancient aircraft on the beach. And that, for all practical purposes, was that. At a time when the average combat pilot's life in France was something like three weeks, there was no chance of much finesse. Pilots were needed in the squadrons at the Front and it seemed to Biggles that he had barely arrived, at Frensham before he received his movement order out to France. He had to collect it from the Adjutant at the Fighting School, and as he stanped his log-book, the Adjutant said casually, 'Oh, by the way, you can put up your "wings". You've passed. Well done!' Not yet eighteen and with less than fifteen hours flying to his credit, 2nd Lieut James Bigglesworth had suddenly become a fully-fledged pilot in the Royal Flying Corps.

When he reached France his first posting was to 169 Squadron stationed near St Omer in the north of France. He had been hoping for a scout squadron, flying the latest Sopwith Pups, and he was somewhat disappointed to discover that in 169 they were still equipped with the lumbering two-seater F.E.2 pusher biplanes. They were reliable enough and easy to fly, but they were underpowered. Their top speed was a laboured eighty miles an hour, and already the German Albatrosses had the edge on them. Indeed, that autumn was a testing time for the Allied air forces. The Germans had a new device allowing their machine-guns to fire forward through the propeller, and at a time when the German ground forces were bogged down in the trenches of the Somme, their airmen were hard on the offensive, particularly in the small area from St Omer up to the Belgian coast where Biggles found himself. As early as that July, ten German bombers had attacked the British Lines at Festubert in broad daylight. Boulogne was raided, and just a few days before Biggles reached his Squadron, 8,000 tons of ammunition were destroyed in a daring midnight raid on the British base at Audruicq.

Squadron No. 169 was in the thick of things. Losses had been heavy and beneath the atmosphere of forced cheerfulness which seemed to be the order of the day, morale was bad. Conditions at St Omer were grim – so grim in fact that Biggles himself was almost killed within minutes of arrival. He had reported to the Adjutant – who was distinctly off-hand with him – and was strolling over to the Mess, when he heard an aeroplane approaching. He took no notice, thinking that it was one of the Squadron coming in to land, but he heard a sudden whistling noise and a moment later was thrown to the ground by a violent explosion. This must have saved his life, for the aircraft was in fact a German scout plane, making a sortie from its base across the Lines, and having dropped its bomb, it then went on to rake the airfield with machine-gun fire.

Biggles was indignant, and rather shaken, but the members of the Squadron treated this mishap to the new boy as an enormous joke.

'Jerry must have heard that you were coming, old boy!' remarked the Adjutant drily. 'Obviously popped over to give you an official welcome from the Kaiser. Probably as well he didn't get you though. We're getting rather low on pilots.'

This was all too true, for later that same afternoon 169 lost its Commanding Officer. The poor man died of wounds after bringing back his badly shot-up F.E.2, and it was the new C.O., a difficult, bad-tempered man called Major Paynter, who officially welcomed Biggles to the Mess of 169 that night. It was an uncomfortable occasion, which Paynter's words did little to relieve, and afterwards there was a lot of horseplay and heavy drinking – the inevitable reaction to the losses and the strain the Squadron had to bear, and Biggles heard somebody remark, 'Good God, they're sending us schoolboys now!'

Someone else suggested taking Biggles' trousers off (the traditional method in some regiments in those days of putting young subalterns in their place). But this was firmly stopped by the Second-in-Command, a major by the name of Roberts. 'No time for that sort of tommy-rot,' he shouted. 'We've too much work to do tomorrow, and Bigglesworth here is due to fly with Way as his observer. Time you got off to bed, my lad.' As Biggles followed his advice, Roberts said tactfully, 'Don't take too much notice of what's happened here tonight. Everyone's a bit strung up. You'll be all right, and Way will keep an eye on you. Do as he says, and you won't go far wrong.'

Hardly surprisingly, Biggles had little sleep that night, and all next morning as he stayed on standby for his first operational flight, he suffered badly from an attack of nerves – one of the few occasions that he ever did. But luckily Lieutenant Way realised how he was feeling and did his best to put him at his ease. Way was a down-to-earth New Zealander, and although barely twenty-one himself was already one of the most experienced observers with the R.F.C. His pilot had been killed two days earlier, but he was admirably calm as he explained the drill for the patrol – the way the flight would keep together, how he would operate the two machine-guns in the aircraft's nose, and the necessity to keep as high as possible above the enemy. 'Just keep the old bus in the air, and stay glued to the Flight Commander's tail,' said Way. 'I'll do the rest.'

It sounded easy, but as the hours ticked by Biggles' nervousness grew worse. He tried to think about the General and his brother, Charles, but even that was not much help. But he couldn't help remembering the remark about schoolboys – it made him angry and his anger kept him going. He ate no lunch, and then, just after two o'clock, the order came – take-off in ten minutes' time. His debut as a combat pilot had begun.

He still had his outsize flying coat, and all but tripped over it as he swung himself aboard the plane, but once inside the cockpit all his worries left him. Way gave him the thumbs up from the forward cockpit, a mechanic swung the big propeller, and as the Beardmore engine thundered into life, something in Biggles came alive as well. He was no longer worried or concerned with death, and suddenly he felt at one with the machine. As he opened up the throttle and the aircraft started to roll across the field, he was caught up in a sense of real exhilaration. It was a grey, wet afternoon, with low cloud shrouding the horizon, but as the tail lifted and the biplane rose above the poplars at the far end of the field, Biggles felt his spirits lift with it.

After his doubts and fears it seemed extraordinarily easy. The Flight Commander's plane was there ahead of him to follow, the F.E.2 was flying beautifully, and for some twenty minutes they were circling above the airfield as they climbed to 7,000 feet. Then the Commander dipped his wings and Biggles saw him turn towards the east. His first sortie over enemy territory had started.

As the three planes sailed on in perfect formation, Biggles could soon see the long brown scar of the Front Line trenches in the neat countryside below. That was where men were fighting in the mud and misery of Northern France, but on that perfect autumn afternoon it was impossible to grasp – even when he saw a group of round black blobs suddenly appear a few hundred yards ahead. He counted them – five, six – and suddenly there was a flash quite close to the left wing-tip followed by a dull explosion and a rush of air which made the biplane buck. He almost panicked as he thought that he would lose control, but he soon pulled the aircraft back on course, and as he did so Way turned round, grinned at him and shouted something.

Biggles could not hear him but he knew what he was saying: 'Archie' – enemy anti-aircraft fire. A full-scale barrage, and by the look of it, too close for comfort. But there was nothing to be done except ignore it. The Flight Commander was still holding his position, and, a little nervously by now, Biggles did the same.

Then he saw that Way was standing up. The anti-aircraft fire had ceased, and his observer had his Lewis gun in readiness over the side of the cockpit. He fired a short burst – probably to warm the gun and stop it freezing up, thought Biggles, who could only see the other aircraft of the flight and the empty sky above. Then Way fired again, a longer burst this time, and Conway, the observer in the nearest F.E.2, was also firing.

This had Biggles puzzled. He could still see nothing but clear sky ahead, but Conway was signalling, waving and pointing downwards. Way waved back, then leant out of the cockpit to aim the Lewis gun straight down. Biggles craned his neck to see what he was firing at, and with shocked amazement saw a green aircraft with swept-back wings immediately below them. But what held his attention were the two black Maltese crosses glaring at him.

Everything seemed to happen in slow motion then. The German plane – an elderly two-seater Taube used for reconnaissance – tried to bank away, followed by another burst of fire from the Lewis gun, and Biggles saw the figure in the rear cockpit stand up and collapse as the bullets hit him. The plane slipped sideways and its left wing crumpled like tissue paper. As it spun towards the countryside below, one of the crew fell out. Biggles watched him turn and turn, then disappear.

That brought Biggles back to his senses very swiftly. The Flight Commander turned his plane abruptly, making Biggles bank the F.E.2 so sharply that he almost went into a spin himself. Luckily he still had sufficient height to put the plane into a dive and then pull out, as he chased back towards the Allied Lines, following his leader.

It was then that the real sense of exultation caught him. The wind was streaming past his face, the engine roaring, and he had just experienced his first 'kill' in the air. He felt no pity or remorse for the figure he had seen spin down to earth – it was too unreal for that. This battle in the air was an exciting game – and he had felt himself invincible.

He saw a green Very light fired by the Flight Commander, signalling the end of the patrol, and then the airfield was below them. Biggles made a perfect landing, and when the plane had rolled to a halt he shouted his congratulations to his observer.

'Good shooting! You got that Taube beautifully. I didn't realise that it was there until you'd hit it.'

Lieutenant Way took his goggles off, and gave Biggles a thin smile.

'I didn't really get the Taube. That was Conway's. I got the other one.'

'What other one?' said Biggles warily.

'The blue and yellow Fokker that was after us,' Way said in his soft New Zealand accent. 'Didn't you see the blighter? He almost got us. He was with another Fokker, black one. Conway got him as well. I'll have to buy the man a drink.'

Biggles was feeling slightly dazed by now – no longer the dare-devil combat ace that he had felt himself to be whilst coming in to land.

'How many were there, then?' he asked.

'Heavens, man! Didn't you see them? There were seven all told – a whole Hun patrol. We sailed through the middle of them.

Why else d'you think the Flight Commander turned our noses back so fast?'

He laughed and Biggles felt extremely foolish, but Lieutenant Way was a kindly man at heart and, slapping Biggles on the back, he said, 'Don't worry, youngster. You flew damned well, and you'll soon get the hang of things. Huns take a lot of spotting till you get the knack. Now come and have a spot of tea. I think we've earned it."

And so it was that over tea and army biscuits Biggles celebrated his first 'kill' in the air – of an aircraft he had never even seen.

Biggles could not afford to be an innocent for long. He was learning in a school where few who made mistakes survived, and he was constantly spurred on by the feeling that the other members of the Mess were laughing at him – they had christened him 'the schoolboy wonder'.

The German Air Force was maintaining its superiority, and Biggles was soon flying across the Lines three and four times a day. To survive one had to know one's job, and at a time when the average life of a British pilot was three weeks, Biggles was managing it very well. He insisted that he had a lot of luck, and 'the schoolboy wonder's luck' became a byword in the Squadron. Once he returned with a German bullet-hole in the flap of his leather flying helmet; another time a German Halberstadt had Biggles at its mercy, and then its guns jammed (Biggles insisted he could still remember the look of fury and disgust on the German pilot's face as he went diving past). But luck apart, Biggles was a born combat pilot, and within three weeks of his arrival at 169 he was earning the grudging admiration of his brother officers.

Despite this, Biggles continued to feel out of things – just as he had at Malton Hall. This was partly age – he was still only seventeen and a half at the beginning of 1917, and all the other members of the Squadron seemed considerably older. As at school, he made efforts to conform. He started smoking, attempted unsuccessfully to grow a small moustache, and would join in with any high-jinks that were going in the Mess. Yet, however hard he tried, Biggles was all too aware that he was a loner still.

In some ways this was an advantage. Pilots are individualists at

heart and Biggles always felt that in the last resort he had no one
to rely on but himself. On the other hand, it was now, in his most
impressionable period of all, that Biggles consciously adopted the
slang and manner of his older brother officers. It was a *persona*
that he never lost – indeed, as the years went by, he would
become something of a caricature of an old style pilot from the
R.F.C. But in that hard-pressed winter that he spent at St Omer,
Biggles still appeared a rather earnest, overgrown schoolboy with
a cheerful word for almost everyone and a fanatical love of flying.

   This passion never left him. Most of the older pilots in the
Squadron ultimately tired of flying. If they were lucky and
survived their first few months with an active-service squadron,
their nerve would usually begin to go, and generally only the
toughest or the maddest fliers went on to become the famous aces
of the war.

   Biggles was different. Partly through temperament – and
partly too because of the extraordinary series of adventures that
soon diverted him from Front-Line flying – Biggles never did
become a famous ace. He was not a natural killer, and he flew for
the simplest of reasons – because he loved it and believed that the
happiest place on earth was the cockpit of an aeroplane.

Towards the end of 1916, the British forces in the north of France
were finally bogged down. The weather was as bad an enemy as
the German army, as fog and ice were added to the hazards of a
combat pilot's life.

   Allied Headquarters had been hearing rumours that the
enemy was massing to attack along the narrow segment from the
Belgian border, but clear-cut information was urgently required
– information which only aerial reconnaissance could provide.

   Even in decent weather this sort of reconnaissance was
hazardous. The German base at Vanfleur was forty miles behind
their Lines, and although the F.E.2s were ideal for this sort of
operation, as their low speed and stability made them the perfect
spotter planes, they were also hideously vulnerable. The generals
were demanding detailed information – numbers of rail trucks in
the sidings, news about arms dumps and troop formations, all of
which meant that the aircraft would have to spend several
minutes flying dangerously low across the town.

When the request came through from High Command, one of the most experienced pilots in the Squadron, a Captain Littleton, was given the job. He failed to return. So did Lieutenant Blake, another veteran of 169. But although two planes were lost, there was no question of abandoning the task; it was now the turn of Biggles' flight.

Mapleton, the Flight Commander, refused point blank to ask for volunteers. 'I'm not letting anyone commit suicide just because he considers it the right thing to do,' were the words he used. Instead he suggested that all three pilots tossed for it, the odd man out to go. Inevitably, the odd man out was Biggles. Way appeared understandably concerned. Mapleton's talk of suicide was not exactly calculated to give much encouragement to the chosen victims, but Biggles seemed delighted, for he had reached that dangerous point of all young fliers where confidence had started to outrun experience. He seemed to have a charmed life in the air and felt no fear. Flying was still a game, and even the warnings and the grim briefing from the C.O., Major Paynter, failed to dampen his spirits.

Paynter suggested that they flew at dawn next morning, but Biggles showed his contempt for Paynter's advice by insisting on that very afternoon.

'Jerry is always waiting for a dawn patrol,' he said. 'Less opposition in the afternoon.'

The C.O. agreed but warned them to watch out. 'Reports from Intelligence suggest that Richthofen and his merry men have moved up to the airfield at Douai, and there are already more Boche combat planes there than anywhere else on the Western Front.' He smiled quizzically. 'I tell you this to cheer you on your way.'

'Well, if we've got to go, we might as well get it over with as soon as possible,' Way remarked to Biggles when they were safely out of earshot.

Biggles was irrepressible, and twenty minutes later he was giving the F.E.2 full throttle, and the sheds and hangars of the Squadron H.Q. were receding in the rain beneath them. It was filthy weather all the way – rain, broken cloud, and at 8,000 feet ice was soon forming in the cockpit (twice Way fired short bursts on his Lewis guns to stop them icing up). In some ways, however, the weather was a blessing. The cloud gave cover and it would be a very eager German who took his aircraft up in such conditions. And in fact, some forty minutes after taking off, Biggles and Way had reached their destination without incident.

Then came the tricky bit. Biggles had difficulty finding a break in the cloud and had to bring the aircraft down to 2,000 feet before he and Way could see a thing below then, and at that height the eighty-mile-an-hour F.E.2 was something of a sitting duck for the German anti-aircraft guns. Not that this made the slightest difference to our hero. One of the earliest lessons he had learned was that the only way to deal with 'Archie' was to ignore it. 'If a shell has your name on it, too bad,' was his philosophy. But as the aircraft sailed slap through the middle of the German barrage, even his equanimity was shaken, and the aircraft bucked and bucketed as the German gunners got rather too close for comfort. Biggles took what evasive action he could manage, banking the F.E.2 and doing his best to twist and turn across the target – none of which made his observer's task any easier. But Way was meticulous, and as the lumbering aircraft flew across Vanfleur at little more than 1,000 feet, he had a great deal to record. The sidings of the goods yard were full of flat trucks, each with a German field gun plainly visible. Shell were being loaded further on, and there were stores and motor vehicles, whilst outside the little town were row on row of tents for troops that would reinforce the big attack.

In those days before aerial photography much depended on the accuracy of the observer, and it was clearly urgent to get detailed news of this big German build-up back to the Allied High Command. So whilst Biggles' instincts were to get out of Vanfleur now as speedily as possible (and how he wished he'd had a bomb or two to drop on the ammunition dump outside the station), Way was insisting on a further flight across the town just to make sure that he had everything recorded on his note-pad. Biggles reluctantly agreed and, bringing the aircraft almost down to rooftop level now, started the return journey over the town.

This time all hell broke loose, not only from aircraft guns, but also from German soldiers in the streets, who took pot shots with their rifles at the aircraft with the unmistakeable red, white and blue roundels on its wings. Miraculously, she came through unscathed – apart from some tell-tale bullet-holes around the cockpit, and shrapnel gashes in the wings – and Biggles decided they had tempted providence enough for one wet afternoon and that it was time for home.

Easier said than done. As he began to put the aircraft into a slow climb and turn her nose south-west, the German guns below fell silent, and suddenly he saw the reason. Out in the clearing sky that lay between the F.E.2 and home were twelve black dots which, even as they watched, grew larger. German Albatrosses! Against such opposition Biggles' F.E.2 had as much chance of surviving as a cow faced with a pack of hungry lions.

But he still possessed one lingering advantage – the blanket of low grey cloud that stretched north of Vanfleur to the Belgian coast. If they could reach it, there was still a chance of giving the faster German planes the slip.

For the next few minutes it was touch and go, with Biggles speeding for the cloud-bank at full throttle, and the German triplanes closing in. Biggles could see by now the Squadron numbers on the fuselage of the leading aircraft, and then, suddenly, they were in the cloud. It was like flying straight into a dense grey fog, an eerie, silent world in which the German planes could never hope to find them.

There was no question now of flying south towards St Omer, for their best hope of dodging their pursuers still lay in the protection of this interminable bank of cloud. So, Biggles flew north-west by his compass, hoping in the end to reach the Belgian coast, then follow it down towards Dunkirk and home.

At first it seemed as if this plan would work. The German aircraft had no hope of finding them, and after studying his map and calculating distance from his flying time, Biggles decided they would soon be over the Belgian coast, and cautiously brought the aircraft down below the level of the cloud.

'Great!' shouted Way as they reached clear air beneath the cloud-bank, for there on the horizon lay the sea with a pale blue sky beyond. Biggles gently eased the aircraft to the left and started the slow journey back to Base. Two things were worrying him by now. The first was his petrol level. The F.E.2's maximum endurance was three hours, and they had already been airborne more than half of this. The second worry was an enemy patrol. In this clear sky by the coast the F.E.2 would have no hiding place.

For twenty minutes all seemed well. The pale blue winter sky began to darken with the approach of evening, and Biggles kept the aircraft's nose along the white line of the breaking surf beneath, whilst Way kept a sharp lookout for an enemy. But as always happens, trouble came when least expected.

From the map, Biggles had calculated that they would soon have reached the point where the Front Line met the sea, and was already looking forward to getting back in time for dinner, when Lieutenant Way shouted out a warning and swung his Lewis gun towards the water. Biggles followed the direction, only to see the dark shape of an Albatross heading towards them from the mist. At the same time, something made him glance in the opposite direction: another Albatross was swooping towards them for the kill. The two scout planes, out on their evening patrol, were evidently working together and launching a beautifully-timed dual attack on them.

Way did his best to head them off by firing manfully at each aircraft, but the odds were obviously too great, and the F.E.2 was no match for the synchronised machine-guns of the German planes. The distances began to narrow, and above the racket of the engine and the Lewis gun, Biggles could hear the whine of the two approaching Albatrosses. They were daring fliers to approach so close, and at the point where it looked as if collision was inevitable, Biggles yanked at the joystick and sent his aircraft zooming upwards. A second later came an appalling crash from just below. The aircraft shuddered in the explosion and was hit by small bits of wreckage, and as Biggles peered down he saw what had occurred. The two German pilots must have taken simultaneous evasive action to avoid collison, but had done it in the same direction and had met each other head on. There were no survivors, and as the F.E.2 lumbered on unharmed, Biggles could tell himself that he and Way had just had one of the luckiest escapes of the war.

But talk of escape was slightly premature. St Omer was still a good half hour away, the light was failing and suddenly the engine faltered, coughed, and then cut out. Biggles held the aircraft steady as it started to plane down towards the sea, and for a while he thought that he would even make the beach. No such luck. Like an extremely tired seabird the old F.E.2 glided towards the waves, bounced on the water and then subsided in a shower of spray. Luckily the sea was very shallow, and Biggles and Way, their flying jackets jettisoned already, were able to wade ashore unhurt and make their way towards the sand dunes up beyond the beach.

It was as well they did, for at this point they had no idea on which side of the Front Line they had landed, but they soon found out when they heard German voices echoing along the beach. An enemy patrol had ventured out to investigate the crashed British aircraft. Luckily the light was fading quickly by now and the Germans were delayed by their attempts to search the plane. During this time the two British airmen made good their escape along the dunes, dodging between the shadows and the banks of high sea-grass that gave them perfect cover.

Soon they were halted by barbed wire, and as they lay hidden, trying to make out just what lay ahead, they heard a German working party digging a few hundred yards ahead. There was no longer any doubt of their position. They had reached the Front Line – and were lying on the German side of it.

Both men were wet and very cold – conditions not exactly calculated to bring out the best in Biggles – and it was Way who then decisively took charge.

'Nothing for it, I'm afraid,' he whispered. 'Either we swim, or spend the remainder of the war in a German prison camp.'

Swimming had never been much of a speciality with Biggles. To tell the truth, he loathed the water and it required the grim alternative of prison even now to make him think of it. Fortunately Way was a powerful swimmer – 'Hang on to my collar,' he told Biggles as they slid into the icy waves.

The swim appeared to last for ever, and but for Way, Biggles would undoubtedly have drowned. Luckily the Lines were fairly close together, and the current flowed towards the south. After what seemed a wet eternity, Way turned towards the shore, and Biggles felt the sand again beneath his feet.

They scrambled up the shore and then a voice rang out – '*Halte-là!*' It was a French patrol and they were safe at last.

It took another hour and a half to get back to the Mess at St Omer by road, and when they arrived, in borrowed French uniforms, they were something of a sight. But they received a hero's welcome, and that very night Way's information from Vanfleur was en route to the generals – who, for once, made good use of it.

Adventures such as these appealed to Biggles, for his attitude to war remained a very private one. Apart from his passion for flying, which nothing could deflate, he still regarded the war as something of a personal crusade. But during the early spring of 1917, the war in the air began to change, particularly for hard-pressed 169, and Biggles started to become uneasy about what was happening. As he put it when he talked about it later, 'All the fun suddenly went out of it and it became a very beastly business – like the war itself.'

Part of the trouble was the growing strength of the German opposition, which, with faster planes, and sound Teutonic tactics, was sending out massed patrols against which the isolated F.E.2s had little chance. In answer to this the Allied Air Command switched 169 to night-bombing duties – a task which hardly suited Biggles. It was hazardous, impersonal work, and although he continued to fly with Lieutenant Way, and on one memorable April night joined in a mass attack on the Richthofen headquarters at Douai, Biggles did not enjoy it, and made no secret of the fact.

He was at his best when faced with an instant challenge, and was still very much the boy who had taught himself to survive in the forests of Garhwal. Although relations between Biggles and Major Paynter were as bad as ever, the C.O. must have recognised something unusual in him, since it was now that he chose him for a very special mission, which required rather more than the everyday pilot's skills. Biggles was still barely eighteen at the time, but this mission was to prove of key importance to him, both as a foretaste of the sort of high adventure he would follow in his life, and for the introduction that it gave him to the man who would help to shape his destiny. This was a tall, emaciated-looking, steely-eyed Intelligence major attached to Wing Headquarters. His name was Raymond.

Paynter introduced him to Biggles in his office, and Major Raymond, in that clipped, laconic way he had, explained that the Allied Secret Service had a little problem. The German army was bringing up reinforcements over a bridge across the River Aisne near a town called Aille. Several air attempts to bomb the bridge had failed, and because of the urgency it had been decided to try sabotage. Raymond had found a Frenchman from the district who was highly recommended by the French High

Command as one of their top saboteurs, but he had to be landed near the bridge – by night, of course, and without arousing the German guards. The F.E.2s were ideal for this sort of work – they were slow and could practically land and take off in a cabbage patch. How, Major Rayond asked, did Biggles feel about it?

'No problem, sir!' said Biggles easily.

'Oh, and there's just one other thing I should have mentioned,' added Raymond. 'Under the rules of war, if they catch you or the Frenchman they're perfectly entitled to shoot you both. They probably will. Say if you'd rather back out now.'

Biggles shook his head.

'Capital,' said Raymond. 'Say nothing of this to anyone of course, but be prepared to leave at a moment's notice'.

It was next day, just as Biggles was finishing dinner in the Mess, that he was called again to Paynter's office, and Major Raymond introduced him to a small round Frenchman wearing a bowler hat.

'Here's your passenger,' he said. 'Take-off in half an hour's time. Good luck!'

It was so casual that the Frenchman might have been a civil servant who required flying back to Base. He spoke little English and seemed a most unlikely saboteur. They discussed their mission briefly; despite his broken English the little man appeared extremely competent, and had a brief-case with him. 'Dynamite,' he said cryptically when Biggles stared at it.

'How is he planning to return?' Biggles asked Major Raymond.

'Oh, that's his business,' he replied. 'He has his own ways of getting back across the Lines.'

'Why don't I wait for him?' said Biggles.

'Far too dangerous. They'd be bound to spot you.'

Biggles accepted this, but was worried at the thought of this fat, heroic little Frenchman – who rather reminded him of his old friend Captain Lovell – having to risk the guns and wire of no man's land.

'Tell him I'll return for him at dawn,' he said. 'We'll make a rendezvous and I'll be there.'

'On your head be it if you want to take the risk,' said Major Raymond.

It was a tricky piece of flying, for plainly there was no room for error, but luckily Biggles had already had a chance to reconnoitre the bridge in daylight earlier that morning, and to memorise the landmarks and the field near the river where he had to land. Luckily there was a moon – and Biggles had a knack for this sort of precision flying.

He gave the thumbs up to the Frenchman – and the Frenchman, from his seat in the front cockpit, solemnly raised his bowler hat.

The flight took less than half an hour, and Biggles was relieved that the German anti-aircraft guns took no notice of this solitary aircraft crossing the Lines at 5,000 feet. But he was taking no chances. He could not risk alerting the German guards on the bridge, and before he reached the long pale ribbon of the Aisne, he cut his engine and came in to land in a slow and silent glide.

It was the sort of landing every pilot dreads. Biggles had no way of knowing if there were trip wires stretched across the field, or if a German ambush was already waiting for them. But they were lucky, and the bus-like F.E.2 made a perfect three-point landing.

'Six a.m. sharp, I'll be there,' whispered Biggles as the Frenchman, with considerable agility, heaved himself and his black bag over the side of the cockpit and landed on the grass.

'*D'accord*,' he answered. Biggles watched the bowler hat go bobbing off across the field, and waited nervously until the Frenchman reached the shelter of the hedge before starting up the engine. There was a row of trees at the far end of the field, and the wheels of the F.E.2 scraped through them as it took off in the darkness, turned and sped for home. This time there was some anti-aircraft fire and Biggles wondered if the Germans had been put on the alert for him.

He had five hours to wait before returning, and it says much for the state of Biggles' eighteen-year-old nerves that within ten minutes of landing back at base, he was rolled up in his bunk and instantly asleep. The next he knew, his batman, holding a cup of tea, was shaking him on the shoulder and saying sternly, 'Five o'clock, sir. Time to rise and shine!'

It was a cold and cheerless morning, and Biggles began to wish that he had taken Major Raymond's advice and let the Frenchman find his own way back. But a promise was a promise, even if it meant rising at that unearthly hour. His aircraft was refuelled and waiting, and soon he was across the Lines and heading for the Aisne as dawn was breaking. He followed his earlier routine, cutting his engine and gliding in towards the field, and then glanced at his watch. Six o'clock exactly. 'How's that for timing!' he thought to himself.

Already there was sufficient light for Biggles to survey the landscape, and as he did so something caught his eye – a movement in a nearby field. He looked again and suddenly made out, in the shadow of a line of trees, a row of horsemen – German cavalry. By now he was approaching the rendezvous, and was just about to switch on his engine and escape from what was obviously a trap, when something else caught his eye – a figure in the middle of the field, waving at him. His man was obviously there and waiting for him to take him off to safety. At whatever risk, he felt he had to land and pick him up.

He took a swift glance at the German cavalry in the nearby field. They had spotted him, and were already galloping to where he aimed to land, but the figure in the field was still waving at him.

'Can't let the fellow down,' thought Biggles to himself. 'He'd never trust an Englishman again.' He pushed the joystick forward, started the engine to be ready for an instant take-off once the Frenchman was aboard, and aimed for the centre of the field.

But as he swept in to land, a strange thing happened. A second figure darted from the edge of the field and sprinted towards the waving man. Biggles could see he had a gun. There was a flash, the first man fell and as the aircraft rumbled to a halt Biggles could see the man who had fired more plainly. He wore a large black bowler hat.

'Bonjour monsieur,' the Frenchman shouted cheerfully. 'Like all you English, you are only just in time.'

'But who's the man you shot?' shouted Biggles above the roar of his engine.

'A German agent. They must have known you were coming and he was trying to decoy you down.' The Frenchman heaved himself aboard as Biggles opened up the throttle. 'Off we go, *mon vieux*, unless you wish to end up at the wrong end of a German firing squad.'

Biggles required no second bidding, for by now the first of the

German horsemen were barely forty yards away, whilst bullets from their carbines buzzed like angry wasps around the cockpit. There was nothing for it but to fly straight at them, hoping they would have the sense to scatter – which to Biggles' satisfaction was exactly what occurred.

'The Boche cavalry's no match for an F.E.2,' he chuckled to himself as he soared above the milling horsemen, waved debonairly at them with a well-gloved hand, banked the plane and headed off for home and the three-course breakfast that he knew was waiting for him in the Mess.

'If Way has finished off the Cooper's marmalade,' he told himself, 'I'll kill the wretched fellow.'

Once back at Base – after Biggles had performed his customary immaculate three-pointer – the little Frenchman gave a courtly bow and said, 'My thanks, *jeune homme*. You saved my life and taught those filthy German cavalry a lesson they won't forget. I trust we'll meet again.'

'Delighted to have been of some assistance,' Biggles modestly replied, and watched as the little man went trotting off towards a waiting Staff car. Suddenly he almost envied him, Frenchman and civilian though he was, for he was certainly extremely 'game' – even old Captain Lovell would have admitted that – and in the middle of this massive European war, he was managing to live a life of high adventure. During that night's brief contact with him, Biggles had experienced excitement such as he had never before known. Compared with him the fellows in the Mess appeared extremely dull, and even though the Cooper's marmalade had not been finished, Biggles felt restless and dissatisfied. He had a brief word of congratulation from Major Raymond, but that was all, and though he knew that thanks in part to him the bridge across the Aisne was totally destroyed, Biggles feared that this would be the last he would ever see of the world of sabotage and Air Intelligence.

During the weeks that followed, Biggles' relations with the remainder of the Squadron – particularly with Major Paynter – deteriorated rapidly, although Lieutenant Way did his best to intercede for him.

'The boy's all right,' he'd say to Paynter. 'He's just a bit too eager and reckless, but the fact remains that he's the best damned flier we've got.'

But Paynter now referred to him quite openly as 'the schoolboy wonder', and pointedly refused to recommend him for the M.C. which Biggles had obviously earned. 'He just thinks this war is a confounded game,' Paynter would grumble. 'He needs to be taught a lesson.' Others would say he was a lunatic, a glory-seeker, an adventurer, and though Way attempted to get through to Biggles – 'Calm down,' he'd say, 'just take it easy, and for God's sake be a little tactful with the others,' – Biggles refused to listen. The truth was that sensitivity and tact were not in his vocabulary.

In his attempt to 'teach the boy a lesson', Paynter now put him on the most routine of tasks – 'art obs' – artillery observation, shuttling back and forth across the Lines and radioing targets for the guns. It was hazardous – the F.E.2s were sitting ducks for the German *Jagdstaffeln* in the neighbourhood – and it was also deadly boring, particularly for anyone of Biggles' temperament. After three weeks of this he lost his temper. It had been a particularly frustrating day, with Biggles giving 'fixes' on a German battery, which the English Artillery continually missed. Any other pilot would have shrugged his shoulders, cursed the gunners and retired to the Mess for a Scotch and soda. But not Biggles.

No sooner had he landed back at Base, than he shouted at Lieutenant Way, 'I'm sick to death of this. We're going to deal with that battery ourselves.'

Way urged caution, which was understandable as he had to sit in the front cockpit whatever the escapade Biggles embarked on, but Biggles was emphatic.

'Refuel the old bus, and stick a pair of 112-pounder bombs on the racks. And make it snappy!' shouted Biggles to the Flight Sergeant. While this was going on, he got on the Mess telephone to the Artillery. 'I'm sick and tired of giving you ham-fisted idiots instructions all afternoon and then watching you bungle them,' he shouted. 'I'm going to deal with that blasted battery myself.'

(It was only later that he realised he was talking to the Colonel – not that it would have made a scrap of difference in the state he was in.)

It was a crazy venture from the start, for by this time the enemy was thoroughly alerted, and had ringed the battery with anti-aircraft guns and filled the sky with fighters. But nothing would stop Biggles now. Way saw his set, white face, and decided not to argue – even though the sky seemed to be one vast inferno.

Biggles attempted no finesse this time, but flew straight at his target, ignoring everything – the shrapnel that came zinging through the wings, the rifle fire directed from below, the threat of German Albatrosses in the sky above. After three weeks of 'art obs' he knew this section of the Front like his own back yard, and long before he reached the German battery he had put the F.E.2 into a straight dive from 6,000 feet.

It was a moment of supreme excitement, the sort of moment Biggles had begun to live for, with the wind tearing past his goggles and screaming in the guy-wires of the plane. The anti-aircraft fire was all around them, and Way was returning fire with his Lewis gun, scattering the German gunners from the gun-pits. Once again, time stood still and every detail etched itself on Biggles' memory. Down, down he went, the Beardmore engine thundering and the ground hurtling towards him. Way had long given up all hope of getting out alive, when Biggles eased back the joystick, jerked at the toggle to release the bombs, and felt the exhilarating lift from the impact just below as the German guns exploded. Honour was saved, and three weeks' boredom was atoned for. Now let the Germans do their worst!

In fact it was not the Germans that Biggles had to fear. Apart from a close shave with a formation of twenty Albatrosses, the journey back to Base was uneventful. But once he landed the real trouble started. The Artillery Colonel had already been in touch with Major Paynter to complain about the brash young officer who had called him a ham-fisted idiot. (The fact that the same young officer had saved innumerable lives by silencing the German battery scarcely came into it.) The Artillery had been insulted, and Major Paynter was already waiting on the tarmac – fuming.

'Recklessness,' 'overstepping orders,' 'endangering an aircraft and the life of a brother officer' – these were the spluttered words that Major Paynter used to describe Biggles' exploit. And, having reprimanded him, he added just one further touch of senior officer's pettiness.

'You will return this afternoon to the scene of this unfortunate affair, taking a camera with you. I shall require a photograph of the battery you bombed upon my desk by one hour after sunset. Is that clear?'

Biggles saluted, and held his tongue, knowing that there was little point arguing against a martinet like Paynter. But Biggles had never grown used to reprimands from anyone, and that day was probably the nearest he ever came to mutiny. Just the same, the Major had his photographs before sunset.

This exploit rather brought things to a head in the uneasy relationship between Biggles and the rest of 169, for by now there were two clear parties in the Mess. The larger, led by Major Paynter, was opposed to Biggles and its main aim was to 'cut him down to size', as one of them expressed it. And the smaller party, led by Lieutenant Way, while admitting most of Biggles' faults, insisted that his skill and courage more than made up for them.

'Of course the boy's a lunatic,' said Way in a discussion in the bar that night, 'but he flies like an angel and he kills Germans. You can't condemn him just because he doesn't drink and hasn't got a sense of humour.'

For several days the arguments went on, and then, in that dreadful early summertime of 1917, all argument became superfluous as every man in 169 suddenly found himself with more important things to think about. The British High Command had launched the great, ill-fated 'push' that ended in the slaughter of Paschendaele, and 169 was thrown in as well, providing non-stop ground support for the advancing British troops.

This was the grimmest fighting 169 had ever seen – for Biggles, it would always be the low point of his life. For days on end the Squadron kept up unremitting pressure on the enemy, bombing and strafing troops, artillery and anything that moved in German territory. Single planes were flying nine and ten sorties daily, and the wear and tear on men and on machines was frightful. It was as if the war in the air had suddenly come down to earth, and no one could escape the noise and stink of battle. Losses were heavy – four of the Squadron's aircraft failed to return in the first three days of the fighting – and even Biggles' iron nerve began to waver with the strain. In his sleep he seemed to hear the rattle of his Lewis guns and see the nightmare faces of the troops he killed. He knew for certain that it would only be a few days before he joined them.

He had one slight consolation. Owing to the damage to machines, he had been given a new Bristol Fighter as replacement for his battle-scarred old F.E.2. It was a faster aircraft – and more of a match for the German Halberstadts and Albatrosses – and flying it revived his earliest ambitions to join a first-rate combat squadron in place of all this uninspiring work supporting the Artillery and Infantry. So Biggles began to make inquiries about a transfer. But before they came to anyhting the inevitable occurred – on one of his sorties from St Omer, the Bristol was hit by anti-aircraft fire, the engine badly damaged, and Biggles and Lieutenant Way were forced to hike across the mud of no-man's-land before returning to their Squadron two days later.

It was the loss of the Bristol Fighter which really spelt the end of Biggles' time with 169. He was without an aircraft, much of the Squadron was in hospital – or dead – and he was barely on speaking terms by now with Paynter. So when he was suddenly presented with the offer of a posting to a brand new squadron, No. 266, at Maranique, he jumped at it, even though it meant foregoing two weeks' leave in 'Blighty' to which he was now entitled.

When he told Way of his decision his old observer laughed. 'I always said that you were mad. This proves it.'

'Why?' said Biggles, who was genuinely surprised at his reaction. 'Who on earth would lose the chance of flying Sopwith Pups just for a fortnight's lousy leave in England?'

'I would, for one,' laughed Way, 'but off you go and try not to be too daft. You won't have me to keep an eye on you.'

Biggles was instantly at home in 266, which had a very different atmosphere from the squadron he was leaving. Instead of the irascible Major Paynter, there was an easy-going Dubliner called Major Mullen as Commanding Officer, and from the very start he seemed to sum Biggles up.

'I've heard a bit about you, James my lad,' he said. (In all the months that Biggles was with 169, Paynter had never once addressed him by his Christian name.) 'And on the whole I think that I approve of what I hear. But all the same you need to learn the difference between foolhardiness and courage. Also I insist that all my pilots are fully trained to fly their aircraft before I let them loose upon the enemy. This is a squadron of professionals. Remember that. Now come and have a drink!'

During the next ten days Biggles spent all his time getting acquainted with his new aeroplane, the single-seater Sopwith Pup. This was the aircraft which seasoned pilots called 'near perfect' and 'impeccable', and Biggles soon agreed with them. After the heavy old F.E.2, the Pup was light, fast and wonderfully manoeuvrable, and with its forward firing Vickers gun the pilot could take on the German Albatrosses on equal terms. Everything depended on the pilot's skill, and a few days' flying the Sopwith was all that Biggles needed to recover from the gruelling weeks in 169. Here in his brand-new cockpit he felt renewed and ready for whatever fate still had in store for him.

Major Mullen personally checked Biggles out before allowing him to fly in action – and even then the mission that he gave him was a relatively painless one, flying cross-country back to his old base at St Omer to make arrangements with the Aircraft Repair Section for returning a reconditioned fighter plane. No trouble was expected, but as a matter of routine the Vickers gun was loaded and the plane given its full load of fuel – which in the circumstances was just as well. Shortly after take-off, Biggles spotted Allied anti-aircraft fire above the Lines – sure sign of a German aircraft in the vicinity. The shells were bursting high, at something like 15,000 feet, and they were considerably off his course. But although Biggles had no orders to engage in combat, it was not in his nature to miss a chance of 'bagging' a German combat plane, particularly when he was flying a brand new Sopwith Pup which he had never before tried against the enemy.

He instantly changed course – forgetting all his orders about reaching St Omer – and, aiming for the German section of the Lines, soon had 10,000 feet upon his altimeter, from which height he could now make out the German aircraft clearly. It was a Rumpler two-seater – something of a rarity which the Germans used for high altitude reconaissance – and Biggles had no hope of catching it. For several minutes the two planes were flying parallel, with the Rumpler having the advantage of 2,000 feet in height, and showing not the slightest sign of yielding it to the

solitary Sopwith Pup. But then the temptation to attack must
have beome too much for the German pilot, for suddenly Biggles
saw the Rumpler bank, then dive towards him, firing a long and
ineffectual burst. This was a great mistake, for the Rumpler lost
its tactical advantage, and the Pup was more manoeuvrable than
the big two-seater. The German pilot must have seen this, for he
rapidly veered off and made for home – but not before Biggles
had the chance of one long decisive burst of machine-gun fire in
return.

It was really a forlorn hope, for the Rumpler was
theoretically well out of range, but Biggles' luck was in. One of his
bullets hit the observer in the rear cockpit, and another must
have struck the engine, for he saw the Rumpler's propeller stop,
and as he swung the Pup into a dive to deliver the *coup de grâce*, the
German pilot raised his hands in a gesture of surrender.

This was an unheard-of thing to do. 'Rather death than
dishonour' was supposed to be the motto of the German pilots,
and Biggles could not help despising such cowardly behaviour.
On the other hand, it gave him the chance of capturing a
German aircraft single-handed. He signalled to the German
pilot, pointed to the Allied Lines, and, just to show that he meant
business, fired a short burst above the Rumpler – which instantly
obeyed his orders. For the next ten minutes, as the Rumpler
glided down, Biggles kept buzzing round its tail just to make sure
there were no tricks. It made a perfect landing in a field – with
Biggles in his Sopwith Pup close alongside – and, thanks to some
British troops who were there to greet the German, he was
prevented from damaging the plane.

This was accounted an impressive coup for Biggles, since
intelligence had been hoping for a captured Rumpler for some
time. The field where they had landed was not far from base at
Maranique, and whilst Biggles was waiting for the ambulance to
arrive for the injured German observer, the C.O., Major Mullen,
drove up in a staff car with, of all people, Major Raymond in the
seat beside him.

Mullen was effusive in his Irish way, heartily congratulating
Biggles on his capture, but Major Raymond was inscrutable as
ever.

'Ah, young Bigglesworth,' he remarked, peering at him
through his monocle. 'Still doing the unexpected, I perceive.

You'd better watch out, or you'll soon be working for Intelligence yourself.'

He smiled knowingly – and Biggles wondered what this strange man really meant. Not that he had much time for speculation as the very next day he found himself fighting for his life in combat with some of the greatest German aces of the war. He admitted later that as a newcomer to this sort of fighting, he was lucky to have escaped alive.

It all started unexcitingly enough, when Biggles found himself detailed to take part in a routine dawn patrol. There were five Sopwith Pups, led by one of the most experienced pilots in the R.F.C., a beetle-browed Ulsterman called Mahoney. The first hour of the patrol was uneventful. It was a lovely late-summer morning, and with the aircraft flying perfectly, an azure sky above and nothing but the distant rumble of the guns below, the war seemed very far away. Then Mahoney saw a British spotter plane on the far side of the Lines engaged in combat with three German Albatrosses, and suddenly the hunt was on.

This was the most exciting moment of an engagement – when the Flight Commander dips his wings, and all five aircraft, engines screaming, swoop down in perfect formation onto an enemy below them. Biggles was in his element, although it was soon quite clear that the pursuers were just too late. The British spotter plane had plummeted to earth, a blazing wreck, and the three Albatrosses were already streaking off to Base – with several miles' headstart on the Pups.

Biggles was in the rear-left position of the formation, and as he started easing his aircraft out of its dive, something made him glance behind. Just why he did this he would never know. Perhaps it was some instinct that he learned in the jungle as a boy. Certainly it saved his life, and the lives of the remainder of the flight. Diving down behind him out of the glare of the morning sun, was a German high patrol of twenty Fokker triplanes.

Again he relied on instinct now. None of the other British planes had seen the Germans and Biggles had no way of warning them. There was no time for second thoughts as Biggles kicked the rudder bar, and trusting that his Pup would stand the strain, swung the sturdy little aircraft round on its axis. It was a move of total desperation for he was now flying straight through the middle of the packed formation of the enemy, but as sometimes happens in emergencies, his desperation worked. For several seconds Biggles thought that he must surely crash head-on with the leading triplane, and for that moment, faced with what seemed certain death, his mind was as clear and sharp as it had been when he faced his tiger in Garhwal. He had no sense of fear and held his plane unwaveringly on course with his machine-gun chattering away before him.

Suddenly it was all over. The triplane that was roaring down upon him swerved and sailed past, missing his wing by inches. The rest of the formation followed in their tight-packed dive, and Biggles was aware of the gaudy patterns of their fuselages as they went flashing past. The triplane that had nearly hit him was bright scarlet.

By now Mahoney and the remainder of the flight had seen what was happening and had split formation to engage the enemy. Biggles swooped back to join them, and for twenty minutes the dogfight raged. A further flight of Bristol Fighters soon joined in, the sky was full of isolated aircraft diving, weaving and pursuing one another, and Biggles was aware of firing, then swerving off, then firing again at any target that came near him.

Then suddenly the fight was over – almost as soon as it began. The aircraft had lost height in the *mêlée*, and Mahoney, now alarmed to find his aircraft well over German territory, signalled to disengage. Most of the German squadron had disappeared by now, and half an hour later Biggles was landing safely back at Base.

This was his first experience of a full-scale 'dogfight' in the air, and it left him strangely unaffected, even when Mahoney landed, slapped him on the back and cheerfully congratulated him.

'Great work, my boy!' he said, and smiled his strange crooked smile (all broken teeth and shaggy eyebrows), 'You realise who you nearly got?'

Biggles shook his head.

'The bold bad Baron! Von Richthofen in person! He was in that scarlet triplane that you nearly hit. It isn't every day you meet him and survive to tell the tale.'

By lunchtime the full story of the fight was in. Two of the Pups had failed to return and three of the Bristol Fighters had been shot down as well. According to observers on the ground, the Germans had lost seven aircraft.

'Not bad for a morning's shooting,' Major Mullen said to Biggles and Mahoney in the Mess. 'I'd better buy you both a drink. I think you've earned it.' There was no mention of the two dead members of the Squadron. Like their aircraft, they had been 'written off' already. There was no point at all in being sentimental.

Biggles, however, found it difficult to dismiss them quite so lightly. Perhaps this was a sign of strain. Perhaps he should have had that fortnight's leave when it was offered. It had been all right while he was actually in the air, but now he had a sense of dreadful let-down and depression. He had seen far too much of war and death in the last ten months since he had been in France. Besides, he was haunted by the thought that the two pilots ought not to have died, and that the battle they had fought that morning had been a terrible mistake. Von Richthofen and his men had laid a trap for them; the flight had sailed into it, and but for luck and Biggles' quick reactions, not two, but all five members of the flight would have fallen to the German Spandaus.

This was the thought that preyed on his mind, and finally he brought himself to mention it to Major Mullen. Had he been Major Paynter, this would have been interpreted as one more sign that 'the boy wonder' was once more 'getting above himself', but Mullen was intelligent enough to spot the genius in Biggles, and make allowances accordingly.

'Trap?' he said. 'You think the Huns had set up a trap for you this morning?'

'Certain of it, sir,' said Biggles quickly. 'I think the whole thing was arranged. The first three Albatrosses were a decoy to lure us right under the noses of Richthofen's squadron.'

' huh!' said Major Mullen thoughtfully, 'You may be right.'

'Whether I am or not, I think we ought to try something of the sort upon the Hun.'

'And how do we do that?'

'In India they would use a goat as a decoy to catch a tiger while the hunters waited in the tree above. I think we could do the same, but it'll need several squadrons. One squadron would attack across the German Lines in the direction of Douai and hang around long enough to bring Richthofen and his boys out in pursuit. Then they would lead them back across the Lines where we would have two further squadrons flying at 12,000 feet waiting for them. With any luck the Huns would have split formation by then and we could even catch the stragglers as they made for Base.'

'You think that it would work?' asked Major Mullen.

'I think it's worth a try – and I wouldn't mind another crack at Richthofen, to tell the truth,' said Biggles.

This was the beginning of the celebrated 'Big Show', which three R.F.C. squadrons finally staged against the enemy some two weeks later, with Major Mullen leading 266 in person. Earlier in the afternoon a group of F.E.2s had lured the German 'circus' up from their field at Douai, and Biggles had the satisfaction of being in the first of the formations of Sopwith Pups which swept down on the two unsuspecting triplanes as they were coming in to land at Douai. Neither had a chance against the fire-power of nine British aircraft firing together, and they broke up before their pilots could have realised what hit them.

It wasn't particularly sporting, but Biggles never had believed in sport at school, and it made even less sense in the air. He often used to say that the jungle near Garhwal was a better training ground for combat flying than the playing fields of Malton Hall, for in the cockpit, just as in the jungle, only one rule applied, the cruellest and simplest rule of all – kill or be killed. 'That was the rule von Richthofen and his fliers always followed – and so did we. So both sides knew what they were up against.'

Certainly, that afternoon the British pilots did their share of killing, and seven of the German triplanes were officially accounted for at no loss to the British squadrons.

'Highly satisfactory,' was Major Mullen's verdict on the whole affair, and Biggles' reputation as a 'lunatic' began to change. He was becoming cunning – 'one of those fliers who can use their brains,' as Major Mullen said approvingly to Mahoney in the Mess that night.

'Perhaps he won't kill himself after all,' replied the Ulsterman.

'I wouldn't count on that,' said Mullen.

But during that late summer with 266, Biggles' charmed life continued. Throughout the long patrols, the dogfights and diversions, he seemed almost indestructible. Mahoney christened him 'the machine', and now there began to be something faintly inhuman in the way he fought. His flying was near perfect. His instinct never seemed to fail him in the thickest dogfight, and however near he flew to death, his boyish smile would never falter. He used to say his one regret was that he never came face to face again with the scarlet triplane of von Richthofen.

But beneath the confidence and schoolboy eagerness, something was going wrong.

Mahoney, who was an understanding man, was probably the first to spot the signs of what was happening.

'Ease up, young Biggles,' he would say. 'Come out and have a drink with me tonight in Maranique. We could even find ourselves a couple of nice girls. A woman would do you good.'

But Biggles always grinned and made the same excuse. 'There aren't any nice girls left in Maranique, and you can't mix drink and flying.'

'I can.' Mahoney would reply.

'You're lucky. You're an Irishman!' Biggles would answer gravely, and next morning he would always be the first man down for dawn patrol, and when bleary-eyed Mahoney shambled across the tarmac Biggles would smile at him and primly shake his head.

'Rough night, Mahoney?' he would shout. And Mahoney, most tolerant of men, would softly answer.

'Wonderful! I found a lovely girl and she's got a sister who can't wait to meet you.'

'Later, when I'm not so busy,' Biggles would reply as his engine started up. And Mahoney would wonder how much longer Biggles could go on without cracking up.

The truth was that Biggles, in his single-minded way, was still in love with flying. He remained scared of women, and all the feelings and emotions which might otherwise have found an outlet in a normal love-affair were centred on his Sopwith Pup. Dedicated, chaste as any novice monk, he had no knowledge of the world, and precious little knowledge of himself. He had no real friends, no hobbies and no vices – and there was no give in his lonely, locked-in nature. Mahoney saw this but he could not communicate with Biggles now. All he could do was wait, and hope the boy would not destroy himself.

In the autumn of 1917, Squadron 266 was re-equipped with Sopwith Camels – a more powerful, more lethal aircraft than the Sopwith Pup, but one that took a lot of flying. Once again Biggles proved himself a virtuoso pilot, and seemed to have adapted to this latest aircraft faster than anybody in the Squadron. For several weeks he flew it with his usual skill, and then at the beginning of October the whole Squadron was involved in a dawn patrol that turned into one of the most vicious dogfights anyone had ever seen. It was appalling weather right across the Front and 266 was ambushed by two German squadrons far across the German Lines.

As usual, Biggles' nerve sustained him through the battle and at one point he was in the thick of things with twenty German triplanes in the crowded sky around him. He fought like an automaton, looping and diving and evading certain death, with his twin Vickers guns blazing at the enemy. He had no recollection of how many German planes he had hit, and then, as often happened in a dogfight of this sort, the enemy appeared to vanish. The cloud closed in around Biggles, and he was flying on his own. Then he noticed that a bullet had destroyed his compass.

Suddenly, he was scared. It was an emotion he had never felt in an aeroplane before, and it shook him. He had no idea of his position or direction, and felt lonelier than ever in his life before. At first he could see no landmarks, but then, miraculously, there was a break in the cloud and below him he could make out another Sopwith Camel. Presumably it knew where it was heading, and Biggles followed in a shallow dive which brought him out below the bank of cloud. By now the other plane had disappeared. Then he saw it, still descending, and as he overhauled it he could see the reason. The propeller was no longer turning and its pilot was already looking for a place to land.

This was not difficult, for the countryside was a patchwork of neat green fields, and as Biggles circled overhead, he saw the leather-coated British pilot make a perfect landing, clamber out, then fire his Very pistol at the plane to stop the enemy retrieving

it. For Biggles there was only one thing to do – rescue the pilot –
and in a moment he had landed by the blazing wreck and was
beckoning to him. As the man came running to the plane, Biggles
recognised him. It was Mahoney.

'Jump in, you idle Irishman,' he shouted, for he had spotted a
lorry-load of Germans driving down the road to find out what
had happened.

'Thank God you're a little 'un, Biggles my boy,' the fourteen-
stone Mahoney answered as he squeezed his great bulk into the
single cockpit with Biggles somehow wedged beside him. It was a
bumpy take-off, and the German troops were firing by now, but
the overloaded Camel was soon soaring above the startled enemy
and then up into the mist towards the safety of the British Lines.

On that journey back to Base, Mahoney noticed something
strange about Biggles. His hand was trembling and his teeth were
tightly clenched. He spoke not a word, and when they landed
back at Maranique, and Biggles was surrounded by a crowd of
half the Squadron on the tarmac to congratulate him on the
rescue, he still said nothing. He was still trembling and when
Major Mullen saw his ashen face he recognised the signs.

'Off to bed with you, James my boy,' he said. 'You look done
in.'

'I'm fine,' said Biggles gamely.

'You're nothing of the sort,' said Mullen. And that evening,
when he saw him in the Mess, the Major said, 'Ah, James, I think
it's time you had a little leave, and Mahoney agrees with me.'

'But sir, I don't want leave. I want to go on flying.'

'I don't care what you want, I'm ordering you a fortnight back
in Blighty. And take my advice, while you're there enjoy yourself.
There are more things in life than aeroplanes.'

3

Women and War

Biggles did not particularly enjoy his leave. It was over a year since he had been in England, and he felt out of place in London during that fourth winter of the war. He was now eighteen and a half, and since leaving school his entire life had been spent in the fighting and the danger of the Western Front. It had hardened him beyond his years. It had also narrowed him. Flying had become his life, and he had no conception of what pleasures there could be beyond the cockpit and an evening in the Mess.

'I was incredibly green still in those days,' he admitted later. 'When I stepped off the train at Victoria, London was like a foreign city and I was completely lost. I was staying in a small hotel off Piccadilly, but I knew nobody and had never been so lonely in my life.'

Mahoney had told him to enjoy himself, but he had really no idea how to go about it – and wasn't sure he wanted to, to judge by what he saw around him. He went to a musical comedy at The Lyceum, and was very bored. He nearly had a fight with three Australians who called him 'Blondie' – Biggles was in mufti at the time – and suggested he should join the Boy Scouts and defeat the Kaiser. He dined alone one evening in the Carlton Grill and felt outraged at the soft life of the wealthy, overfed civilians around him. As he was leaving, one fat lady in a low-cut evening dress gave him a white feather, for which he thanked her and replied that he would treasure it. One of the hotel porters even offered to

63

find him what he called 'a nice young lady to keep you company', but the overpainted harridan who finally appeared and promised him 'a lovely time' would probably have proved too much even for Mahoney's somewhat basic tastes. For somebody as fastidious and virginal as Biggles, she appeared repellent, and when he had disengaged himself – no easy task – he quietly resolved to stick to aeroplanes, for as he put it later, 'they seemed prettier and far less trouble than the female sex'. He also decided there and then that he had had enough of London, and for the remainder of his leave went off to his schoolboy place of refuge – old General Bigglesworth's in Norfolk.

By now his M.C. had come through. It was officially awarded for his rescue of Mahoney, and although like all Front-Line fliers Biggles pretended to despise such decorations – 'sent up with the rations' was the usual way they referred to them – he could not resist wearing the brand-new ribbon on his uniform. He had been promoted Captain as well, so that when he stepped off the little train at Norwich he felt that in the General's eyes he had finally atoned for leaving his Rifle Regiment for the R.F.C. He had almost evened up the score with his distinguished brother too.

Not that the General seemed to notice, for the old man was now in roaring form and spent the entire evening over dinner grumbling about the war, the generals, and particularly the politicians. Their chief offence was that they had apparently turned down the General's own attempt to re-enlist. He was in his seventies by now, but had dyed his hair – 'it looked extremely odd', said Biggles – and had stumped up to Whitehall and tried to join the fray. 'It must have been that blithering Lloyd George,' he shouted. 'What does a Welsh mountebank like that know about the principles of war? He's scared that men like me will show him up for the fraud he is. No wonder that we're in the mess we're in.'

But with the port, the old man calmed down sufficiently to notice Biggles' M.C. ribbon and congratulate him. But even then poor Biggles' triumph was short-lived. 'Pity, just the same,' the General said, 'that you didn't stay put in a decent regiment like your brother Charles. He's doing very well, I hear. Just won the D.S.O. in that muck-up on the Somme, *and* been promoted Major. Grand chap, your brother!'

It was the same old story. Charles had beaten him again, but

Biggles wisely kept his disappointment to himself and turned the conversation to the other members of the family. Throughout his time in France he had heard nothing of his father, but the General kept in touch with him. 'Poor old chap,' he said (although in fact John Henry Bigglesworth was a good twelve years younger than the General) 'dreadful trouble with malaria and his heart's affected. Last I heard from him he was on his way back to the U.K. When you're over next you'll see him.'

Biggles wondered if he wanted to. He had managed for so long without a father that the whole idea of coping with him now was not attractive. It was his mother that he really longed to see, but naturally the General had no news of her, and for the remainder of the week that Biggles spent with his uncle there were other things to occupy his mind. The pheasants were magnificent that year, but to the General's disappointment, Biggles had little taste for shooting them. 'I think I've had enough of shooting in the last few months,' he said. The General shook his head as if to say the boy was going soft. The General also had a new invention with which he was terrorising the whole neighbourhood – a radio-controlled anti-aircraft rocket. 'Like most of the old boy's brainwaves, it was a trifle premature,' said Biggles later. 'Probably as well it was. If it had really worked there'd not have been much future left for chaps like me.'

After his time in Norfolk, Biggles still had a few days before returning to his Squadron, and had planned to see the Laceys at their house in Sussex. He had not had much time to write to them whilst at the Front, and had no idea what to expect when he went down to Lewes. His Aunt Priscilla had been somewhat guarded on the telephone, but he was looking forward to seeing his absent-minded botanising uncle once again, and even his spoiled young cousin, Algy. Rather to his surprise, his uncle met him at the station with an ancient pony trap that had been taken out of moth-balls, since the motorcar was laid up for the war.

Lord Lacey seemed as vague and bumbling as ever with his long dundreary whiskers and his big checked overcoat. For a while he chatted on about the scandalous way the local farmers had been ploughing up the Downs. 'Never a thought for the effect on the flora of the district. Still, such is war, and one must make one's sacrifices.' Biggles agreed that it was very hard, and then his uncle suddenly said, 'Your dear Aunt thought that I should break the news to you so that it wouldn't be too great a shock.'

'What news?' said Biggles, thoroughly alarmed.

'We have a visitor – or should I say a guest. Someone we haven't seen for years. My sister, Catherine – that is to say, your mother.'

Biggles' heart began to pound as fast as if he were facing twenty Fokker triplanes in a dogfight.

'My what?' he said incredulously.

'My dear boy,' said his Lordship. 'I do realise the shock that this must be for you. And I realise how you must feel, but life has not been easy for her. She is a widow now. Her husband died last year in France and we have offered her a home at least until the war is over.'

Biggles was completely lost for words. This was the moment he had dreamt about for years, the longed-for rediscovery of his beloved mother. But now that it had come he wasn't sure he wanted it.

'What is she like?' he asked at last.

Lord Lacey smiled. 'She's changed a lot, but underneath I think she's probably the same as ever. Life never really can defeat people like your mother.'

'Thank God for that,' said Biggles quietly.

She was waiting in the drive to greet them, and at first he barely recognised her. The mother he remembered was the youthful, fair-haired goddess who had come to kiss him goodnight every evening in the nursery. Now she was a plump, grey-haired matron in a dark-green overcoat. Could it possibly be her?

He jumped down from the trap, and for a moment they stood staring at each other.

'James?' she said tentatively.

'Mother,' he replied, not certain if he should laugh or cry, and then they were in each other's arms.

'Thank God I've found you!' she exclaimed.

Biggles' rediscovery of his mother did not turn out to be as joyful an affair as he imagined, and though it would be pleasant to record an idyllic reunion after all the years that they had been apart, it did not happen.

'Perhaps deep down I still resented her for leaving us,' Biggles admitted in old age when he brought himself to talk about it all. 'And I suppose that I reminded her of many things that she would rather have forgotten.'

The truth was that they were strangers. Biggles had been living for so long with the image of a dream-like mother that he was not prepared for the reality. For Catherine Lacey – or the Widow Duclos as she had now become – was as dominating and tiresome as ever, but she no longer had the beauty which had previously disguised her faults. Even that first night at the Laceys, over dinner, she managed to annoy her new-found son.

'But surely, James,' she said, 'the Flying Corps is not particularly smart. I think that I must do my best to get you transferred to the Guards.'

'I'd rather that you didn't,' he replied.

'Oh, but why not?' she asked quickly.

'Because I happen to love flying,' he replied.

'Young Algy's just the same,' said Aunt Priscilla, trying to change the subject slightly. 'Since he's joined up, the only thing he wants to do is get a transfer from the Grenadiers to the R.F.C.'

'How very strange of him,' said Catherine, coldly.

Later, as she kissed her son goodnight, she smiled and said, 'Now that I've found you, darling James, I think the time has come to take you firmly in hand. You really do need looking after.'

How those words echoed in his ears for the remainder of his leave! For years now he had managed on his own and really pleased himself in everything he did. But now he had a mother, this had changed. Nothing was sacred any more – his friends, his underwear, his overdraft, and even his sex-life.

'James, darling, you are so uncouth,' she'd say and flash her brilliant smile at him. 'You need a really nice girl who'll take your mind off this beastly war.'

'I'm not so sure I want one,' he replied.

'So like your father,' was her answer, and before he left for France, Biggles endured interrogation upon almost every subject he held dear to him.

So it was probably as well that his leave ended when it did, and as he stepped aboard the Channel ferry he did so with a sense of freedom and relief. No more loneliness in London, no more comparisons with his brother Charles, and – for a time at least – no more questions from Mama!

'Biggles, my boy, you look exhausted,' said Mahoney as he slunk into the Mess that night.

'Did you find yourself a lovely girl?'

Biggles shook his head. 'No such luck! I found myself a mother, and now the Huns will come as quite a rest. Thank God for the enemy!'

For the next few days it was exhilarating to be back and flying once again. Despite the filthy weather and the depressing progress of the fighting in the trenches, Biggles had never felt so happy since he first joined 266. His old Sidcot flying suit was waiting for him like a faithful friend, and while he was away the mechanics had fitted a new Bentley engine into his Sopwith Camel. She flew like a bird, and as he took off on his first patrol he was like a man renewed. The strain and tension of the weeks before his leave were over, and more than ever now he felt that this was the only life he wanted. London, relatives, and those fat civilians he had seen on leave bored or disgusted him. He wanted nothing but the freedom of the skies and the excitement of the day's adventure.

But it was a slack time now for 266. There were two new Camel squadrons in the sector, clamouring for action on their own account. Mahoney was content to let them have it, but for Biggles life without its daily dose of action would have been unbearable.

'You know what you are, James my lad?' Mahoney said.

Biggles shook his head.

'A bloody flying addict. It's worse than taking to the bottle. You should watch it and relax.'

This was something Biggles could not do, and during the Christmas period he was continually nagging Major Mullen for some fresh assignment. Sometimes he got one and was happy. Twice he was 'lent' to Colonel Raymond (as he was now – he had been promoted) for a night-time 'drop' of Allied agents into Belgium. Both trips went off perfectly, and the excitement helped to keep the Bigglesworth adrenalin flowing. These operations also helped keep Biggles in the Colonel's eye. He even dined with him one night, and for the first time Biggles found that that cold strange man was almost human.

'Happy, Bigglesworth?' he asked, as he swirled his pale gold vintage brandy in a glass the size of a small goldfish bowl.

Biggles shrugged his shoulders.

'Life gets a little dull at times,' he said.

'Does it indeed?' the Colonel laughed. 'We'll soon change that for you. Ever thought of working for Intelligence?'

Biggles was instantly on his guard.

'Not if it means the end of flying,' he said quickly.

'Good Lord, no! That's the last thing we would want, but I'd like to think that we could call upon you for, shall we say, some more demanding operations if the need arose.'

'I'd enjoy that, sir,' said Biggles.

'Splendid,' said the Colonel.

But there was no immediate result of that evening's conversation. Christmas came, all operations ceased, and then the routine of the ordinary patrols continued.

Christmas was a trying time for Biggles. He never had enjoyed it as a festival. He disliked Christmas pudding, and the carols and the horseplay in the Mess embarrassed him. There was a parcel from his mother, which contained cigars, a novel by Ouida and two sets of woollen underwear. This was bad enough, but worse still was the Christmas letter he received from Aunt Priscilla. His cousin Algernon, she wrote, had got his transfer to the Flying Corps and had finished his basic training. He was already on his way to France, and she had pulled strings with the Air Board to have him sent to 266.

'The boy has always looked up to you,' she wrote, 'and I know that you will do your best to keep an eye on him. He's very young, and I would like to think that you will be an elder brother to him.'

Major Mullen roared with laughter at the news.

'Elder brother! That's a good one, James my boy!'

'But sir,' said Biggles, 'you must do something about it. The boy's a frightful weed, a real mother's darling. He's called Algernon Montgomery – and, by God, he looks like it!'

'Well, he can't help what he's called, poor fellow, and if he's as you say, he clearly does need looking after. I think you'd better have him in your flight.'

'My what?' said Biggles, suddenly aghast.

'James, remember you were young yourself once, and they say that blood is thicker than water.'

'Algy's isn't,' Biggles answered grimly, and stormed out of the Mess.

The following afternoon Algernon arrived. Biggles himself had just returned from a sortie over no-man's-land. For the third day running he had missed a German Halberstadt reconnaissance plane he had been after, and as he stumped across the tarmac in his flying gear, he was not in the best of tempers. A truck had drawn up beside the hangars and a lanky, freckled youth with overlong fair hair was strolling cheerfully towards him, peaked cap worn jauntily on the back of his head.

'Biggles!' he shouted. 'Wonderful to see you. The Mater told me you'd be here.'

Biggles stopped, and eyed him with disfavour.

'Lieutenant Lacey, I presume,' he said.

'Of course,' the youth replied, but Biggles cut him short.

'My name is Captain Bigglesworth,' he said icily. 'I am your Flight Commander. Get your kit to your room, report your arrival to the Adjutant, and meet me in the Mess in twenty minutes' time. I want a word with you.'

It was unusual for Biggles to pull rank on a younger flier in this way, but he had been thoroughly put out by having his young cousin wished upon him by his dominating aunt. There was also something about young Algy that annoyed him. But luckily, by the time they met in the Mess, Biggles had simmered down, deciding he must give the boy a chance.

He bought him a drink (Biggles noted with approval that he asked for ginger ale), then asked him how much flying he had done.

'Ten hours in Camels, fourteen in Avros,' he said proudly.

'Jumping Jehosaphat! Ten hours in a Camel and they think you're fit to face the enemy. Listen laddie, and listen carefully. Forget what they taught you back at training school. You start learning combat flying now with me. The Huns we're up against are von Kirtner's circus – Fokker triplanes. They're not as good as Richthofen's gang – you can thank your lucky stars for that. But they're mean and dangerous, and you can't afford mistakes. Tomorrow I will take you out to see the Lines, and I insist on certain rules. Rule number one – keep position in formation.

You'll be on my left, and stick there at all costs. An isolated plane is easy meat. Rule number two – keep your eyes peeled, and always watch the sun. That's where the opposition comes from if it gets the chance. And rule number three – if a Hun does get on your tail, don't try to get away. You won't. Go for him instantly. Give him everything you've got. Try and ram him. You'll see how quickly he'll get out of your way. And one last thing, if you ever meet a Hun head on, you don't give way. In 266 it isn't done. Leave it to him to give way to you.'

Algernon Montgomery seemed slightly dazed by all this good advice, and next day Biggles called him early for their tour of the Lines. He was not expecting trouble, and in fact had tended to exaggerate the risks from Kirtner's fliers. But as the two Camels took off from the airfield and headed east, Biggles was disturbed to see the banks of scattered cloud across the German territory – ideal cover for a lurking enemy. But Algernon Montgomery was on his best behaviour, keeping position close by Biggles' wing-tip as if his life depended on it. Once or twice Biggles glanced back at him, and the boy smiled and waved in return.

For half an hour they flew along the Lines at about 7,000 feet, with Biggles pointing out the all too familiar landmarks – a stream, a wood, an abandoned village, with the fearsome desolation of no-man's-land beyond. Apart from some lazy puffs of anti-aircraft fire, there was no sign of opposition – until suddenly, less than a mile away in an opening in the clouds, Biggles spotted six Fokker triplanes flying in tight formation. Had he had Mahoney with him, he would have plunged into the attack, but with a greenhorn pilot like his cousin, it was far too risky. Instead, he dipped his wings as a signal, dived straight towards the nearest bank of cloud and turned for home – trusting Algernon would follow.

He did nothing of the sort, and when Biggles looked behind he saw to his horror that he had disappeared. He turned back instantly, climbed, and flew out from the cloud – in time to see his cousin's aircraft far below following the German triplanes.

'He's raving mad,' he said, and set off in pursuit, but even as he did so the distant aircraft disappeared into a further bank of cloud, and it was pointless to continue.

'Poor silly idiot,' he said, and somewhat callously began to wonder what on earth he'd write to Aunt Priscilla. 'A hero's

death', or something of the sort. Biggles was getting rather used to
writing letters to his pilots' next of kin, and had a standard set of
phrases he could use.

When he landed, Major Mullen was already waiting on the
tarmac.

'Where's Algernon?' he shouted. Biggles shook his head.

'Copped it, I'm afraid. Chased off in pursuit of half a dozen
Fokkers. I'd warned him. Sorry sir, but there it is.'

But even as he spoke, there came the unmistakable engine note
of a Sopwith Camel, and through the low cloud came an aircraft
with the Squadron's markings.

'Looks as if you wrote him off too early,' Mullen said. 'Perhaps
you'd better deal with him yourself.'

'It will be a pleasure, sir,' said Biggles savagely.

Algernon Montgomery seemed quite surprised at Biggles'
fury.

'Daft young puppy!' Biggles shouted. 'Next time you feel like
suicide, please do it somewhere else, and not in your aircraft.
We're short of Camels, but we can do without lunatics like you.
What did you think that you were up to?'

'Having a crack at them, sir! They were the first Huns I'd ever
seen, and I'm afraid that my excitement got the better of me.'

'Did it indeed? You're lucky to have escaped alive.'

'But I got one.'

'Got what?'

'A Fokker. Shot it down. It was at the tail-end of the formation,
and with all that cloud around he can't have seen me. It was a
fluke, of course – more luck than judgment, sir.'

He smiled happily, and despite himself Biggles began to
wonder if he could possibly be telling the truth.

'How d'you know you shot it down?

'I saw it fall – on the edge of that square-shaped wood on our
side of the Lines.'

'We'll check. But get this straight, Algernon my boy. In future,
when I say that you stay put I mean exactly that. You
understand?'

The boy nodded. 'Sorry sir,' he said.

'Well,' said Biggles as he sat with Major Mullen and Mahoney,
having his customary pre-lunch gin and orange in the Mess
beside a blazing fire, 'I just don't know what to make of him.

Either he really did shoot down that Hun, or he's the biggest liar in creation.'

'He might have done it,' Mullen said. 'It has happened.'

'But not to Algernon,' said Biggles. 'He's too soft to shoot a dicky-bird, let alone one of von Kirtner's triplanes.'

'Well, we'll just have to wait and see. Taking him with you on the dawn patrol tomorrow morning?'

Biggles nodded.

'Then for God's sake drum into his idiotic head that he's to stick to you this time whatever happens.'

'If it's the last thing that I do,' said Biggles grimly.

Biggles was in a pensive mood next morning as he led his flight toward the German Lines. Reports had reached the Squadron Office that a German aircraft had indeed crashed in flames exactly where his cousin said. 'So he may be a damn fool, but at any rate he's not a liar,' he said to himself. 'At least that's something.' A more serious matter on his mind was that enemy air activity was starting to increase again. There had been reports that Kirtner's circus had been reinforced and warnings to all British combat pilots in the sector to expect trouble.

For a while there was no sight of it. The clouds of the previous day had dispersed, and with the pale blue sky and wintry sun the world held a totally deceptive air of peace. Even the ever-present anti-aircraft fire had taken the day off, and Biggles was humming to himself when he saw the enemy. There was no question of evading them this time, even if he'd wanted to, for they were flying straight towards them, six Fokker triplanes with the green and white insignia of von Kirtner's circus. 'Three Britons to six Huns,' Biggles muttered to himself. 'About the right odds I should say!' He waved to Healy on his right and Algernon on his left, then dipped his wings and roared head-on towards the enemy.

It was the sort of fight that Biggles liked – a test of nerve and flying skill where everything depended on split-second judgment. If anything would really test his cousin, it was this. The great temptation in this sort of battle was always to over-react, to fire too soon, to dodge too rapidly, and he could see the wicked flashes of the Spandaus on the leading German plane already firing towards him. He clenched his teeth and held his fire a moment longer as he kept the nose of the oncoming aircraft firmly in his sights and curled his finger round the twin triggers of his Vickers guns.

By now he could feel the Spandau bullets striking home into the Camel's body. The aircraft shuddered, then at last he fired – one long and deadly burst that sent the Fokker zooming down with a plume of black funereal smoke spewing from its shattered engine. 'One down and five to go!' said Biggles to himself. But even as he said this there was a resounding crash that drowned the roar of Biggles' engine. Away on his right, Healy's Camel had just collided head-on with another Fokker, and the two planes, blazing and entwined in death, were spiralling to earth.

'Good fellow, Healy,' Biggles said, and raised his hand in a gesture of farewell. 'Four of them to two of us. A bit close for comfort now!'

He glanced out of the corner of his eye for Algernon, and was delighted – and surprised – to see him still glued in position twenty yards behind his wing-tip. Then they were in the thick of it again, with all four remaining German pilots out for blood. Biggles had no time to see how Algernon was faring. A second Fokker fell before his guns, and for a moment he glimpsed Algernon diving to evade a persistent German on his tail.

Then Biggles realised that he was on his own – and trapped. The three remaining enemy aircraft had encircled him. Two had climbed above him and were waiting to dive down for the kill, taking it in turns until he was destroyed. He realised that there was no way out.

He shrugged his shoulders. He couldn't think of a better way to go, and was glad that Algernon had escaped. The leading Fokker was now at the beginning of its dive, and heading straight towards him, Spandaus blazing, when suddenly another Sopwith Camel flashed towards it. It had come out of nowhere, and the Fokker zoomed aside to avoid disaster. So did the next plane, and the next, as the Camel rocketed across the sky then roared alongside Biggles. He recognised the pilot then – Algernon Montgomery.

By now the remaining Fokkers were in disarray. Biggles was almost out of ammunition, and before they had a chance to regroup for the attack, the time had come to make for home. He raised his hand above his head, signalling a return to Base, and the two British aircraft turned in unison and dived towards the British Lines.

Biggles landed first, and jumped down from the cockpit to meet Algernon as his plane rolled to a halt.

'Just what do you think you were doing?' he said as Algernon removed his helmet. 'Flying like a flaming lunatic! That's not the way to stay alive.'

'Well sir,' said Algernon a trifle sheepishly, 'you said the only way to fight was to go in with everything you've got. That's what I was doing.'

Biggles nodded. 'I was very glad to see you, but why didn't you fire? I didn't see your guns in action once.'

Algernon looked still more uncomfortable at this.

'I'm sorry sir, I couldn't. You see, my guns were jammed. Dud cartridge and I simply couldn't clear it.'

Biggles stared a moment in amazement.

'You mean to tell me that you came back into that dogfight with your guns jammed?'

'Well, you had said I was to stick with you whatever happened. I'm sorry if . . .' But before he could finish, Biggles had thrust out his hand.

'You'll do, Algernon,' he said. 'Thanks for what you did. And you can call me Biggles.'

This was the beginning of a lifelong friendship, for the two cousins really had a lot in common. Superficially they made an ill-assorted pair, for Algy – the 'Algernon' was swiftly dropped – was a gangling six foot two, whose freckled face and slightly vague expression formed an instant contrast to the compact frame and solidly determined face of Biggles. But the contrast in their appearance was to become part of their appeal, and soon they formed a sort of double act in 266.

Algy followed up the exploits of his debut with the Squadron by proving himself a virtuoso pilot. He lacked the killer's instinct and the sheer aggressiveness of Biggles, but was in fact a far more stylish flier. Also, his somewhat goofy manner was something of a disguise for a very shrewd head, and in battle he was absolutely fearless. He picked up the elements of combat flying as swiftly as

Biggles had done, and before long the two of them were quite inseparable – both in the air and on the ground. Soon they were practising tactics together, and they worked out a routine which ultimately accounted for the lives of many of the enemy. On the ground they became like two devoted brothers – Biggles the dominant one, and Algy his devoted confidant and crony. Algy was the perfect foil to Biggles, for where Biggles was quick-tempered, and impatient to a degree, Algy was the gentlest and most easy-going of souls, cautious where Biggles was hot-headed, and essentially a loyal and devoted character, who never quite recovered from his earliest hero-worshipping of Biggles.

'In those days,' he explained, 'Biggles was extraordinary. The first thing that struck you about him was his energy. He was a sort of human dynamo – he never seemed to tire and the tougher things became, the more he liked it. Also, he had incredible enthusiasm. Nothing appeared to get him down, and once he had started on a mission, nothing on earth would stop him. Of course he could put people's backs up, and always called a spade a spade, but I hate to think what would have happened to 266 without him. Then, of course, there was his Secret Service work. People forget that underneath that rough-and-ready manner he adopted, he was in fact a very clever operator and as cunning as they come. Colonel Raymond was the first to spot this and he relied on him increasingly during those last months of the war.'

One of the strangest – and the most far-reaching – of these Intelligence operations which Biggles carried out for Colonel Raymond cropped up fairly soon after Algy joined 266. This was the Marie Janis business which always has been one of the great conundrums of the Biggles' saga. For, apart from being his first full-scale operation on behalf of British Intelligence, it also involved Biggles in his first real love-affair. No one will ever know quite how much suffering it caused him, nor how much the shadowy, romantic figure of this beautiful and ruthless woman continued to dog him in the years ahead. This was the one subject on which Biggles himself invariably clammed up, but according to Algy, Marie was the key to the whole controversial subject of Biggles' romantic life. Strangely enough, Biggles did permit Captain Johns to give a brief but incomplete account of the affair in one of his earliest books on his exploits in this period, his invaluable *Biggles, Pioneer Air Fighter*, but the Official Secrets Act

– and Biggles' reticence over what was clearly a most painful subject – served to prevent the full story being told. There will always be an element of mystery to the whole affair, but things can now be said and certain all-important facts included in this fascinating story.

It all began by chance, the sort that every pilot fears – a sudden engine failure in the Sopwith Camel that Biggles was ferrying back to Maranique from the Supply Depot at St Omer. Twenty miles or so from Base the new engine suddenly cut out, and Biggles made an immaculate forced landing on the edge of the large forest of Clarmes. It was a perfect day, and he walked to a nearby house for help, where the door was opened to him by what Captain Johns described later as 'a vision of blonde loveliness'. As Biggles presumably approved of this description, we can take it that this was the first impression Marie Janis made on him. She was then in her early twenties and a photograph taken of her later more than confirms her beauty – enormous eyes, a heart-shaped face, and an expression that was hard, sensual and coquettish. Biggles was attracted from the start. Marie's reactions must seem more debatable.

She asked him in and made a fuss of him. Her parents were away, and she was living on her own with two servants. Biggles soon telephoned to Maranique for help with his aircraft, and while he waited, Marie offered lunch, which he accepted. Biggles was nineteen, and his experience of women all but non-existent. His mother's original desertion had left him shy and wary of the female sex in general; but beneath the shyness he was uncomfortably romantic, far more so than his closest friends suspected. Just as he had dreamed for years of rediscovering his beautiful lost mother, so he now dreamed of finding his perfect woman. Marie Janis filled the bill, for everything about her seemed romantic – the old farmhouse with its beams and stone floors and delicious smell of cooking, her being totally alone in this peaceful countryside in the midst of war, and also, of course, the element of chance that had brought them so romantically together.

For more than a year now, Biggles had been facing daily death, and this golden-haired young girl was offering a glimpse of happiness beyond the horror and the threat of war. Mahoney would have seen it all in very basic terms, but there was

something touching in the way this fearless veteran of the skies
was so vulnerable and trusting when it came to love. Marie spoke
English (although Biggles' French was excellently now) and she
explained she had an English mother and a Belgian father.
Where were her parents? Biggles asked. Her mother, she replied,
was dead, and her beloved father had been trapped behind the
German Lines and was condemned to live in Belgium, much
against his will.

Biggles was sympathetic. Did she ever hear from him? She
shook her head. Poor girl! He took her hand. She made it clear
that she was grateful for his sympathy, and kissed him tenderly to
show her gratitude. They walked through the orchard arm in
arm – and by the time the car arrived from Maranique to take
him back, Biggles was in love.

His whole life changed abruptly. Previously he lived for flying,
but now his Sopwith Camel had a rival – Marie Janis. Instead of
having dinner in the Mess and then retiring early after a rubber
or two of bridge, Biggles would borrow the uncomplaining Algy's
motorcycle, and go roaring off to visit her. The second time they
met, he took her out to dinner at the nearby village, but usually
he ate at home with her, and before long they were meeting every
day. They were undisturbed, the food and wines delicious, and
soon the inevitable occurred.

Biggles reproached himself for this. 'I was a swine, Algy,' he
confessed to him years later. 'I should have had more self-control,
and more respect for her.' But as one looks at the photograph of
Marie Janis, one rather wonders if either would have saved him.
The lovely Marie obviously knew what she was doing when she
admitted Biggles to her bed. Whether Biggles did, one doubts.

Nobody knows much about Biggles as a lover. No letters that
he wrote survive, and all his friends are too discreet to tell the
truth – even if they know it. He was certainly extremely
sentimental. He was good-looking and had stamina above the
average. Those brief dramatic rages he expended on the enemy
when his blood was up show that beneath the Boy Scout manner
he was emotional and even passionate. And as he was taught the
arts of love by this gifted Belgian girl, several years his senior, it
would seem probable that the picture we have of Biggles as the
sexless man of action is inaccurate.

All this is supposition. What is undeniable is that for several weeks Biggles and Marie were lovers. Then the first shadows started to obscure their happiness. To start with they were nothing very much – the vaguest questions and most generalised inquiries. 'Where did you fly this morning, *mon chéri*?' and 'Where was the Squadron yesterday that you were twenty minutes late in visiting your Marie?' Biggles was as aware of the demands of strict security as the next man, but in his slightly fuddled state he put these questions down as part of her adorable concern for him. Then even he began to grow suspicious.

By now she had started asking him quite detailed questions in which no ordinary young Belgian girl in her right mind could have been interested – 'Biggles, darling, what is the operational ceiling of the Sopwith Camel with a supercharged Bentley rotary engine?' or 'My beloved, when will you be receiving this new combat plane, what is it called, the Sopwith Snipe?' Biggles tried to put the dreadful thought behind him, but soon it could be ignored no longer. Either Marie was preternaturally concerned with aeronautics – or she was a spy.

It shows how deeply Biggles was in love – or at any rate infatuated with her dimpled body – that even then he did his best to dodge the truth. He would give non-committal answers, bring her tender gifts, and hope that this growing nightmare in his private life would go away. Of course it didn't, and when things had reached the point where Marie would actually refuse to make love unless she received the information she required, Biggles decided he must act.

Several times their conversation had got round to the question of her father – how much she missed him, how sad it was he couldn't cross the Lines, and where he was living now. Finally, Marie explained that as far as she knew he was still in his old family home, the Château Boreau, near a small village called Vinard.

'A pity that you can't communicate with him,' said Biggles. Tears filled her lovely eyes.

'Perhaps I could help,' he said. 'We often fly that way. It shouldn't be too difficult to drop him a message.'

'But wouldn't it be dangerous, dearest one?'

'A little – but if it made my darling happy, it would be worth it.'

'You would do that for me?' she whispered.

'Anything at all,' he answered with a sigh.

And so it was all arranged. Marie would write a letter to her father, and Biggles on his next patrol would drop it on the Château Boreau. He could have been forgiven even now if he had dropped the letter without telling anyone and made the most of Marie's gentle gratitude when he returned.

But when it was a choice between his country and the woman he loved, Biggles was not a man to take the easy way. His duty was self-evident. That same night Marie gave him a letter for her father, written in her forward-sloping hand on purple paper, Biggles returned to Maranique, then telephoned Colonel Raymond at Wing Headquarters.

It was late, well past one o'clock, but the Colonel rarely slept, and within the hour had driven all the way to Maranique. Biggles explained the situation – not without embarrassment – but the Colonel was an understanding man at heart, and something of a man of the world himself.

'Dashed tricky situation for you, Bigglesworth,' he said. 'But you have acted as I hope that I would myself. Let's see the letter.'

As Biggles took it from his pocket his heart was beating. Colonel Raymond deftly steamed it open, then studied it for several minutes with his magnifying glass. Finally he nodded.

'As I thought,' he said. 'The bitch has used invisible ink – the oldest trick in the business.'

'Sir,' said Biggles, 'I would rather that you didn't speak of her like that.'

The Colonel was about to mutter something, but thought better of it.

"Sorry Bigglesworth,' he said. 'Shouldn't have said that to a brother officer. All the same, this Mademoiselle Janis is obviously a spy. To tell the truth, we've had our eye on her for quite some time, but never have been able to prove a thing. You realise of course what this Château Boreau is?'

Biggles shook his head.

'Headquarters of German Field Intelligence. Now listen carefully. I think our backroom boys should do a little work on this letter to the so-called Monsieur Janis. Change things around a bit, and then you can deliver it exactly as arranged.'

'And what about Marie?' said Biggles, suddenly concerned. 'You'd not do anything to her?'

'Course not, Bigglesworth. We're not like the Huns. We don't shoot women spies – at least, not if we can help it.'

But even as he spoke, there was something steely in the Colonel's glance that made Biggles realise the dreadful danger that was threatening Marie. For whatever she had done, whatever she had planned to do, he loved her still.

Next morning Biggles was off extra early on his dawn patrol. Algy flew with him for a while, but at a signal the two fliers parted, and Biggles turned north, towards the frontier and the little village of Vinard. He had no difficulty locating the Château Boreau. It was a red-brick building with a pointed, high slate roof. Biggles flew round it once at little more than 200 feet. At first there was no sign of life, then an old man tottered out across the lawn and waved. Biggles zoomed down towards him, then took the letter from his pocket, kissed it tenderly, and threw it from the cockpit with a weight attached to bring it down to earth. He saw it flutter down and the old man picked it up.

All the way back to Base Biggles was in a state of turmoil. What on earth should he do?

As a stern patriot, he should clearly let the woman that he loved go off to face the punishment she had richly earned. But, even as he thought of this, he pictured the grim smile on Colonel Raymond's face – and a firing squad at dawn. It was unthinkable, and yet he knew for certain now that this would happen to Marie unless he acted. He also knew that if she died he would be responsible, and that he could never live with such remorse.

He was back in Maranique in time for a late and somewhat dismal breakfast. Algy had landed ahead of him, and Mahoney was already telling him about his previous night's exploits with some girl he had picked up in town. By an uncomfortable coincidence, she too was called Marie. It was a very common name, but it was enough to make Biggles' mind up for him, and without waiting for his toast and marmalade he dashed back to his quarters, and five minutes later was once more in the air, and flying north. He had not far to go, and within ten minutes he was flying over the all too painfully familiar roof of Marie's house. There was the orchard where he had kissed her, the white front door, the bedroom window which had witnessed the happiest moments of his life. He circled low around the house, and suddenly the front door opened. Marie appeared. She was wearing the dress he loved – a blue and white creation that showed of her splendid bosom to perfection. Recognising Biggles' aircraft, she waved happily, but instead of waving back, he dropped a note. An hour later, when two men from Colonel Raymond's secretariat arrived to pick her up for questioning, Marie Janis had already left.

If Colonel Raymond had his own suspicions over what had happened, he kept them to himself. 'First rate, Bigglesworth,' he said, 'I realise how difficult it was for you, but the spy ring's broken up, and a lot of useless information has been fed to German Field Intelligence in that letter you delivered to the Château Boreau. Rather a pity that the bird herself had flown by the time we went to pick her up. Still, possibly it was just as well. Always a nasty business, having to deal with women.' And Biggles, who could still imagine that beloved face, eyes bandaged, facing twelve British rifles in a prison yard at dawn, silently agreed.

A few days later, Biggles received a letter. There was no address, and the postmark was obscure. Inside was a sheet of purple paper, and he recognised the writing instantly.

'Thank you my darling Biggles. What a pity that this beastly war has come between us, but we will meet again, never fear. All my love, Marie.'

Biggles' decisiveness, his self-control and his ability to think clearly in a crisis, were not lost on Colonel Raymond, and it was shortly after the Marie Janis business that Biggles finally threw in his lot with the British Secret Service. It was something that he was always reticent about. This was partly habit – no secret agent worth his salt feels happy throwing off the veil of secrecy. But in Biggles' case, I feel that there was something more than this, a real contradiction that ran through his character and troubled him.

For the fact was that Biggles, thanks to heredity and the strange traumas and training of his childhood, was ideally suited to being a spy. Even as a child he had learned to mask his feelings from his father. His adventures in the jungles and bazaars of India had taught him to blend into any background and had given him a taste for secrecy and personal adventure. Then, as he had to accommodate himself to life at Malton Hall, Biggles the loner was again disguising all his fantasies and feelings in his desperate attempts to conform in a minor English public school.

This was what Colonel Raymond – with uncanny insight – must have realised. What he failed to see was the other side of Biggles, the side of him Algy Lacey called 'the good Boy Scout' – the fearless, incorruptible, straight-talking character who pretended to be far simpler than he was. This side of Biggles was at its best in the middle of a dogfight, for as he once said, 'A Camel, blue skies and plenty of Huns are the height of my ambition, and I hope to find them all in France.'

Generally he did, but early in the spring of 1918 he became crucially involved in the strange adventure with the British Secret Service which took him away from 266 for several months, months during which he found himself playing the distasteful part of a double agent against the background of the Middle East. He played it brilliantly, as one can see from Captain Johns' account of the mission which he entitled – somewhat to Biggles' chagrin it appears – *Biggles Flies East*. Indeed, Biggles became enrolled in that exclusive band of British agents who have actually been awarded an Iron Cross by the Germans. But Biggles would always shy away from telling us about the affair. 'Messy business,' he would say, and light a cigarette as if the whole adventure were discreditable. For him perhaps it was, but in fact it probably did more to help the Allied war effort than any of his battles in the skies. That might have worried him as well.

Biggles' part in the affair rested originally on his close resemblance to an Englishman called Brunow, who not long before was cashiered from the R.F.C., and had made contact with the enemy to work as a German spy. Colonel Raymond, who had been observing Brunow closely since his disgrace, finally convinced the members of the British Air Staff Intelligence of the possibilities of substituting one of his own men for Brunow – and selected Biggles for the task.

It was a long and hazardous affair. (Readers who wish to study it in its complexity are referred to Captain Johns.) But it involved Biggles in the task of infiltrating German Intelligence in Palestine, and he did this so effectively – and in the process flew a captured Sopwith Pup so skilfully – that he was awarded the Iron

Cross I have referred to. (He always pretended that the award embarrassed him; nevertheless, he kept the medal and Lord Lacey tells me it was among his effects when he died.) Throughout this mission Colonel Raymond was in Cairo, and for a period Algy worked with him, specially seconded from 266 to provide back-up support for Biggles in the field. Largely thanks to Biggles, the whole German effort to involve the Arabs in a diversionary revolt against the British was aborted.

Apart from its place in history, this mission to Palestine is interesting for the light it throws on the development of Biggles' character. It was his first real chance to demonstrate his true skill as a double agent, and he exhibited the same fearlessness and iron nerve that he had shown in combat with the enemy in France, and the whole adventure shows that Biggles had by now become a man of fairly ruthless cunning when the need arose.

But despite his success, Biggles affected to dislike the Middle East and the intrigue and spying that he found there. 'The whole area is rotten with the canker of espionage,' he said – forgetting that he was no mean hand at espionage himself – and he told Raymond that he could hardly wait to return to battle on the Western Front, 'and the wholesome fighting in the air'.

All this apart, this mission to the Middle East had one further memorable feature – it brought Biggles face to face with the man who would be his bitterest opponent in the years ahead, the Prussian known as Hauptmann Erich von Stalhein. Biggles remembered him in those days as 'tall, slim and good-looking in a rather foppish way', despite the double duelling scar disfiguring his cheek. He had recently been wounded with his regiment in France and was still limping and using a stick. From the moment Biggles first clapped eyes on him, he found something sinister and threatening in this dark-haired Prussian with the monocle and brooding eyes.

Von Stalhein was acting as Chief of Staff Intelligence to the incompetent Count von Faubourg, Station Commander of the German air station at Zabala where Biggles found himself. He never had much difficulty tricking Faubourg, but from the start von Stalhein was another matter. Biggles realised von Stalhein was suspicious of him. 'He sensed that I was phoney. Anybody else would have had me shot at once, but that was not the way von Stalhein operated. You see, he was an old school Prussian

officer, and he still adhered in those days to the rules of the game –
fair play and all that. Mind you, he changed his ideas somewhat
in the years ahead, but although von Stalhein proved to be the
most diabolical opponent I've ever met, and cunning as a snake,
he always managed to remain something of a man of honour.'

In Palestine this proved to be very much the case, with Biggles
and von Stalhein acting out a deadly duel of wits, in which the
Prussian never quite succeeded in discovering the proof of
Biggles' double-dealing. Nor, one must add, did Biggles ever
manage to unmask von Stalhein when the tables turned, and the
Prussian – already a virtuoso master of disguise – played out the
part of the commanding El Shereef, elusive as the wind as he rode
behind the British Lines on his magnificent horse. By the end of
their encounter Biggles and von Stalhein had clearly recognised
each other as the lifelong adversaries they would prove to be,
and in a strange way they seem to have valued each other. They
and they alone had been a match for one another. They had been
the true protagonists in this sinister affair, and when it ended –
and it seemed as if von Stalhein must have perished when his
plane was hit by British anti-aircraft fire – Biggles felt, not
elation, but a curious regret. Yet even then, something must have
told him that the von Stalheins of this world are not killed that
easily, and that somehow he would meet him later on. But before
he could learn the truth about von Stalhein's fate, Biggles was
back at Maranique with Algy where, to his relief, life and death
were cleaner and less complicated than in the cess-pit of the
Middle East.

For Biggles the last months of the war passed rapidly, as the
routine of combat flying with 266 continued. The risks and the
adventures were still there, but already, so it seemed, the
pioneering days of air fighting were behind him. It was a life of
regular patrols, reconnaissance, and aerial support for bombing
raids. Biggles, who was now one of the veterans of the R.F.C.,
could have moved on to take command of a fresh squadron of his
own, but he resisted this, even when promoted Major, late that
summer. He was not interested in command – nor, for that
matter, in pursuing fame and glory for their own sake. (His
inborn aversion to publicity explains why he never allowed

himself to be made into one of the wartime 'aces' by the popular press. He always insisted it was 'tasteless' to boast about the number of enemy planes he had shot down, and never would reveal how many 'kills' were to his credit.)

He was wounded once that summer – caught in the shoulder by a bullet from one of von Kirtner's triplanes in a surprise attack on the airfield at Maranique. He was furious at this. 'If I'd been in the air, I'd only have had myself to blame, but there I was standing on the tarmac and all I heard was the rattle of machine-gun fire, and then I woke up in hospital.' It was officially a 'Blighty wound' – qualifying for a month or two of easy convalescence back in Britain – but he convinced the doctors that this wasn't necessary, and was up flying in a fortnight. Somehow he learned which aircraft from von Kirtner's circus was responsible for the attack. It had a blue and white striped fuselage, and according to Wing Intelligence was flown by the well-known German ace, Graf von Ranke. From then on, Biggles waged a personal vendetta. Every time he flew he kept his eyes skinned for the Fokker triplane with the blue and white striped fuselage, but it seemed to be eluding him. Algy saw it once in a large formation north of Lille.

'You didn't get the blighter, did you?' Biggles asked anxiously. Algy shook his head.' Sorry, old scout, I missed him.'

'Thank God for that,' said Biggles fervently. 'I've still got something to settle with the Graf. I wouldn't have forgiven you if you'd robbed me of that satisfaction.'

In the old days, this sort of humourless desire for revenge would have been unthinkable in Biggles, but the long dragging agony of war was changing him. So had the treachery of Marie Janis, and the intrigue and sordidness of his mission to Palestine. Had it not been for Algy, it is by no means certain what would have happened, with the grim obsessive mood that seemed to have overtaken Biggles now. But Algy helped to keep him human, for Algy had what Biggles lacked – a real sense of humour – and he would always make fun of him if he saw him getting too wrapped up in himself.

'Biggles, old son,' he would say, 'you're getting boring.' And Biggles, who would have jumped on anybody else who spoke like this, would generally grin sheepishly and say, 'Sorry Algy. Didn't realise. I'll have to watch it.'

But despite Algy's influence, Major Mullen started to get worried about Biggles by the end of summer, and when Biggles was promoted Major, and awarded the D.S.O., he did his best to have him seconded back to England for a period with a training squadron. When Biggles found out he was furious, and finally had the order changed. But the damage had been done. The rumour had got round that Biggles was beginning to crack up, and he, in his pig-headed way, was set to prove that he was doing nothing of the sort.

This mood of his grew worse when, early in September, news arrived about his brother Charles. He had been killed with his battalion on the Somme, and although Biggles had never really liked him, he convinced himself he had a duty to avenge his brother's death.

Algy did his best to talk sense into him – to no avail. Biggles was still seeking Graf von Ranke's Fokker, but as well as this he now believed he had a private battle with the German Air Force. Little else mattered to him, and although his flying was as masterful as ever he started taking risks that he would never have dreamt of doing earlier. Other members of the Squadron started to fight shy of flying with him, but this never seemed to worry Biggles – and Algy always kept an eye on him.

Then came reports that Graf von Ranke's Fokker had been seen again. Wing Intelligence confirmed that the Graf was still piloting the aircraft, and Biggles sought him like a hunter for his prey. Twice he missed him, and then finally one autumn morning he and the Squadron were on support patrol, deep over enemy territory, when they were pounced upon by twenty enemy aircraft. They were Fokker triplanes with the markings of von Kirtner's circus, and in the midst of them Biggles suddenly made out a blue and white striped fuselage.

This was the moment he had waited for for months, and even as he gripped the triggers of his Vickers guns and hurled his Sopwith Camel in between the milling aeroplanes towards von Ranke's Fokker, he could feel the dull ache in his shoulder reminding him of his wound. His jaw was set, a red glow blazed before his eyes, and he could clearly see the leather helmet of the man he hated. Nothing else mattered now, and as he dived towards his enemy he took no notice of the other German planes around him, nor did he even bother now to glance behind him.

Despite his speed it seemed an age before he felt close enough to fire.

'Swine,' he kept muttering, 'filthy low-down swine!' He was scared of one thing only – that von Ranke might escape him. But the German must have realised his fate was sealed, for just before Biggles fired he turned in his cockpit, and Biggles saw fear on his face. Biggles squeezed the triggers, and a stream of flaming lead tore through the blue and white fuselage. A wing flew off, the aircraft keeled to one side, and as Biggles zoomed above the doomed aeroplane, he saw von Ranke's body tumble from the cockpit and go hurtling down.

But Biggles' vengeance was short-lived. While he was struggling with his bucking plane and trying to avoid the debris from his enemy, there was a crash and his instrument panel shattered. A cruel pain seared his left leg, and even as he swung himself around to see his new opponent, a fresh hail of tracer fire lashed the Camel's fuselage. There was a triplane on his tail, diving down from the sun to avenge von Ranke in his turn. Biggles knew that he was finished – and only had himself to blame. Had he not been so desperate to kill von Ranke, he would not have made this elementary mistake. He made one wild attempt to get away, yanking at the joystick and kicking at the rudder bar, but the plane failed to respond and the pain in his leg was now excruciating. Another blast of tracer hit the aircraft and it began to burn, then fell into a spin. He felt himself going down and down, and knew that he would crash.

Almost by instinct now, he made one final frenzied effort to wrench the aircraft from its spin – and miraculously it began to work. The engine was still functioning but he was barely more than 100 feet above a wood. Once more he pulled the joystick, but the plane continued on its downward path. A row of poplars rushed towards him, and he just had sense enough to raise his one undamaged leg up to his chin, fold his arms across his face, and await the impact.

There was a horrendous crash, but the branches of the trees had dulled the impact, and more by instinct now than anything, Biggles clawed his way from the wreckage – just in time. As he stumbled from the plane the petrol tank ignited and in seconds what had been a Sopwith Camel was a blistering inferno.

He tried to run, but his damaged leg buckled beneath him, and he had to crawl to get as far away from the blaze as possible. He pulled off his blood-stained goggles, and as he did so saw a group of men running towards him. They were wearing field grey, and silently surrounded him. So this was it. There was nothing he could do to avoid spending the remainder of the war in a German prison camp – if he ever got there in one piece. For, as he raised his hands and tried to struggle to his feet, one of the Germans came towards him, kicked him in the side and shouted, '*Schweinhund flieger!*' Biggles recoiled with the pain but managed to bite back his cry. The German raised his foot to kick again, but a command rang out, and he turned away. Biggles saw a slim young officer who had just got out of a Staff car. He had the Iron Cross at his neck, and as he walked towards the troops they drew themselves erect, and stood firmly at attention.

The officer saluted Biggles.

'Bad luck,' he said in English. 'Are you in any pain?'

Biggles shook his head. 'A scratch,' he answered, 'nothing more.'

The officer continued to regard him with an expression of uncertainty upon his face.

'Well,' said Biggles through his teeth, 'let's get it over with. Perhaps one of your men would help me. I've always wondered what the inside of your prison camps was like.'

At this the German smiled and shook his head.

'I don't think that is necessary,' he said.

'Why not?' said Biggles through his pain. 'I don't understand.'

'An Armistice was signed an hour ago. I shall do my best to make arrangements to have you repatriated as soon as possible.'

Either from loss of blood or sheer relief, Biggles fainted.

4

Peace

'So what do you propose to do, old fruit?' asked Algy ruminatively.

'Dashed if I know, and that's a fact,' said Biggles, sipping his third pink gin that morning. 'Had thought of trying to stay on. The old country'll always need an air force, I suppose, although you wouldn't think so from the way they're treating us. Breaking up the Squadron like this, slinging the aircraft on the scrap-heap – and the pilots too! Now that we've won the war for them, the blasted politicians think they can treat us all like so much obsolete equipment. Frankly, old boy, it makes me sick!'

Biggles glowered through the window of the Mess at Maranique as rain swept across the airfield. The Armistice was three weeks old, and apart from a dismantled Sopwith Camel on the runway there was no sign that this had ever been one of the most active combat stations in the war. Mahoney was already off on leave in Paris, and several of the other pilots in 266 Squadron had opted for a swift return to England in their eagerness to leave the war behind them. Biggles would probably have joined them, but his leg wound had confined him to a hospital bed at Base for the last fortnight, and he was still on crutches. The leg was on the mend, but his spirits remained distinctly low. Algy had stayed behind to be with him, but even his devotion was becoming just a little strained by Biggles' bitterness.

'You really had considered signing on?' asked Algy.

Biggles shrugged his shoulders with impatience.

'I talked it over briefly with the C.O., but he wasn't hopeful. He said he'd recommend me – which was nice of him, all things considered – but he added that I'd have to drop back in rank to a Lieutenant, even if the Air Board took me on. He didn't seem to think they would.'

'Holy mackerel! They'd be off their flaming chumps to turn down a flier with your record.'

Biggles shook his head.

'By no means, Algy lad. Those Whitehall warriors don't much care for individualists like us. It'll be a peacetime air force, and they want nice safe reliable characters to serve in it. Which I imagine rules us out. Not that the situation really arises anyhow. This blasted leg wound stymies my chances. I'm already thinking that poor old Charles was not all that unlucky popping off like that. He'd had a dashed good war – and if this is peace, he's best off out of it.'

A look of consternation spread over Algy's habitually complacent countenance at these gloomy words.

'You don't really mean that Biggles?' he exclaimed.

Biggles smiled wanly, and at the same time signalled the Mess waiter for another drink.

'Afraid I do, old scout! For almost as long as I remember I'd been looking forward to the war ending but now, my God, I'd give a lot to see a pack of Fokker triplanes over yonder.'

Algy leant forward, fixing Biggles with his pale blue eyes.

'Biggles,' he said, 'forgive me addressing you like the proverbial Dutch Uncle, but I think the time has come to pull yourself together. Self-pity gets you nowhere, and I think we've had enough of it. You're young. You've got your life before you and there's no point getting maudlin just because the old Squadron's breaking up.'

Algy was not a man for speeches of this sort and a heavy silence greeted his effusion. Then Biggles placed his hand on his cousin's arm.

'Thanks, Algy. You're quite right, as usual. This confounded wound has got me down. There's no point wanting the impossible. One must be realistic. What do you suggest?'

'It's dashed difficult, I know,' said Algy, 'but I've been giving quite a bit of thought to the future over the last few months. The

Mater seems to think I should go into the Diplomatic Corps.'

'And could you?' Biggles asked him quickly.

Algy's boyish smile returned as he grinned at Biggles.

'Can you see me as an ambassador?'

'Frankly, no, old thing, I can't.'

'No more can I. There's always chicken-farming. Lots of the chaps are doing that. How's about chipping in with me and buying a few hundred Rhode Island Reds?'

For the first time in several weeks, Biggles laughed.

'Or an ostrich farm,' he said. 'The eggs are bigger, so we'd have bigger profits. No, but seriously, just what are chaps like us to do?

'Well,' said Algy pensively,' 'it seems that you and I are rather similar. The one thing we really know about is flying – and the one thing we still demand from life is real adventure. It shouldn't be impossible to combine the two.

'Absolutely,' Biggles said, 'but how?'

'By using our imagination.'

Three weeks later Biggles and Algy were installed in what were euphemistically described as 'bachelors' apartments' in Mount Street, Mayfair. The rent – £300 a year – had appeared exorbitant to Biggles, but Algy, practical as ever, pointed out the need for what he called 'a good address'. 'We must begin as we intend to continue,' he explained. 'Absolutely no point slumming it in Kensington just to save £50 a year. Here we're within walking distance of the Ritz, and the Carlton Grill is just around the corner. Can't think of a better place to set up shop.'

By this time, Biggles' leg was almost healed, and though he limped and used a walking-stick, his spirits had revived. He liked the little flat – he had his own small 'den' where he kept his log-books and trophies from the war, along with his faithful Sidcot flying suit, his goggles, and a small armoury of various offensive weapons. Algy had found the perfect housekeeper – a policeman's wife of uncertain age called Mrs Symes. ('As long as she can grill a steak and keep her mouth shut, she's all right by me,' said Biggles typically.) The whole arrangement seemed to have reconciled him to the shock of breaking with his beloved

Squadron. It had been a wrench leaving Maranique and bidding a last farewell to that battlefield above the desolation of the Western Front. He had felt naked out of uniform, and missed the routine of the dawn patrols, but in his heart of hearts he knew that Algy had been right – and was duly grateful to him. He was even starting to do something he had always thought impossible – enjoying living in the heart of the metropolis.

'You'll soon turn me into a confounded cockney,' he said to Algy as he limped cheerfully down Piccadilly en route to meet Mahoney for a farewell dinner at the Café Royal. (Mahoney was off to Kenya to plant coffee. 'Glad that you're leaving the fleshpots to do something for the Empire,' Biggles told him.)

There was still one matter of concern for Biggles – money. Algy had been more than generous, as he could well afford to be. His grandfather, the fiery old Lord Lacey, had died immensely rich from the somewhat dubious profits of his Governorship, and had set up a succession of abundant trusts for all his heirs. Somewhat unfairly in the circumstances, Biggles did not qualify for any of the Lacey wealth. The old man's refusal to forgive his daughter for her marriage continued beyond the grave. But Algy already had the interest on the money, which amounted to an income of several thousand pounds a year, and he insisted on sharing some of it with Biggles.

'After all, old chap, it's family money and you're one of the family. Can't have you penalised because the old man didn't like your father.'

Biggles saw the logic of his words, and was duly grateful, but it went against the grain to be dependent on his cousin, even though Algy was the most generous and discreet of men where money was concerned. This made him all the more determined to make the joint activity on which they had now embarked a genuine financial success.

The idea behind it all was Algy's really, and the two cousins had discussed it at great length during their final days at Maranique.

'Why don't we set up together as independent pilots? The only thing we know about is flying, and now the war's over there is bound to be a need for characters like us who'll fly anywhere at any time, and do anything – provided it's within the law.'

'What'll we do for aircraft?' Biggles had inquired warily.

'No problem there,' said Algy. 'The government has several thousand it no longer needs. They're almost giving them away.'

'And maintenance? Neither of us is what you'd call a skilled mechanic.'

'By the counter-clockwise aircrew of Icarus, you're an optimistic fellow, I'll say that for you,' replied Algy with a laugh. 'What about the mechanics that we had with 266? Finest bunch of experts on the Western Front. They could have made a mangle fly. For a fiver a week we could have the pick of them.'

'And an airfield?'

'Well, to start with we could garage the old bus at Brooklands.'

'One final question, Algy lad. Who's going to foot the bill – until the shekels start rolling in?'

Algy smiled. 'Who d'you think? Our old horror of a grandfather. He left a special legacy for my eighteenth birthday. Five thousand ill-gotten guineas, yours truly strictly for the use of. I can't think of a better way of using them.'

The next few days passed rapidly, and suddenly all Biggles' natural zest for life appeared to have returned. Algy had just spent several hundred pounds of his legacy on a brand-new Bentley three and a half litre tourer, and the first journey that the cousins made in it was down to the Royal Aircraft Establishment at Farnborough. Biggles had had no difficulty arranging with the powers that be to purchase a government surplus warplane – 'without its armament of course', as the Wing-Commander in Whitehall had quickly added – and they spent a happy morning at the famous R.A.E. 'shopping around for something suitable', as Algy put it.

Their first thought had been to find a good, all-purpose aircraft – 'something solid and reliable' said Biggles – and the first plane they looked at was a long-range Vickers Vimy heavy bomber. Neither was very taken with it, despite Biggles' sensible insistence that they could use it to fly freight and passengers and make their fortune.

'It isn't really us,' said Algy, and Biggles knew that he was right. All their experience had been with combat planes, but these were only single-seaters and they obviously required more

than that. Biggles explained the problem to Jim Halcrow, one of
the most experienced test pilots with the R.A.E. He was a short,
bald, somewhat silent man, but he had known Biggles of old and
was anxious to be helpful.

'Well,' he said, scratching his non-existent hair, 'there is one
aircraft that might suit you. Still rather hush-hush, I'm afraid,
but come and have a look.'

He led Biggles and Algy to a separate hangar, heaved back the
sliding door, and walked towards a brand-new biplane standing
on its own.

'Phew!' said Algy. 'That's more like it. What a beauty! But
what is it?'

'Looks like a Snipe,' said Biggles cautiously.

'It was a Snipe,' said Halcrow smiling to himself, 'but we've
been altering it a bit – for the R.A.F. As you see, she's got twin
cockpits, extra tanks and there's a new 500 horse-power Bentley
engine. Goes like a blinking bomb!'

'What did the R.A.F. want her for?'

'Long-range anti-submarine patrols. She's got a range of 1,500
miles. But now that the war's over, it won't go into production.
This is the prototype. Why don't you make a bid for her? You
might be lucky.'

'That's the plane for us,' said Algy.

'I think I'd better start to pull a few more strings in Whitehall,'
Biggles said. 'It could be difficult, for she's probably still on the
secret list, but if there's anything that influence can do, by God,
I'm doing it.'

Jim Halcrow grinned.

'You do just that, and I'll do what I can to put a good word in
for both of you down here. I'm fond of the machine and would
like to think she'll go to someone who'll look after her.'

Biggles and Algy were excited now and felt their morning at
the R.A.E. had been well spent. But there was still one more
surprise in store for them before they left. They had already said
goodbye to Halcrow and were walking through the workshops
when a voice called out, 'Good Heavens! It's the Major!'

Biggles looked round, and saw an oil-stained apparition
beaming at him from behind a stripped-down aero-engine.

'Suffering cats!' he ejaculated, 'If it isn't the inimitable Nobby
Smyth. And what on earth might you be doing here, my lad?'

Former Flight Sergeant Ronald Smyth, 266 Squadron's legendary chief mechanic, rubbed an exceptionally greasy hand on the seat of his even greasier set of overalls before accepting Biggles' proferred palm.

'Slave labour, sir!' he said, and grinned as Biggles had seen him grin when asked for the impossible during the heat of battle. 'I had to find myself a job when the Squadron folded up. It's not like the good old days, but it's better than working in some blasted garage. And what would you and Captain Lacey both be up to in these parts?'

'Trying to buy ourselves an aeroplane – and also trying to find a good mechanic to look after it. You wouldn't know of one by any distant chance?'

'Well as it happens, sir, I do,' said Smyth, with an even wider grin. 'When do I start?'

Algy never did discover quite how Biggles managed it, but within a week negotiations were completed and the converted Supersnipe – as Biggles called the plane – was standing on the tarmac of the Brooklands airfield, her brand-new paintwork gleaming in the bright spring sun. Biggles and Algy had already had considerable discussions on how the aircraft should be registered.

Biggles had tried to insist that it belonged to Algy, but he wasn't having that.

'Suffering seacows!' Algy had replied. 'What would I ever do if my sainted mother found out I'd bought an aeroplane? I'd have hell to pay. No, Biggles, we're in this together. We'll form a company and register the aircraft in its name.'

'What name?' asked Biggles pensively.

'Well,' said Algy, 'as far as I can see there's only one name that'll really do.'

'What's that?'

'Biggles and Co.,' said Algy cheerfully. 'Then if Mama gets wind of what I'm up to, I can put all the blame on you.'

And so it was that the extraordinary firm of Biggles and Company first saw the light of day.

Like the majority of companies, Biggles and Co. found it uphill work to get established. With the ending of the war there was a glut of former fliers desperate for work, and our two heroes had their work cut out to scrape a living. But at least they managed to keep flying – even if it meant doing the lowliest of jobs. For several weeks they worked from Heston Airport as part of an air-taxi service, and at weekends offered 'joy-rides' at five shillings a passenger. They flew at fêtes and fairs. They worked with a stunt parachutist called Rix – until he lost his nerve – and they did aerobatics for the fun of it. All of this barely paid Smyth's wages and the petrol, but it kept them occupied and happy, and they were young enough to rough it for a while, especially with Mrs Symes to mother them whenever they returned to Mount Street. Then, at the end of March, Biggles and Algy got their first big chance, as they had always known they would. What was surprising was the form the offer took, and that they owed it to the last person either would have dreamed of – Algy's father.

The strange affair began one Saturday. Biggles and Algy had been down at Brooklands, working on the aircraft, and they were late returning to the flat. Mrs Symes was out, but she had left a note for Algy.

'Phew,' he said to Biggles as he read it. 'It's the old man on the war-path. I'm to telephone him urgently. If I know the Pater that means one thing only – trouble.'

'Better face it like a man,' said Biggles, laughing at the expression on his cousin's face. 'Just have a good stiff drink and get it over with,' and pouring him a mammoth whisky soda, Biggles pushed the white-faced Algy to the telephone and closed the door. Two minutes later, Algy re-emerged, but instead of looking shattered, he was cock-a-hoop.

'Well,' he exclaimed, 'the dear old boy is not as daft as we thought he was!'

'That's not saying very much,' said Biggles drily.

'But seriously, it's quite incredible! He knows about the Supersnipe and what we're up to, and far from disapproving, he has work for us.'

'What sort of work? Gathering cowslips from the air? Tell him it's the wrong time of year.'

'Biggles, your levity is quite uncalled for. It sounds just the sort of job we're looking for – flying some botanist friend of his to Switzerland.'

'From where?' said Biggles cautiously.

'It was a bad line, and he couldn't tell me any more than that, but I said we'd both go down for lunch tomorrow and he'll brief us then. Could be the start of something interesting.'

'It could,' said Biggles.

It was a fine spring morning, and the dark green Bentley bowled along the Brighton Road like the thoroughbred it was, but Biggles' mood was anything but sunny. Unlike Algy, who delighted in his motorcar, Biggles was always bored by any mode of transport other than an aeroplane. Also, he was feeling guilty. He knew that his mother would be staying with the Laceys, and he also knew that he had been neglecting her. But the truth was that she always managed to infuriate him now, with her perpetual fussing over petty details, her tactlessness and chronic snobbery. Besides, as he realised, she was often right – and that was worse.

But it was not just the thought of lunching with his mother that had so upset him. He would have been hard put to explain just what it was, but something worried him about this project that his uncle was suggesting, and the fact that Algy was so thrilled about it somehow made his premonition darker still.

'Well,' said Lord Lacey, when they were all seated round the enormous luncheon table, 'it's good to have you two boys safely home again.'

'Amen!' said Biggles' mother fervently. (She was still attired from head to toe in mourning for his brother, which Biggles thought excessive in the circumstances.)

'And what's all this your father tells me about this aeroplane of yours?' said Aunt Priscilla to her son. 'I for one would have imagined that you'd had enough of the beastly things while you were out in France. I still think you should be a diplomat, Algernon.'

'There, there, my dear,' Lord Lacey answered tactfully before a family row developed. 'They tell me aeroplanes are quite the coming thing. And that reminds me. There's this business of Professor Krahenbiehl. Perhaps when the ladies have retired, we can discuss it all.'

'You mean the details are too shocking for the gentler sex?' said Aunt Priscilla.

'By no means,' said Lord Lacey. 'But I think that the details might bore you and Catherine. So if you'll both excuse us ...'

'Well, father,' Algy said when the ladies had departed, 'many thanks for your support. I thought you handled mother wonderfully. But just who is Professor Krahenbiehl, and why does he want to go to Switzerland?'

'Of course, dear boy. I keep forgetting that you're not a botanist yourself. Such a pity! No, Krahenbiehl's an old, old friend of mine, and the world's greatest expert on the mountain orchid. I haven't seen him since before the war. He lives near Frankfurt. But two days ago I heard from him. Miraculously, he has survived, but as he explained in his letter, all his work, his notes, his specimens are threatened by the chaos of defeat. Imagine, there's no heat for his greenhouses!'

'Terrible!' said Biggles.

'Exactly! But there's a way of saving Krahenbiehl and his work for posterity, if he can only get to Switzerland. The Institute at Zurich has invited him, but he must get there swiftly with the best of his collection. Most of his specimens are irreplaceable and delay would be unthinkable. That's where you and this aeroplane of yours come in. How's about it? Krahenbiehl's a rich man and I know he'll make it worth your while.'

Biggles scratched his chin.

'Flying to Hunland,' he said dubiously. 'Could be tricky, and I don't know if we'd get permission. Probably take weeks.'

'Weeks?' said Lord Lacey, suddenly aghast. 'But that's no good. By then the whole collection will have perished, and the loss to science would be quite unthinkable.'

'It's all right Father,' Algy said. 'You can count on us. Cable Professor Krahenbiehl we'll pick him up tomorrow evening.'

'You must be off your rocker, Algernon, dear chap,' Biggles exclaimed angrily.

The two of them were seated by the fire in Biggles' 'den', having just consumed the cutlets and rice pudding Mrs Symes had cooked for them.

'You know quite well how risky it will be. Flights into Germany are rigidly controlled, and if anything goes wrong we could end up with the Supersnipe impounded by the Allies. I'm totally against it.'

Algy looked surprised to hear his cousin talk like this.

'Old scout,' he said, 'are you feeling all right? I mean, it's not like you to go worrying your head about controls. Besides, what can go wrong? The Supersnipe's in perfect nick, thanks to the splendid Smyth, and we agreed that what we wanted was adventure. Why all the fuss?'

Biggles had no reply to this, and shrugged his shoulders.

'O.K.,' he said. 'If you'll drive me down to Brooklands after breakfast, I'll nip across to Frankfurt and pick up the blighter and his orchids by early afternoon. Please tell Mrs Symes that I'll be late for supper.'

Algy flushed at this.

'Now not so fast. Who said that you were going? It was my idea – or at any rate, my father's – and I wouldn't dream of letting you have all the fun.'

'And I,' retorted Biggles, 'am your superior officer. As such it's my decision who should go.'

'Sounds like stalemate,' said Algy with a grin. 'Only one thing for it. We must toss for it – the winner goes.'

Biggles nodded, and producing a half-crown, spun it expertly and slapped it on his hand.

'Heads!' shouted Algy.

And heads it was.

Biggles and Algy were at Brooklands early, and despite his cousin's cheerfulness, Biggles hated to see him go.

'No need at all to worry, dear old chap!' shouted Algy above the roar of the Supersnipe's great engine. 'I'll be home in time for supper, never fear.'

He raised a gloved hand, gunned the engine, and as Smyth pulled back the chocks from the aircraft's wheels, the Supersnipe went sailing off into the morning sky.

Biggles spent a singularly useless day, pottering around the airport, lunching at the club-house, and then driving off for tea with Smyth in Weybridge – anything to pass the time. The shadows on the airport lengthened, and the landing lights went on.

'Captain Lacey will be back any minute now sir, I suppose,' said Smyth.

But he wasn't.

Biggles stayed on at Brooklands all that night and by breakfast-time, with Algy missing still, he decided something must be done. But what? It was difficult to know exactly what to do that wouldn't cause more trouble than it solved, for as Biggles had already pointed out, they had no authority to fly to Germany, and if he sounded the alarm and Algy had simply been delayed en route, there would be hell to pay.

On the other hand, if he had crashed, search parties should be looking for him. Biggles pondered deeply over breakfast and finally decided there was one man in England who could be relied upon to help him. Ten minutes later he was hurling the Bentley up the London Road in search of him.

'Ah, Bigglesworth!' said Colonel Raymond, as Biggles entered the large airy room with its view across the Thames, from which the Colonel ran the Criminal Intelligence Department of New Scotland Yard. 'An unexpected pleasure! What are you up to now that you've left 266? I heard something about you and old Lord Lacey's heir setting up together. Charter flights or something of the sort. Any truth in it?'

Biggles smiled modestly.

'Well, sir, we're a little more ambitious than the usual charter firm. Algy and I are really after something that peacetime life appears to lack.'

'What's that?' asked Colonel Raymond, screwing his monocle in place, and fixing Biggles with his eagle eye.

'Excitement, sir!'

'Good God, man!' said the Colonel. 'I'd have thought that both of you had had enough of that to last a lifetime.'

'It becomes something of a habit,' replied Biggles.

'I suppose it does,' said Colonel Raymond, pensively. 'I'm not certain that I couldn't use you in my line of business. We'll have to see, but in the meantime what can I do for you today? I can't believe you've driven here at this unearthly hour simply for old time's sake.'

'Well, no sir. Since you mention it, I have a little problem and I wanted your advice. It's about Algy ...'

In a few well-chosen words, Biggles proceeded to outline the strange story of Professor Krahenbiehl and Algy's flight to Frankfurt, and as he did so, Colonel Raymond's face looked grim.

'Well,' he growled when Biggles finished. 'I would award your cousin high marks for daring – but none at all for common sense. If you'd only come to me originally, I might have given you a little help – and good advice. Serious business, you know, making an unauthorised flight into ex-enemy territory like this. Most probably he's been arrested and at this very moment is cooling his heels inside a German gaol. And quite right too. Daft young idiot!'

Biggles began to feel his anger rise at hearing Algy thus described, fair though he knew the Colonel's words to be.

'But all the same sir, we can't leave him to the gentle mercy of the Huns. He's an Englishman, and also he's my partner and my friend. Besides, we don't know for certain that he is in prison. He may have crashed – or anything.'

The Colonel's face relaxed at this, and he nodded sympathetically.

'You've a point there, Bigglesworth. First we must ascertain our facts.' He glanced swiftly at his wristlet watch. 'You know the Blazers' Club in St James's? Meet me there for luncheon at twelve-thirty sharp. By then I hope to have the information that we need, and possibly the two of us can work out an appropriate campaign.'

Biggles had often heard of the Blazers' Club, that holy of holies of the Secret Service world, but he had never been beyond its eighteenth-century portals. Discreetly tucked away in a small street between St James's and Green Park, its elegant exterior had scarcely changed from the days when it had been the town house of some long-dead nobleman. Even its subfusc interior – old panelling, dim portraits, solid hide armchairs – gave little hint that here the casual visitor was entering the most exclusive club in London, and for that matter, in the Empire.

Early though Biggles was, the Colonel was already waiting for him in the vestibule. His visage was distinctly stern.

'Well, sir?' asked Biggles, ready for the worst.

'Not here, Bigglesworth. Let us both wait until we're seated at the luncheon table. No point in muddying the gastric juices with premature bad news. Here at Blazers' we pride ourselves on having one of the six best chefs in Europe and we owe it to him to do justice to his art.'

Eager though Biggles was for news of Algy, he could do nothing but possess himself in patience, and it was not until the potted shrimps were on the table, and the Colonel had satisfied himself that the legendary Club claret was at the proper temperature, that Biggles blurted out the question that he had to ask.

'What news of Algy?'

The Colonel shook his head and sniffed the claret for the umpteenth time.

'None,' he said briskly.

'None?' repeated Biggles. 'But there must be something, sir. Some news from Frankfurt, or the report of a crash in Switzerland.'

'I said none, and I mean none,' barked the Colonel. 'I've made the most thorough inquiries across Europe, and I've drawn a blank. Your friend has vanished into the thinnest of thin air. I'm sorry Bigglesworth, but there it is.'

Biggles felt his heart begin to pound.

'Poor old chap,' he said. 'I blame myself. I should have stopped him going. It's entirely my fault. So there's nothing to be done but wait?'

'I didn't say that,' Raymond replied quickly. 'I drew a blank about your friend, but in the process of inquiry I discovered several most disturbing facts.'

'Such as?'

'That Lacey landed at Frankfurt entirely as planned just after two o'clock yesterday afternoon. He refuelled, and took off again some twenty minutes later with a passenger he evidently felt was your Professor Krahenbiehl.'

'And wasn't it?'

Raymond shook his head.

'One of my men, acting on my orders, went to the Professor's house. Professor Krahenbiehl was there – in perfect health, and total ignorance of his so-called flight to Switzerland.'

'Ignorance?' said Biggles. 'That's impossible! I saw the letter that he wrote to Algy's father.'

'Plainly a forgery. It wouldn't have been too difficult to do. You told me that Lord Lacey hadn't seen Krahenbiehl since well before the war. It wouldn't have needed much ingenuity to fake his writing, and it would seem a reasonable deduction that this was done by whoever was aboard the plane.'

'But why should anybody bother?' Biggles asked.

'Good question,' said the Colonel. 'Whoever it was was obviously desperate to get out of Germany and would take almost any risk to achieve his aim. What does that suggest?'

'A war criminal?' said Biggles.

Raymond nodded. 'Or possibly a spy. And there is something else we know about him.'

'Yes?'

'He was acquainted with your family and knew enough about you and Lacey to be certain one of you would take the risk you did. Any idea who it could be?'

'None,' said Biggles. 'Absolutely none.'

'Well, we must try and think, for more than Lacey's safety is at stake. If I'm right – and I'm pretty sure I am – this could be far bigger than either of us dreamt.'

For once in his life, Biggles felt completely at a loss, but at least he now possessed the full support of Colonel Raymond, and through him, of the British Secret Service, as the Colonel was convinced of the importance of the case. But although the search for Algy and the Supersnipe had spread, and every British agent in the field was contacted for urgent information, none was forthcoming. Two days passed – anxious days during which Biggles stayed in London, and had several conferences with Colonel Raymond. The two men racked their brains to discover the identity of Algy's passenger, but neither made much progress. Then came the news that Biggles had been dreading all along. Colonel Raymond telephoned to say that the burned-out wreckage of an unknown aeroplane had been spotted on a mountainside near Freiburg, some forty miles on the German side of the frontier with Switzerland.

'Any sign of survivors?' Biggles asked, trying to disguise the dread he felt.

'No reports of any,' said the Colonel gruffly, 'and by the sound of things it seems unlikely. But it appears pretty clear that it's your aircraft. I'm sorry, Bigglesworth. We'll talk tomorrow when more definite news arrives.'

Biggles felt broken by the news. To think that after all the dangers he had faced in battle, Algy had had to go like this – in a stupid crash against a mountain in bad weather. But that was how it often was. Drysdale, the toughest flier they had had in 266, had been knocked over by a bicycle and killed. Duclos, the legendary Belgian ace, died when he fell off a tram in Paris. At least Algy had gone as he would have wished – at the controls of an aeroplane with all his faculties intact. But what would happen now? Biggles didn't care to think about the future without Algy. Certainly he hadn't the heart to continue Biggles and Co. without him – or to go on flying for that matter.

Oppressed by these gloomy thoughts, he sat drinking in his den till long past midnight, knowing that if he went to bed he would never sleep. It was nearly one, and he had all but killed his bottle of Johnnie Walker when he was roused from his reverie by the shrilling of the telephone in the hall. He let it ring for several minutes, cursing whoever was calling him at that time of night and hoping he would go away. But the ringing persisted, and finally he lumbered to his feet, and took the call.

'Major Bigglesworth? The Continental operator here. I have a call for you from Germany.'

'From where?' said Biggles. But before the operator could reply a distant voice had broken in. It was so faint that he could barely hear, but there was no mistaking its identity. It was Algy.

'Algy, old chap!' bawled Biggles. 'Suffering cats, where are you? I thought you'd had it.'

From the disjointed words that crackled through the telephone, Biggles had difficulty making sense of Algy's story.

'Sorry, Biggles ... crashed ... unhurt ... being held at Freiburg.'

'Where?' Biggles shouted.

'Freiburg ... I'm held hostage ... can't say who ... either they get an aeroplane to fly them on to Zurich, or I've had it ... Freiburg, Biggles. Don't let me down ... they mean business.'

Before Biggles could say another word, the telephone went dead.

'All of my chaps have drawn a blank, I'm afraid, Bigglesworth,' said Colonel Raymond next morning. 'We've been in touch with the police in Freiburg, but with Lacey's life at stake, I had to tell them to go easy. Not that they've any news either.'

The Colonel scratched his head.

'Dashed if I know what the next move is, Bigglesworth. I suppose we sit and wait for Lacey's captors to make a fresh demand.'

Biggles looked grim, and shook his head.

'I don't like the idea of that at all. Think of old Algy, stuck there with some flaming lunatic and thinking each moment is his last. Besides, sir, he appealed to me for help, and I'm his friend. With your permission, I've got to go to Freiburg.'

Colonel Raymond stared across the room. Down below, the Thames was sparkling in the morning sunlight, and as he watched it, this proud, lonely man found himself envying the ordinary people in the street who could enjoy a scene like this without the burden of responsibility he always carried. Finally, he slapped his stainless steel ruler on the desk.

'Right you are, Bigglesworth. I'll back you. Probably I shouldn't – and if anything goes wrong, I'll soon be seeking fresh employment. Please remember that. But we can't leave Lacey without doing something. I'll arrange an aircraft for you and all necessary clearances. Then you're on your own. Don't let me down.'

'As if I could!' said Biggles.

An hour later, Biggles was at Heston Airport, performing the last-minute checks on a long-range Vickers monoplane, lent by the R.A.F. He had borrowed goggles and a flying suit, and at Colonel Raymond's own suggestion had been issued with a ·32 Browning automatic from the armoury. Apart from a thermos flask of scalding coffee, this was all Biggles carried for the long flight to Germany.

Once he was airborne all his worries left him. New though the aircraft was to him, the controls were no problem to a flier of his experience, and before long the English Channel was below him

like a bright blue mist as the monoplane roared on at 15,000 feet.
Then came the patchwork fields of France, and about an hour
later he espied the Rhine, a silver ribbon just below his wing-tip.

'Hunland!' he thought – the stronghold he had fought against
for all those months in France. What devilment was being
hatched there even in defeat? When would that barbarous race
ever learn its lesson? If they had done anything to Algy ... He
ground his teeth and checked his compass. Strasbourg sprawled
below him on the right, and with the mountains on his left
horizon he urged the aircraft on the straight flight south to
Freiburg.

He still had no idea how he would contact Algy, but he
assumed his captors must have prompted him to make the call
and would be soon prepared to introduce themselves. The airport
was a simple field outside the town, with two small hangars and a
runway. He circled it, and at first saw little sign of life, but as he
came in to land, he saw a large black car suddenly race towards
him from the perimeter of the field, and by the time his engine
stopped, the car had drawn up some twenty yards away. It had
darkened windows so that he could not see inside.

He was about to jump down from the cockpit when the driver's
door swung open and he heard a voice he thought he recognised –
a guttural, inhuman voice that stirred vague memories from the
past.

'Bigglesworth, stay where you are. That's excellent. Now, no
tricks please. I have you covered and would hate to have to kill
you now. You will please walk towards me with your hands
above your head. You must excuse me, but I must assure myself
you are not armed. March! Quick!'

But Biggles wasn't being hurried.

'Just a moment! What about Captain Lacey?' he called back.

'He's here with me. See for yourself!' The passenger door
swung open, and Biggles glimpsed a recumbent form, gagged
and tied hand and foot. There was no question who it was.

'O.K.,' he shouted then, 'I'm coming down,' and stepping
from the cockpit he advanced towards the car, his hands above
his head. The far door of the car opened wider now, and a masked
figure emerged, holding a massive Mauser automatic. He limped
slightly, and at that moment Biggles recognised him.

'Von Stalhein!' he exclaimed. 'I thought that you were dead.'

'It would suit many people if I were, but no such luck! A little higher, please. That's better.'

Biggles was conscious of cold, reptilian eyes fixing him through the thin slits of the mask, and despite himself he shivered as he felt the Junker's hands exploring his defenceless body.

'A Browning automatic!' snarled von Stalhein. 'You should have known better, Bigglesworth. Such toys are for children!' and he sent the weapon spinning onto the grass behind him.

'Now we must be swift. There are certain things I want transferred from the car into your plane. You will carry them, and I will keep you covered.'

'Not until you remove the gag from Captain Lacey. You know quite well that that's no way to treat an officer and a gentleman, von Stalhein.'

The Prussian shrugged.

'Very well. There's nothing he can do now anyhow. Captain Lacey, my apologies.'

'Sorry, Biggles,' Algy said when the bandage was removed. 'I should have followed your advice. I wouldn't be in this mess ...'

'Enough of that,' barked von Stalhein. 'Bigglesworth, in the back of the car are six large cases. Place them in the cockpit.'

'Professor Krahenbiehl's famous specimens,' said Biggles.

'You might call them that,' von Stalhein said. 'Hurry now. I'm anxious to be off.'

Biggles went to lift the first of the cases. It was as much as he could do to carry it, but finally he had staggered to the aircraft with all six of them.

'And now?' asked Biggles.

'Into the aircraft please. We will fly due south.'

'I thought you wished to get to Zurich. That's south-east from here.'

'And fly straight into the arms of your Colonel Raymond or one of his employees? Please to credit me with just a little sense, Major. No, we will land at Basel. There is a small airport there, and I have made arrangements to be met. Once that is done all your responsibilities will be over. But don't forget, Major Bigglesworth, I shall be sitting just behind you, and at the first sign of double-dealing I shall blow your head off.'

Biggles nodded.

'And what about Captain Lacey?'

'He can stay where he is. I'm sure he's rather stiff, but otherwise in perfect health. Once we have gone, someone will release him.'

Biggles realised that it was pointless arguing, so after a brief farewell to Algy, he climbed aboard the aircraft, revved the engine, and glanced back quickly to see the muzzle of von Stalhein's automatic just behind his neck. Angrily he opened up the throttle, and the plane soared up the runway on its way to Switzerland.

It was a short, uneventful flight to Basel, but all the way Biggles racked his brains to think of how to outwit von Stalhein. Some things were clear to him already. It had obviously suited the wily Prussian to have had Biggles and the British Secret Service believe that he had died on his mission to Palestine, and since then he had enjoyed the perfect cover for a spy – that of a man his enemies believe is dead. It was a daring plan of his to count on Biggles or Algy to get him into Switzerland under the guise of old Professor Krahenbiehl. But why take such a risk? Biggles could not believe von Stalhein needed to escape from Germany on his own account. Whatever crimes the man was guilty of, he was so elusive and such a master of disguise that he could confidently escape from any manhunt. The answer clearly lay in that mysterious luggage he carried with him. It must be desperately important for a man like von Stalhein to have taken quite such risks to get it into Switzerland. Biggles would have given almost anything for a chance to peep inside those six black cases, but von Stalhein's Mauser was still six inches from his neck, and now that they were coming into land, Biggles required all his energies to bring the monoplane safely into the small mountain airport.

He made his usual perfect three-point landing.

'A stylish piece of flying, Major,' said von Stalhein as the big aircraft rolled to a halt before the airport building. He had now taken off his mask, and, but for the cropped hair and livid duelling scars disfiguring his cheeks, might have been an ordinary businessman.

'Now listen carefully,' he went on. I have everything arranged. The customs men are in my pay, and you and I will take the baggage through without any trouble. Outside the airport my associate is waiting with a car. Once we are gone you are free to do exactly as you like, but until that moment I shall be behind you and will have the Mauser in my pocket. So no tricks, Major Bigglesworth. It would upset me to be obliged to kill so excellent a pilot.'

Biggles nodded.

'You win, von Stalhein – for the moment. But don't think you'll get away with it.'

'Oh, but I think I have already. Now, the luggage if you please. Be careful with it. Be good enough to load it on that porter's trolley, and I must be on my way.'

Biggles had no alternative but to do as he was told. He piled the heavy bags aboard the trolley and, followed by von Stalhein, pushed them past the few officials who were in the airport and out towards a waiting car. He had all but reached it when he heard someone behind him say, 'One moment, sir!'

He turned and saw that a tall, good-looking man with spectacles had approached von Stalhein, and that the Prussian was attempting to ignore him.

'Excuse me, sir,' the man repeated with polite insistence.

'What is it?' growled von Stalhein. 'Can't you see I'm in a hurry?'

'I won't keep you long, sir. Just a small formality. Inspector Luscher, Swiss Federal Police. Your passport would appear to be out of date. Would you mind ...'

It was the diversion Biggles needed, and in a flash he turned upon von Stalhein. A shot rang out – but von Stalhein's aim was faulty now and the bullet went whining harmlessly away. At the same time, Biggles had the satisfaction of landing a good British uppercut onto the Junker's jaw.

'That's for Algy,' Biggles gasped, 'and that's for ...' But before he could land a second blow von Stalhein had wrenched himself away and bounded like a panther for the waiting car. The engine was already running and as the door swung open for him, Biggles had a clear view of the driver. It was a face that he could never in his life forget, a small white face framed in a halo of blonde hair. The driver of von Stalhein's car was Marie Janis.

Not that Biggles had much time to dwell upon the fact, for von Stalhein was still armed, and as the car sped off he raised his Mauser and was about to fire at Biggles. Rage suffused his face and at such short range no one could have missed, but at just that moment Biggles saw Marie raise her arm and grab von Stalhein by the sleeve. She must have shouted something, for the Prussian turned towards her and held his fire. Then the car roared off, leaving Biggles by the roadside with six large suitcases.

'Well, Bigglesworth, twelve million pounds in bullion and assorted currencies. Not a bad haul for an afternoon. I congratulate you.'

The scene was the Adam dining room of the Blazers' Club the following evening, and Colonel Raymond, in full evening dress, raised his glass to Biggles.

'At least the British taxpayer isn't out of pocket for my flight, sir.' Biggles said. 'My one regret is that von Stalhein got away like that. The man's as slippery as a cobra.'

'And as evil,' Algy added. 'I have a score or two to settle with him for the way he treated me. But one thing still puzzles me, sir. Where did the money come from?'

Colonel Raymond smiled as he lit a large cigar.

'You really want to know? I'll tell you. It was part of the hidden funds of the old German Secret Service. Von Stalhein had had access to them since the Armistice.'

'So he was just a common criminal?' said Algy.

The Colonel shook his head.

'To give the devil his due, he didn't want the money for himself. It was more serious than that. From what Inspector Luscher tells me, he was planning to use it to finance an undercover network of German agents inside Switzerland to provide a nucleus of trained spies for the future. The Germans may have lost the war, but the German Secret Service, with von Stalhein at the head, is not so easily defeated. Still, Bigglesworth, your action dealt it quite a blow. Small wonder he was furious when it all went wrong. You were lucky that he didn't kill you.'

'But for Marie he would have done,' said Biggles softly.

'Marie? Oh yes, that girl of yours. Of course,' said Colonel Raymond. 'We should have dealt with her originally when we had the chance. She's dangerous, you know.'

'I don't believe it, sir,' said Biggles.

'I'm sorry, Bigglesworth, I know how you feel about her, but you can't fly in the face of facts. Even when you knew her first she was working for the German Secret Service. Since then she has become one of their most daring operators – and von Stalhein's mistress.'

Biggles was on his feet.

'His what, sir?'

'Now, Bigglesworth, sit down, there's a good fellow,' said the Colonel. His voice was gentle now, but as he spoke to Biggles it was with the firmness of a father talking to his son. 'I know it's hard for you, but you must be realistic. The reports that I have had leave no room for doubt. Why else do you think that she was waiting for him at the airport?'

'Seems pretty obvious to me,' said Algy.

Biggles said nothing.

'More champagne?' asked Colonel Raymond anxiously. 'It's Bollinger 98. Drink up, Bigglesworth, it's very good. And take my advice, forget her. There are more fish in the sea, old boy.'

'But sir, you don't understand. Yesterday she saved my life! You don't forget a girl like that, even if she is a spy. So, with your permission sir, I propose a toast. To Marie – whatever and wherever she may be!'

'I'll second that,' said Algy.

There was a pause as Colonel Raymond stared across the table. Then he raised his glass.

'Marie!' he said.

And in silence Biggles drank to the woman he still loved.

5

Flying High

'Well,' said Biggles, putting his legs against the fender in his den and lighting a gold-tipped Turkish cigarette, 'things are distinctly looking up, Algy my old lad.'

Algy grinned back at him from the armchair opposite and closed his blue account-book with a bang.

'Over £4,000 straight profit on our first year's operations. That's after allowing for depreciation on the aircraft, wages, petrol, every jolly thing. Biggles and Co. has quite a healthy surplus at the bank.'

'Wages of sin!' laughed Biggles. 'Only one thing rather worries me. What are we going to do with all this wealth?'

As Biggles knew quite well, the company had been extremely lucky, thanks in the main to Colonel Raymond's influence. As something of a reward for the recovery of von Stalhein's gold – and as replacement for the Supersnipe – he had persuaded the British Government to make an outright gift of the Vickers monoplane to Biggles and Co. It was through Colonel Raymond also that they had been recommended for a number of lucrative operations. The best of these has been the Cronfelt Bullion job (described in detail by Captain Johns in his book *Biggles and Co.*). This had established the two cousins as couriers extraordinary, fliers entrusted by the banks, diamond dealers and insurance companies to transport valuables around the globe at a moment's notice, and business had been booming ever since. An old protegé of Biggles', 'Ginger' Hebblethwaite, had recently been added to the payroll as an extra pilot, and the company now owned a powerful six-seater plane, the Cormorant.

'We seem to have found ourselves an airline,' Biggles had remarked with barely feigned surprise, and although a regular business was the last thing either of them had intended, Biggles and Co. was running with considerable efficiency. Algy had managed the accounts – and shown quite a flair for high finance – whilst Biggles worked as unofficial operations manager, dealing with customers, keeping an eye on Smyth who serviced and repaired the aircraft, and coping with extra staff whenever the need arose.

Biggles and Algy still flew as regularly as ever, but the truth was that suddenly they both felt slightly bored by all the humdrum details of their life.

'The trouble is,' said Algy, lighting a cigarette as well, 'we're both in danger of becoming blasted businessmen. Money, balance sheets and wage bills – they weren't what we wanted when we started flying. And you, my fat friend, unless I'm much mistaken, are beginning to develop quite a paunch. Really, Biggles my old lad, something must be done.'

'Stuff and nonsense!' retorted Biggles, slapping his midriff, 'stomach muscles of iron. Not an ounce of surplus fat anywhere!'

'All the same,' laughed Algy, 'I think I'd better have a word with Mrs Symes to go easy on the steak and kidney pudding.'

'You'll do no such thing,' said Biggles. 'What we both need is something different, not just a change of diet. Why don't we have a holiday?'

Biggles had never really had a holiday before, apart from his times with General Bigglesworth during his breaks from Malton Hall, and he and Algy were determined to enjoy themselves. Luckily, Ginger Hebblethwaite was more than competent to manage the company during the fortnight they planned to be away, and anyhow, the tail-end of February was a slack period for commercial flying.

'Be glad to be rid of you both,' said the irrepressible Yorkshireman. 'Always hanging round the bar at Brooklands and making the mechanics nervous. Smyth is planning to overhaul the Cormorant once you're off the scene and I'll put the company in order in your absence.'

'What it is to be a genius!' said Algy, grinning. 'Still, it's good to know that Biggles and Co. will be in safe hands while we're gone.'

'And where might you be going to, you old lounge-lizard? I think a walking holiday through the Yorkshire Dales at this time of year would do both of you a power of good.'

'Or a bike ride to John o' Groats,' retorted Algy. 'No, Ginger my old scout, we'll leave the violent exercise to you. I've persuaded Biggles that we owe it to ourselves to holiday in style. Only place a gentleman can go in February is Monte Carlo. A good hotel, a little flutter at the casino, some decent French food. It'll be good for Biggles. He's been dwelling on that wretched Janis woman ever since the von Stalhein business and it'll give him something new to think about.'

'You mean it will give *you* an opportunity to get up to no good, Algernon my boy. I know your sort. But while you're trying to break the bank, be careful that you don't go and break the company instead. Biggles and Co. shouldn't play roulette.'

'Oh, I don't know,' said Algy dreamily. 'A few bob invested in Dame Fortune never did much harm.'

It was a perfect journey to the south. The Bentley had been specially tuned up by Smyth, and as it bowled along the straight French roads with Algy at the wheel, all their cares seemed left behind in wintry London. Just after Paris the rain stopped and by the time they reached Lyons, they were in brilliant sunshine; it seemed that spring had come. Even Biggles, who was ill at ease without an aeroplane to fly, had suddenly relaxed. They dined in style at Mère Brazier's, stayed at the best hotel in town, and made an early start for Monte Carlo, where they arrived in time for lunch.

'Where are we staying?' Biggles asked.

'Little place called the Hôtel de Paris,' said Algy with a grin. 'That's where the parents always stay. The Mater says it's the one place on the Riviera where you can trust the plumbing, so I've followed her advice.'

'But dear old chap, it's the most expensive hotel in the South of France!'

'Biggles, my boy, you're too concerned with filthy lucre. We agreed finance was my department, so leave the sordid details to your old pal Algy. Enjoy yourself. I'm told the lobster here is reasonable, and how about some really good champagne? Nothing like starting as you mean to continue.'

Biggles would have protested further, but Algy's high spirits were infectious. They garaged the Bentley, entrusted their luggage to a porter with a gold and black striped waistcoat, and sat enjoying their champagne on the terrace.

'To think that back in dear old London, everyone's shivering with cold,' said Biggles.

'That's half the fun of this,' said Algy. 'Enjoy it while you can, old boy, it won't last. Nothing really pleasant ever does. Incidentally, how about setting up a branch of Biggles and Co. here in the South of France? I'm willing to make the sacrifice of working here if you'll run the show from England.'

'Extremely decent of you, Algy, but by the sound of it, someone's got here before us.'

As he spoke his voice was drowned in the roar of an aircraft engine, and a sleek blue biplane flashed across the terrace at a height of less than fifty feet, narrowly missed the gleaming bulk of the Casino, then swept across the harbour in a 360-degree roll. Then, amid the 'oohs' and 'aahs' of the people on the terrace, the small plane climbed like a rocket, looped the loop, and then came screaming down towards the ranks of expensive yachts gathered in the harbour. By now half the watchers on the terrace were on their feet, as it seemed certain that the plane would crash. For several seconds it was out of sight, hidden by the promenade and Casino, but instead of an explosion, there was a sudden roar and the glitter of blue wings as the plane pulled out of its dive and flashed past the terrace, waggling its wings and zooming out of sight into the perfect sky.

'Not bad,' said Algy. 'Not bad at all!'

Biggles nodded. 'All the same, I can't stand chaps who will go showing off like that. What do they have to prove? If the silly idiot had crashed it wouldn't just have been his own life down the drain. Dozens could have died.'

'True, master. Very true. But all the same he didn't crash and a spot of showing-off does nobody much harm. I wonder who the hell it was. *Garçon!*' he shouted to the waiter who was hovering behind their table. '*Connaissez-vous l'aviateur?*'

'But certainly, sir,' replied the waiter, in perfect English. 'He is one of your own countrymen. Captain James Gordon-Bell. He is extremely rich. How do you say, a playboy? He has a lady friend who owns a big yacht in the harbour. He does the aerobatics to impress her, so they say.'

'Cor, stone the crows!' said Algy when the waiter was safely out of earshot. 'D'you hear that Biggles? Wasn't he the bounder they chucked out of 266? Dreadful fellow?'

Biggles nodded. 'Couldn't stand him – nor could anybody else. He was yellow too. That's why he got his marching orders. Nerve cracked or something!'

'Well, he seems to have recovered it, and no mistake. But Biggles, surely he was never rich? Unless my memory deceives me he never had two brass farthings to rub together.'

'Absolutely! Most mysterious. But I suggest we direct our attention to rather more important topics than the appalling Gordon-Bell. What did you say the speciality was here? Lobster tails *au gratin?* This sea air's made me feel distinctly peckish.'

Excellent although the luncheon was, the topic of Gordon-Bell could not be so easily dismissed. It fascinated Algy, and as they strolled along the promenade that afternoon, it cropped up again, when a magnificent white Rolls-Royce swept past.

'D'you see that, Biggles?'

'Splendid motorcar,' he replied. 'And a very pretty girl inside.'

'Sex will be your downfall, Bigglesworth my lad. Didn't you see the driver? It was our old friend, Gordon-Bell!'

'Some fellows do have all the luck without deserving it,' said Biggles.

For the next few days it seemed as if Gordon-Bell was dogging them. That night at the Casino he was there, immaculately dressed, and once again accompanied by the woman Biggles and Algy had spotted in the white Rolls-Royce. Beneath the glitter of the chandeliers she was more beautiful than ever. She wore a long black velvet dress, which showed off her blonde hair to perfection. As for the diamond necklace she was wearing, its splendour almost rivalled the perfection of her admirable bust. The *salle privée* that night was crammed with the best of

Monegasque society, but she instantly stood out. So, for that matter, did her companion. Biggles remembered him as a frightened-looking youth from his days with 266, but now, in evening dress, his face tanned with the southern sun, Gordon-Bell was totally transformed.

Biggles and Algy tried their luck at *chemin-de-fer* at the same table as this glamorous couple. Biggles won 200 francs, and then stopped.

'Quite enough for one night, Algy. I'm not the Duke of Westminster – much as I'd like to be. Two hundred francs seems pretty good to me.'

But Algy was less circumspect. He lost on the king of hearts. He lost again on the knave of diamonds. He broke even for a while, but then his luck began to change. After half an hour's play he had a pile of chips worth 2,000 francs before him on the green baize table.

'*Messieurs, mesdames, faîtes vos jeux,*' intoned the croupier, and Biggles nudged Algy in the ribs.

'Enough's enough,' he whispered. 'Take my advice and scarper with the winnings.'

But Algy lacked his cousin's Scottish streak, and at that moment glanced across the table. The woman with Gordon-Bell was nonchalantly placing two thousand-franc chips on black, and as she did so all eyes round the table narrowed at the sight of such a bet.

'*Faîtes vos jeux!*' chanted the croupier again, and on a sudden impulse Algy pushed all the chips he had onto the black as well.

There was a sudden hush, and for just a moment Algy felt the woman's eyes meet his across the table. The other bets were laid, and then came silence as the cards were played. A six of hearts, an eight of diamonds, then an ace of hearts.

'Jehosaphat! You've won, my boy,' said Biggles. But there was still one card to play and by now all eyes were on the croupier as he took the last card from the shoe. He silently deposited it on the table – and a gasp went up from all the players. It was the ace of diamonds, the dreaded 'bird of death' – which swept the board.

Algy shrugged his shoulders philosophically and rose from the table.

'Well, it's not every night a chap can say he lost 2,000 francs.'

'At least we made 200 francs between us,' Biggles said

consolingly. 'Let's go and invest it in a drink. Nothing like a little
alcohol. I think we need it.'

The dramatic end to Algy's winning run started a general
exodus from the table, and as the two friends made their way
through to the main gaming rooms, they came almost face to face
with Gordon-Bell and the woman in black velvet.

Algy smiled awkwardly. 'Sorry you lost like that. Dashed hard
luck. Still, so did I, if it's any consolation.' Then, turning to
Gordon-Bell he added. 'I've an idea we've met before. Algy
Lacey. I was in France with 266 squadron – and so was my friend,
James Bigglesworth.' He held out his hand, but Gordon-Bell
appeared not to notice.

'There must be some mistake, Mr, er, Lacey. We've never met
before.' He gave a brief dismissive nod, took the woman by the
arm, and marched decisively away.

'Phew,' said Algy. 'Collapse of stout party! Do we smell or
something, dear old chap?'

'Perhaps he was scared of your snake-like powers of attraction
for the gentle sex, Algernon, my lad. But seriously, it was
extremely odd. He obviously recognised us both. Perhaps he just
didn't want to be reminded of his murky past, and come to think
of it, I can't entirely blame him.'

'Still,' said Algy with a miserable expression on his face. 'I
don't like being snubbed like that, particularly in the presence of
a woman. Makes a fellow feel a proper goof!'

Biggles slapped him firmly on the shoulder.

'Just forget it, Algy. The champagne bottle calls. Come and
drown your sorrows in the fleshpots of the south!'

But Gordon-Bell could not be dismissed so easily. As Biggles
and Algy sat together in the bar of the Hôtel de Paris, he and his
beautiful companion suddenly swept past. Next day the white
Rolls-Royce was once again purring along the promenade, and
once again the small blue biplane did its aerobatics while they
were drinking their pre-lunch aperitifs.

'Why can't the blighter go away?' said Algy irritably, as all
conversation on the terrace stopped against the roar of the
machine.

'He'll go away for good, if he carries on like this,' replied
Biggles. 'Just look at the idiot now! He wants his head examined.'

Even as Biggles pointed, the small aircraft zoomed up above the harbour in a dizzying climb, rolled, and came screeching down towards the sea, and, as on the day before, people on the terrace suddenly stood up to see what happened.

'I'm getting somewhat bored with this,' said Algy, lighting a Turkish cigarette with his old storm-proof Air Force lighter.

'Why don't we go and eat?' said Biggles.

But, before they could rise, there was a dull explosion from the direction of the harbour, followed by silence – then a hubbub of excited voices.

A woman shrieked, and Biggles shrugged his shoulders.

'Somehow I don't think Mr Gordon-Bell will be troubling us any more,' he said.

When they had eaten, Biggles and Algy strolled down to the harbour, out of curiosity. One of the hotel porters had already told them that the plane had narrowly missed hitting several yachts and had crashed into the sea, and by the time they arrived at the harbour there was already a cluster of small boats in the bay trying to raise the wreckage. There was a pair of divers with their big brass helmets, a barge with a crane aboard, and quite a crowd of watchers on the quay.

'What is it about a crash that always brings the ghouls along to have a look?' said Biggles tetchily. 'Anyone would think that it was entertainment.'

'Well, what are we doing here ourselves?' asked Algy logically.

'We're rather different. After all, we're in the business, which is more than can be said for them!' As he spoke he glared at a group of children who were following the salvage operations with considerable excitement, chattering and shouting as the remains of the fuselage were winched above the water. The wings and tail had broken off, but the blue-painted body of the plane was still intact, and as it was raised and swung aboard the barge, one could clearly see a huddled something in the cockpit, all that now remained of Gordon-Bell.

'Poor silly devil,' murmured Biggles. His face had drained of colour. He had encountered violent death more often than he cared to think, but the sight could still unnerve him. 'Why d'you think he did it?'

'We'll never know,' said Algy. 'The tiniest misjudgment is all it needs.'

'Of course. But why did the crazy lunatic take such appalling risks? It's different if you're up against the Huns – and if you cop it then, that's that. But why on earth destroy yourself for nothing?'

'P'raps he wanted to, old boy. He was a funny character, and I've known it happen. Or perhaps he really did feel he had to show off to that bird of his. That's something even I can understand.'

As Algy spoke, he turned away and Biggles followed him.

'Good Lord,' said Algy suddenly. 'Just look at that. *Cherchez la femme* with a blinking vengeance, Biggles. That woman must be cold as ice!'

There on the road above the harbour wall stood the white Rolls-Royce, with Gordon-Bell's woman at the wheel. She was watching as they drew his body from the cockpit, and calmly smoked a cigarette.

'Paging Major Bigglesworth! Paging Major Bigglesworth!' The voice of the bell-boy echoed round the cocktail lounge of the Hôtel de Paris.

Biggles beckoned to him.

'Yes? What is it?'

'Call for you from London, sir! Waiting on the line.'

Tipping the boy ten centimes, Biggles went off to take the call in the kiosk by the porter's office.

'Ah, Bigglesworth!' exclaimed a distant but unmistakeable voice. 'We've tracked you down.'

'Colonel Raymond!' replied Biggles cautiously. 'How did you know I was here?'

'We have our methods at New Scotland Yard. I gather from my spies that you and Lacey are on holiday. We policemen can't indulge in such frivolities. What's the weather like?'

Biggles told him, knowing quite well that the head of Scotland Yard's Criminal Information Department was not in the habit of making international telephone calls to inquire about the weather.

'Capital! Absolutely capital! I hope the two of you have been making the most of it.'

'We have, sir, and we plan to do so for the next ten days.'

'Of course, of course. But while you're busy sunning yourselves or whatever you do, I wondered if you'd see your way to doing a little job for me.'

'Well,' began Biggles still more cautiously.

'Nothing particularly difficult. Just an inquiry, but as you happened to be on the spot...'

Biggles groaned.

'What's that you said?'

'Nothing, sir. We'd be delighted.'

'I knew you would. It's about a scallywag called Gordon-Bell. Ex-flier like yourself. Living in Monte Carlo. Been hearing some worrying reports from Nisberg at the French *Sûreté*. Wondered if you could tactfully check the blighter out and ring me back. If we can avoid a scandal with a British national it always helps.'

'You're five hours late sir, I'm afraid. The poor devil's dead.'

'Dead! But how?'

Biggles told him. There was a brief silence on the line, and Biggles could picture Colonel Raymond at his desk with that brooding frown he knew so well.

'Sorry, Bigglesworth,' he said at last, 'but this is very serious and I have no alternative but to ask you and Lacey to conduct a thorough inquiry on my behalf.'

'But surely the French police will do that, sir?'

'Indeed they will, and that's what worries me. This is a very delicate affair. Now listen...'

'And so you see, old sport, there was nothing I could say – apart from refusing point-blank. And we owe a lot to Colonel Raymond.'

Biggles looked as sheepish as he sounded but Algy was furious.

'That's no excuse for getting us to do his dirty work for him while we are here on holiday,' he exclaimed. 'I was just planning a day's outing in the Bentley for tomorrow. Thought we might nip across to Italy. There's motor-racing at San Remo.'

''Fraid it'll have to wait.'

Algy shrugged his shoulders.

'O.K. You win, as usual. Now what exactly is this business about Gordon-Bell being mixed up in some racket smuggling cocaine? I never heard such nonsense.'

'I know it sounds improbable,' said Biggles, 'but the Colonel doesn't often make mistakes. He told me that just two days ago the French police in Paris rounded up a gang who were supplying drugs on a scale they'd never known since before the war. Millions of francs worth of the stuff. Most of the characters involved were small-time criminals but it was obvious to Commissioner Nisberg that someone big must be behind it all. Most of the crooks were Corsicans.'

'They usually are.'

'Quite right. Which made him think at first that it was the *Union Corse* – the Corsican Mafia – but it seems that just for once it wasn't. Several of the crooks broke down.'

'I'm not surprised with Nisberg interrogating them. Rather them than me, old fruit.'

'Or me. But the long and short of it was that all of them insisted that the centre of operations wasn't Corsica at all, but Monte Carlo. Gordon-Bell was mentioned and the real headquarters of the whole affair was apparently his girl-friend's yacht, the *Evening Cloud*. The two of them were running the racket together. She's an American, married to some Italian. Calls herself Contessa Torelli, and they've been making trips along the Italian coast, picking up the stuff, then flying it up to Paris in that plane of his.'

'Well, all that's over now,' said Algy. 'Neither our old friend Gordon-Bell nor his aeroplane will do any more drug-running this side of the great hereafter, and I'll take a bet that the lovely Countess is now safely back with her Italian husband, wherever he may be. So what exactly are we supposed to do?'

'Conduct a small investigation of our own. It seems that Colonel Raymond isn't satisfied about Gordon-Bell's demise. I've an idea that Raymond's keeping something up his sleeve about the man, but he asked me if we'd have a look at the wreckage of the plane on his behalf. Probably nothing in it, but you never know.'

The remains of the small blue biplane had been dragged into a warehouse near the quay when Biggles and Algy went to see them early next morning. They had no difficulty with the Monegasque police, thanks to a telegram from Paris, and apart from the presence of a single gendarme they were left in peace to examine the wreckage. Clearly no one else had bothered, but as fliers themselves, Biggles and Algy were both interested in inspecting it. This had been standard practice after any air crash with the R.F.C., and Biggles had had good experience in this sort of air detective work.

'Nifty little bus,' said Algy casting an expert eye over the controls. 'Everything seems in order. Looks as if it was straightforward pilot error that was responsible. Silly devil simply thought himself a bit too clever.'

'So it would appear,' said Biggles, 'but I'm still not entirely convinced. Why should a pilot of his obvious experience and skill crash like that?'

'Search me!' said Algy. 'But in the meantime what do you propose to do?'

'I thought I'd take a stroll up to the morgue – to have a look at what remains of Gordon-Bell. I know that Raymond will ask me if I've seen it. Coming?'

Algy looked uneasy.

'Of course,' he said. 'If you really want me to.'

Biggles looked at him and smiled understandingly. Algy had always been the squeamish sort.

'No point in two of us having to face the unpleasantness. Why don't you go back to the hotel. I'll meet you there for lunch.'

'Righty-ho, Biggles! Oh, and thanks!'

Viewing the corpse was not a task that Biggles relished either, but there was no dodging it, and the police doctor, a gnome-like Frenchman with an enormous belly and elaborate *pince-nez*, was already waiting for him. He was a talkative little man and all the time that he was showing Biggles what he called '*Exhibit numero trois*', he chatted on about the other sudden deaths he had had to deal with. Most of them, it seemed, were suicides. 'Foreigners, monsieur, who visit the Casino, stake all their livelihood on the tables, lose and have nothing left, then – poof!' He clapped his hands together and grinned up at Biggles. 'This poor country-man of yours seems to have been rather similar, monsieur.'

'How do you mean?' asked Biggles in surprise.

'Officially, of course, the death was accidental. That's what I've entered on the police report. But there was more to it than that. Look monsieur!' With a gesture formed by long experience, he flicked back the sheet to reveal the body. The legs were badly smashed, but the head and trunk were more or less intact. 'Here!' said the doctor, lifting up an arm. 'Do you notice anything?' Feeling slightly sick by now, Biggles examined the lifeless limb. On the inside, from the elbow to the wrist, was a row of livid dots.

'You know, of course, what that means?' said the doctor.

Biggles shook his head.

'The poor man was an addict. When I analysed his blood I discovered strong evidence of heroin. It would have made him over-confident and blurred his judgment, and I imagine that that was how he died.'

It was a nasty business, but the discovery of Gordon-Bell's addiction solved a lot of problems – the change of personality from the character they had known, and his involvement in the drug-ring. It also helped explain his wild flying and the manner of his death. The drugs had helped him overcome his fear, then made him increasingly reckless so that obviously his judgment had been impaired.

'Poor silly devil,' mused Biggles to himself as he strolled back across the harbour to the hotel, 'but at any rate I have something to report to Colonel Raymond.'

He looked along the quay and was not entirely surprised to see that the *Evening Cloud* had gone. What did surprise him was that there was no sign of Algy when he got back to the hotel, so he waited in the bar and put his call through to Colonel Raymond.

'Bad business,' said the Colonel when Biggles told him about Gordon-Bell. 'An ex-officer too. Can't think where they get these filthy habits. Tell you the truth, we'd had our eye on him for quite some while. He'd been dabbling in espionage for the Eastern Powers as well. Thoroughly bad hat. Still, *de mortuis* and all that, Bigglesworth.'

'Exactly, sir,' said Biggles. 'No point in judging the poor fellow now he's dead.'

'Quite. Of course, the real villain is that woman friend of his. What did you say her name was?'

'Torelli, sir. Contessa Torelli. At any rate, that's what she calls herself. Appears to have done a bunk. Her yacht has disappeared and nobody has seen her.'

'I'm not entirely surprised,' replied the Colonel drily. 'Still, she's Nisberg's headache and not ours, thank God! She won't get very far. How much longer are you and Lacey planning to stay?'

'Another week, sir – if you'll let us.'

Biggles heard Colonel Raymond chuckle to himself.

'That's a good one, Bigglesworth. Yes of course I'll let you. Very grateful too for all you've done. Have a good holiday. See you when you're back.'

Devoted though he was to Colonel Raymond, Biggles felt understandably relieved to have heard the last of him – for a few days at least – and could hardly wait to tell Algy that their holiday task was over, but there was still no sign of him. Nor was there any message at reception.

'Rum,' thought Biggles to himself. 'Probably spotted something in a skirt, if I know Algy.' He was not particularly concerned. Algy would be back in time for luncheon, that was for sure. In the meantime he would sit on the terrace, drink a *crème de cassis*, and study the crime pages of the *Nice Matin*. It was a treat to have a spot of relaxation in the sun at last.

By one o'clock, Biggles had finished his aper from cover to cover and consumed three *crèmes de cassis*, but there was still no sign of Algy. This was annoying. Biggles was hungry and could smell the aroma of delicious cooking wafting from the kitchens. So it was with some impatience that he approached Gaston, the head porter, to inquire if there was any news of his friend, Monsieur Lacey.

Gaston shook his head. No, he hadn't seen him since he went out two hours earlier. Did he say where he was going, Biggles asked.

'Not exactly, sir.'

'What do you mean, not exactly, Gaston?'

'Well, sir, he was with a lady. Very beautiful too, sir.'

Something about the way the porter spoke made Biggles suddenly anxious.

'Did you recognise the lady, Gaston?'

'*Mais bien sûr, monsieur*,' said Gaston cheerfully. 'It was the friend of the English *aviateur* who died. They went off together in her white Rolls-Royce.'

Biggles no longer felt like eating but there was little he could do. He tried to tell himself that he was getting alarmed over nothing and that Algy was more than competent to take care of himself with a mere woman. Perhaps he was, but all the time he had a vision of the Countess as he had seen her, calmly watching her lover's body dragged from the harbour. Algy would be so much human putty in the hands of such a creature.

Biggles had no alternative but to hang on at the hotel waiting for the telephone to ring. It did – but not for him, and by five o'clock he knew the time had come to make a move.

'But no, Monsieur Bigglesworth. It is impossible, impossible!' exclaimed the local *Commissaire de police*, when Biggles tried explaining what had happened. He was a barrel of a man with pink-rimmed eyes and an immense moustache. 'There is no way in which your friend Monsieur Lacey can have been with the Countess Torelli. Her yacht left Monte Carlo yesterday, and, *entre nous* monsieur, it was not a moment too soon. The French police are after her. A most distressing matter.'

'I know,' said Biggles grimly. 'Most distressing. But that's neither here nor there. The fact is that my friend has disappeared. Gaston, the head-porter at the Hôtel de Paris, believes that he was with this woman. If he is, his life could be in danger. Would you please start inquiries.'

The Frenchman was clearly not accustomed to dealing with characters as resolute as James Bigglesworth. He shrugged, he picked his teeth, he attempted to prevaricate, but Biggles was insistent and, as usual, got his way. 'Very well, monsieur,' the Commissaire said grudgingly. 'I will alert my men. They will be on the lookout for your friend, Mr Lacey. If there is any news I will telephone you at the Hôtel de Paris, instantly.

But there was no news – not until next morning when the Commissaire rang in person, sounding more polite than he had been the day before. The white Rolls-Royce had been discovered – abandoned at the Aeroport in Nice. A man and a woman fitting the descriptions of Algy and the Countess had been at the airport the previous evening. They had hired a small two-seater and flown off.

'Did anyone know where they were going?' Biggles asked.

'They said Toulon, along the coast,' the Commissaire replied, 'but I've telephoned the airport there. They've not arrived.'

'Where are you now?' asked Biggles tersely.

'Why, at the Aeroport of Nice.'

'Would you please wait, Monsieur le Commissaire. I'll be with you in twenty minutes.'

In any other circumstances, Biggles would have enjoyed the Aeroport of Nice. There were palm trees round the perimeter of the field, a pleasant bar, an orange-coloured wind-sock flapping lazily in the sea-borne early morning breeze, but he was not in the mood to appreciate such niceties. Algy was in danger. That was all that counted now.

The Commissaire was there to greet him.

'My apologies, Monsieur Bigglesworth,' he said. 'How do you English say, the bird has flown.' He laughed, but Biggles silenced him.

'Monsieur le Commissaire, this is urgent. My friend, Captain Lacey, is in danger with that woman. As you must know by now, she is a criminal, at the head of a network of other criminals. I intend to find him before it is too late.'

The Commissaire sucked at his moustache before replying.

'That will be difficult, monsieur.'

'Not at all,' said Biggles. 'If that woman could hire an aircraft, so can I.'

'Ah, so you are an *aviateur* as well? That is very good, Monsieur Bigglesworth, but how will you know where to search for him? The Mediterranean is a large pond to search for such a tiny fish.'

'If I know my friend,' said Biggles, 'he would not have gone without leaving me some clue to his destination. I wish to talk to the mechanic who saw them off last night.'

'I already have. He could tell us nothing.'

'Just the same, monsieur, with your permission I would like to talk to him myself.'

The mechanic was a typical Frenchman from the *Midi* – small, wiry, with a slightly puzzled smile. Biggles knew the type, and got on with him at once, particularly when they started talking about aircraft. Yes, he had seen the couple off. The aeroplane? A small, two-seater Darravaux. Its range? Five hundred kilometres normally.

'Normally?' said Biggles. 'Why do you say normally?'

'Well, it was strange, particularly as they said that they were only going to Toulon, but the woman would insist on taking extra petrol. Several cans of it.'

'How much exactly?' Biggles asked.

The mechanic scratched his head.

'About 100 litres. Quite a lot. She was particularly anxious about it.'

'And how far could they fly with all that extra petrol?' Biggles asked.

'Oh quite a way. Eight hundred kilometres at least.'

'That's interesting,' said Biggles. 'Now cast your mind back. Did you hear anything they said?'

The mechanic smiled at this and raised his hands apologetically.

'*Mais non monsieur!* They spoke in English and I have no English.'

'But you don't remember a single word? A name? Anything? Think hard.'

The little man sucked his teeth with concentration. Finally he spoke.

'The Englishman, he did say something I remember. He said it several times, a woman's name.'

'What name was that?' asked Biggles quickly.

'Lily, monsieur. I think he was trying to tell me that he was going to see Lily.'

Biggles racked his brains to think of any woman he and Algy knew called Lily. There had been one in Maranique but she had been married to the local chemist and, well, that was another story. Lily? Lily? There was Lily Pons the opera singer – hardly Algy's cup of tea – and there was the Lily of Laguna. No, nothing there. His mind went blank, and yet he was positive that if only he could think straight that simple female name must hold the clue he needed. He discussed the problem with the Commissaire, but he had nothing to suggest except for a notorious nightclub called Chez Lily in Antibes.

'Sounds just the sort of place he would enjoy, but he'd hardly need to fly there with a double load of fuel aboard.' As Biggles spoke these words they gave him an idea.

'Monsieur le Commissaire,' he said, 'have you a large-scale map of this whole area of the Mediterranean?'

'Of course,' replied the Commissaire. 'There is a very good one in the office. Come and see for yourself.'

'Now,' said Biggles, as he looked down upon the map, 'the mechanic tells me that with the extra fuel abroad, the aircraft can fly 800 kilometres.'

The Commissaire nodded, and Biggles continued thoughtfully, picking up a pair of compasses from the navigation desk.

'Suppose I set these compasses to exactly 800 kilometres against the scale of the map, then draw a circle with its centre here in Nice – its perimeter will mark the furthest distance that the plane can reach.'

'*D'accord*,' said the Commissaire nodding sagely, as Biggles began to draw.

'We can obviously ignore the French mainland as she wishes to escape from France, so where does that leave us?' He traced his finger along the lower part of the circle he had drawn. 'They could just about reach the Spanish border here south of Perpignan, or anywhere here in southern Corsica. That's possible, but somehow I feel Italy's more likely. She has an Italian title and must know the country. The only question is whereabouts along this line in Italy?'

The Commissaire shook his head as if all this was far too much for him, and Biggles spent several minutes studying the map in silence. The names of the main Italian cities were familiar to him – from Venice in the east, down through Gubbio and Perugia to the coast below Grosseto – but none of them suggested anything to him, and it would obviously take days to search so large an area. Then suddenly the Commissaire thought Biggles had gone mad, for he gave an enormous whoop of joy, seized him by the arm, and yelled excitedly in English.

'I've got it! Algy dear old boy, I've got it! Here monsieur, for Pete's sake, have a look at that!'

He jabbed a finger on the map, but the Commissaire shook his head in mute incomprehension.

'What does it say?' shouted Biggles.

'Isola del Giglio,' said the Commissaire wearily. 'An island off the coast of Italy. What's so special about it, monsieur?'

'The name,' said Biggles. 'What does it mean, *Giglio?*'

The Commissaire shrugged his shoulders.

'How should I know, monsieur? I'm a policeman, not a linguist.'

'It means Lily!' shouted Biggles. 'The Island of the Lily. I'll bet a brand-new Bentley to a pair of braces that that's where dear old Algy is.'

Twenty minutes later, Biggles was in the air, at the controls of a long-range Breguet biplane, heading south-east towards the coast of Italy.

Only one thought obsessed him now – would he still be in time? Before leaving, he had taken the precaution of putting through a quick call to Colonel Raymond, who had promised to do everything he could from London, including calling his old friend, General Maltesa, head of the Italian *Carabinieri* in Rome.

'He's a good egg, Maltesa, but you know that the Italians aren't renowned for speed. If you value Lacey's life, I would suggest you get to Giglio in double-quick time yourself. I've been talking to Nisberg about this Countess friend of yours. A very dangerous lady. Several murders to her credit under an early alias, and cunning as a snake. The network that she ran in France is broken, but she has other interests and accomplices and will already be planning some fresh devilment or other. Once Lacey has served his purpose to fly her out of France, I'd not give much for his chances of survival with a woman like the Countess.'

'Over my dead body,' muttered Biggles.

'Better make sure it isn't,' replied Raymond before ringing off.

It was a perfect day and suddenly Biggles was in his element again. The sea was amethyst, the plane was flying like a bird and, but for the knowledge that his friend was still in danger, Biggles would have been happier now than at any time since his holiday began. Even Algy's plight seemed less desperate now with the engine roaring steadily ahead and the wind singing in the guy-wires of the sturdy biplane. Corsica was below, its mountains

rising from the sea, and Biggles took the aircraft up to 15,000 feet.
Then there was sea again, with nothing but the occasional small
boat below to show that he was even moving. The hands of the
dashboard clock ticked by. He checked his course against his
compass bearing, and suddenly land appeared, a grey smudge
low on the left horizon. Ten minutes later it had turned into an
island, slap on course. Giglio – the island of the Lily.

He had no plans except to find a landing place and then to let
events take whatever course they pleased. With this in mind he
brought the aircraft down, and circled the tiny island at 500 feet.
There was no obvious sign of life, apart from two fishing boats at
anchor in the little harbour. He flew inland, following the line of
a cart-track to the centre of the island. There were odd cottages
and isolated farms but little else – and nowhere for an aeroplane
to land. Then suddenly he saw what he was looking for – towards
the northern tip of the island was a large white house, with a
rough field behind it. To the ordinary mortal it would have
appeared quite unremarkable but Biggles' practised eye saw
something that he recognised at once – tracks on the ground that
could be made by one thing only, an aircraft taking off or
landing. He banked and flew round behind the house. There
were two parked cars and further on a path that led to a natural
harbour by the rocks.

'So that's where the *Evening Cloud* goes when she's not at Monte
Carlo,' he murmured. 'O.K. Algy, here we come!'

With this he banked again, roared across the house, and then
came in for a perfect three-point landing.

He had been expecting some reaction, and gripped his
automatic as the plane rolled to a dusty halt, but there was not
the faintest sign of life. He jumped down from the cockpit and
began to walk towards the house – still nothing happened, and
the place seemed silent as the grave. He shouted. No one
answered. The house was shuttered, but when he tried the front-
door it opened and he entered. It took a moment for his eyes to
accustom themselves to the dim light in the room beyond.

'Good God!' he suddenly exclaimed with horror.

There were four people in the room sitting around a table. All
had been tied firmly to their chairs. Three of them were men he
had never seen before, but the fourth was wearing a black dress
and had long blonde hair. All of them were very dead. Biggles

was stunned at first and then his instinct was to get away from this house of death. But he had come here to find Algy, and was not leaving till he had.

It took him several minutes more to search the house, gun in hand, but there was not the faintest sign of life. In one room was a large laboratory, where presumably the drug ring had once had its factory. In another was a radio transmitter, but of Algy, and the unknown murderers of the quartet in the dining room, there was not the faintest sign.

Biggles started shouting, 'Algy! Algy!' Total silence followed. Then suddenly he did hear something – a tapping noise from somewhere underneath his feet.

He called again and once more the tapping seemed to answer, but when he looked around the room all he could see was the stone-flagged floor of the ancient kitchen. He called a third time and now managed to locate the sound. It seemed to issue from somewhere near the fireplace, and when he looked there closely, he could see a large stone slab that did duty for a hearth. He pulled at it. It moved. He pulled again, and underneath it he could see a narrow flight of steps descending into darkness. Using his pocket torch to show the way, he lowered himself through the cavity and found he was in an old wine cellar underneath the house. There, bound hand and foot, and tightly gagged, lay a dishevelled figure – Algy.

'My dear old chap!' gasped Biggles with relief. 'However long have you been lying there?'

A muffled groan issued in reply, and Biggles carefully removed the gag.

'Biggles, old boy,' said Algy weakly. 'I thought you'd never come.'

'Whatever happened?' Biggles asked, when they were safely out of the house.

'I'm not too sure myself,' Algy answered. 'That woman tricked me into going with her. She said you'd been delayed and had asked her to drive me down to meet you.'

'A likely tale,' growled Biggles. 'Still, go on.'

'When I realised she had tricked me, it was too late. She had a gun. She forced me to fly her here – and that was that. As soon as we arrived I was trussed up by her merry men and shoved into the cellar.'

'But what about the killings? How did they occur?'

'Haven't the foggiest, old chap, and that's a fact. All that I heard was a lot of scuffling and shouting around lunch-time. She started screaming something in Italian and there were shots. That was all. Next thing I heard was the sound of shutters being closed and doors slammed. I'd say there were half a dozen men, judging by the noise. Italians, and they all seemed pretty worked up, I can tell you. They must have cleared off straight away. Who d'you think they were, old boy?'

'Members of some rival gang, I'd say. Either the Mafia or the *Union Corse*. I shouldn't think we'll ever know for sure. That lady friend of yours had obviously got herself a lot of enemies. If you ask me, you were lucky to be in the cellar. Had they known you were there, they'd certainly have done for you as well.'

'Well, that's something I have to thank her for,' said Algy, managing a grin. 'But Christopher Columbus, what a dreadful way to go!'

'If ever anyone deserved it,' answered Biggles, 'it was your friend the Countess. She was a murderess, a gangster, and she had ruined countless lives through drugs. Take my advice and save your pity.'

Algy nodded.

'All the same,' he said regretfully, 'it does seem a confounded waste. She was a very pretty woman.'

'Algy, Algy, will you never learn?' said Biggles. 'Now, let's get going. I think we'll leave the Countess and her three friends to the Italians. They can do whatever's necessary. I've had enough of your island of the Lily, thank you very much – and we've still got six whole days in Monte Carlo.'

Five minutes later, the biplane took off with a roar and headed back to France.

6

Gone to Timbuctoo

'Just can't think what the trouble is with Biggles,' said Algy
wearily. 'Crotchety, bad-tempered, off his oats. Nearly bit my
head off yesterday just because I lent the Bentley to Deborah.
Dammit, Ginger, Deborah's a spiffing driver and it is my
blinking motor-car!'

Ginger nodded sympathetically.

'Well, you know what the old boy's like. He's very set in his
ways and has been counting on you to drive him over to
Mahoney's for the old Squadron reunion. These things mean a
lot to him, and we had to take a taxi in the end. Apart from the
expense, I think he'd hoped that you'd be there.'

'But Ginger, it's ridiculous. I've got to be allowed some private
life. And all this sentimental dwelling on the good old days –
frankly it bores me rigid!'

'Now, now, Algy, that's not fair,' said Ginger loyally. 'Biggles
is a great believer in *esprit de corps*, and with Mahoney back from
Kenya it was obviously important to him. I think you should
have gone as well.'

'Jeepers!' exclaimed Algy. 'Now you're turning against me
too. You know what I think, Ginger? We're all getting old.
There's Biggles coming up for his thirtieth birthday next month.
The old brain-box is softening with age.'

He tried to laugh, but Ginger cut him short.

'Now listen, Algy,' Ginger said, wagging an admonitory finger underneath Algy's nose. 'I want to hear no more of this. Whatever you and Deborah get up to is your own affair, but I won't hear anybody criticising Biggles. And frankly, Algy, it comes very ill from you of all people. Biggles has had a lot of worries lately and it's up to us to rally round. Remarks like that don't help at all.'

Algy looked suitably sheepish at the Yorkshireman's plain speaking.

'Sorry, Ginger! Just forget I spoke. But all the same, it is dashed difficult for a chap.'

Deborah Carstairs-Lomax was a lovely girl. Of that there was not the slightest doubt. Six feet tall, and golden-haired, she managed to combine the profile of a Roman goddess with the strongest female forehand drive in the Home Counties. Biggles had christened her 'the Valkyrie', and from the start had been considerably in awe of her. It wasn't just her size, although she did over-top him by a good half of her splendid head, and Biggles always had been touchy on the subject of his lack of inches. She was also one of the 'new women' of the Twenties. She had a mind of her own – and spoke it at the slightest provocation. She was independent, and God help anyone who tried to stop her doing as she pleased. She knew exactly what she wanted – and she wanted Algy Lacey.

'Just can't think why,' Biggles had remarked to Ginger in the course of one of their slightly worried conversations on the subject. 'It's not as if our Algy's very keen on tennis, or literature, or any of those "interests" she's always banging on about.'

'Sex is very strange,' said Ginger solemnly.

'Sex, my old Aunt Fanny! I can't believe that Algy's ever had a chance of you-know-what with *that* young lady. Ice from the navel downwards! No, old chap, that lady's set her sights on one thing and one thing only – becoming Lady Lacey.'

'You really think so, Biggles?' replied Ginger, as if such a notion in a woman was quite inconceivable.

'Think so? I'm certain, dear old boy! A title's a very funny thing, and some women will do anything to end up with a handle to their name. Can't understand why poor Algy doesn't see it too.

The poor chap's being kicked around like a blasted football. Not interested in flying any more. No time for any of his old chums. Dreadful, Ginger, simply dreadful how a stalwart bloke like Algy can succumb! But you realise what it'll mean if it goes on?'

'No, Biggles, what?' asked Ginger.

'The end of the old firm, of course. Biggles and Co. just won't survive with that young lady in the woodwork.'

Biggles' words shocked Ginger Hebblethwaite, not least because he had recently been thinking much the same himself. The mid-twenties had been good to Biggles and his friends. None of them had felt like settling down and they had managed to achieve that life of constant flying and adventure which had been their aim when they set up Biggles and Co. after the First World War. There was hardly a corner of the globe they had not visited. Early in 1923 they had been working on retainer for an oil exploration company in British Guiana and had dabbled in the gold prospecting business in the hinterland of that extraordinary country. They never made their fortunes, but they had more than covered their expenses and by the following year had moved on to Bolivia, where for several months they worked in conjunction with Wilkinson, an old friend from the R.F.C. who was currently instructing the newly-formed Bolivian Air Force. While in Bolivia, they had a brush with bandits who had captured the daughter of the President, and, after rescuing her, moved on to the forests of the Amazon in search of a legendary blue orchid. After this they witnessed revolution in Colombia, mayhem in Panama, and warfare in Brazil. Early in 1925 they were in the islands of the Pacific, searching for enormous pearls. They visited Formosa and Japan. For several months they had been piloting a sea-plane up the cannibal-infested Sepik River, again in search of gold, but they failed to find it. They had spent several months intriguing against a Russian spy called Nikitoff in India, and had made their adventure-packed return to England via Persia and the Middle East. The details of these wandering years are given in the pages of *Biggles Flies Again* by Capt. W. E. Johns.

Throughout these years of travel and adventure Mrs Symes had faithfully maintained the Mount Street flat for them, whilst Algy's Bentley had been laid up awaiting their return in a corner of the hangar down at Brooklands. But none of them had dreamt of settling down, and even after Biggles and Co. returned and set up base in Mayfair once again, the assignments and adventures continued to arrive so thick and fast that no one really had a chance to think about the future. Smyth, their inimitable mechanic, finally succumbed to matrimony, but his wife – a Lyons Teashop manageress from Peckham – was an independent-minded lady who intended to continue her career, and hardly seemed to notice when her spouse was absent. Ginger was happy wherever he could find an aeroplane to fly, while Biggles asked for nothing out of life except that the adventures should continue. The fortune that he dreamed of finding was still eluding him, but this was possibly just as well. Great riches would have worried him, and he was perfectly content to leave the financial affairs of the company to Algy. Women appeared to concern him even less these days. He never spoke of Marie Janis, but Ginger's theory was that the shock of her defection to von Stalhein had turned him permanently against the female sex in general. This was not entirely true. Biggles *was* susceptible to women, but he was also very cagey and discreet and probably preferred the cockpit to the boudoir. Any permanent relation with a woman, as he knew only too well, would spell the end of the sort of life he loved, and this was simply not a sacrifice he was prepared to make. But Algy was different. He was inclined to fall in love, and long before the glamorous Miss Carstairs-Lomax was on the scene there had been several very narrow squeaks – the dashing daughter of the Bolivian President, a teenage widow in Brazil, a nubile Japanese from Okinawa. With each of them it had appeared as if his end had come, but every time a fatherly talk from Biggles and a few hours' flying had done the trick. Algy was one of those lucky individuals who can fall out of love as easily as they fall into it – and he was always vulnerable to Biggles' mockery on the subject – until now. In the old days, the idea of a real row between the chums would have been inconceivable, particularly over the subject of a woman. But recently they had come dangerously near it, for the business of the Bentley was by no means the only friction caused by Algy's lady love. When Biggles had referred jokingly to 'the Valkyrie', Algy had said tersely, 'Biggles, I'd ask you not to refer to Deborah like that.' When Colonel Raymond had requested help with an Interpol investigation which involved flying to the north of France, Algy had finally backed out because Deborah was in the finals of the Sussex Ladies' Tennis tournament at Hastings. There had been further trouble when Algy had refused to go with Biggles to the Hendon Air Show on the grounds that 'Deborah just wasn't all that interested in aeroplanes'.

Tact had never been Biggles' strongest suit, and whilst he would do anything for Algy when in trouble, he expected absolute devotion in return. Indeed, the truth was that Biggles was an autocrat who couldn't bear the idea of anybody challenging his authority over his little group of friends – and this was where the real trouble lay. But for Ginger's constant efforts to smooth things over, Biggles and Co. would certainly have broken up that spring – and even now the Yorkshireman was having his work cut out 'just keeping the show on the road', as he referred to it.

Biggles' approaching birthday suddenly appeared a godsend – and Ginger made his mind up to exploit it to the full.

'Listen, Algy,' Ginger said conspiratorially, 'it must all come as a great surprise.'

'If you say so, dear old chap,' replied Algy, stifling a yawn,' but birthdays never have been Biggles' cup of tea. To tell the truth, they always used to bore the old thing stiff.'

'But this is different! Biggles will be thirty and it's a sort of milestone in a fellow's life. I really think we owe it to him to do something that will soften the shock of growing old.'

'*Tempus fugit* and all that, Ginger! Yes, I suppose I see your point. I'll ask Deborah to choose him a new tie from Liberty's. She's got simply splendid taste and it's time we had a change from that Old Maltonian one he always wears.'

Ginger shook his head.

'No, Algy, that just won't do. We must do this properly.'

'Not a tie, old sport? Perhaps some socks then. The little woman bought me a very dashing pair the other day to go with my plus-fours. They'd be just the job for Biggles.'

Once again Ginger shook his head.

'Well what the heck then, Ginger? Gentleman's Relish, cocktail biscuits, or how's about a bottle of his favourite Bollinger champagne?'

'Algy,' said Ginger, looking profoundly serious, 'you don't seem to realise that this is an occasion we should celebrate in style. A chap's only thirty once in his life, and we really must do something to show Biggles how much we appreciate him.'

'So what do you suggest?' asked Algy dubiously.

'I'm not too sure, but I do feel we should really push the boat out.'

'You mean a jolly old party? What about the Café Royal? They do one very well, and Biggles rather looks upon the place as a sort of home from home. We could have lashings of champagne, all his old chums and the surviving members of the family. Might cheer him up a bit.'

Ginger shook his head. 'Algy, for goodness sake,' he said. 'You should know Biggles better than that. It would embarrass him to death. Speeches, great hordes of people – that's not his thing at all.'

'Well I don't know then,' Algy replied, snorting with exasperation. 'Why don't we take him off to Timbuctoo?'

Ginger paused thoughtfully before replying.

'You know, Algy,' he said finally, 'I really think that that could be a frightfully good idea.'

Once the idea of Timbuctoo was mooted, Ginger began to work on it with his customary dedication. Algy, of course, had no glimmering of what his essentially facetious suggestion had begun, and would probably have been quite put out if he had. But luckily for everyone, his romance was taking up almost all his tme and Ginger had the field to himself. His main conspirator in the project was the invaluable Nobby Smyth, and before long the whole extraordinary plan started taking shape.

The essence of it all was that it had to take the form of a surprise, so everything was done in secret – provisions for a fortnight's expedition were carefully laid in at Brooklands, the Cormorant was overhauled, the latest air charts of the Sahara obtained. Ginger was the most methodical of men and was determined that nothing should go wrong. An afternoon was spent at the Army and Navy Stores, purchasing mosquito nets, water-purifying pills, and a patent toilet set for travellers. A bakery in Curzon Street prepared a birthday cake – in the shape of an aeroplane, with thirty candles. As part of French Sudan, Timbuctoo was administered by the French. The French Consulate raised no objection to the trip, and was helpful over the question of accommodation.

'No,' the French Consul-General explained to Ginger, 'there is unfortunately no real hotel in Timbuctoo, but we have what we call a *campement* – a sort of rest house in the city built to accommodate occasional travellers. I'm told it's somewhat primitive, but if you're really set on going, you can at least be sure that all of you will find a bed.'

'That's all we need,' replied Ginger cheerfully. 'It sounds the perfect place for what we want.'

'But what exactly *do* you want, monsieur?' asked the puzzled diplomat.

'A place to hold a birthday party,' Ginger answered, pulling a somewhat rueful face. 'You see sir, I have a friend, a rich, eccentric Englishman, who's made a bet that he will celebrate his birthday out in Timbuctoo. And so you see ...'

'Ah-hah!' replied the Frenchman, brightening at once. 'A bet, monsieur. I understand.'

'A telegram?' groaned Biggles with his mouth half full of kidneys and fried bread. 'Really, Mrs Symes. You might have waited until after the repast. Always trouble, telegrams! And trouble's very bad for the digestive juices – particularly at this unearthly hour of the morning.'

He pulled a face and opened the yellow envelope with the butter knife.

'Well, old chap, what is it?' asked Algy inquisitively from the far side of the breakfast-table. 'Tell us the worst. Your mother's coming up to stay?'

'Not that, thank God,' said Biggles quietly, as a look of deep preoccupation spread across his face. 'No, this sounds rather interesting. It's from our old friend, Jacques Nisberg from the Paris *Sûreté*. He's in the Southern Sahara of all incredible places.'

'What on earth's he doing there?'

'Investigating some expedition that has disappeared in the desert. It seems he wants help.'

'Good grief,' said Algy, nobbling *The Times* while Biggles' attention was diverted. 'These Frenchmen really are the bitter bottom. Next thing they'll be asking us to blow their noses for them. The Sahara's their responsibility, so why the heck pick on us?'

'Because, old fruit, the bally expedition's British. Don't like the sound of it at all.'

'Oh come now, Biggles,' exclaimed Algy. 'Surely you can't be seriously considering going? You've never liked the desert – and besides, it's your birthday tomorrow.'

'Birthday be blowed,' said Biggles angrily. 'When have I ever let a birthday interfere with what is obviously our duty? Algy, old lad, our countrymen are probably dying of thirst or being massacred by tribesmen, and you talk of birthdays.'

'I can't help that,' said Algy, 'I've promised Deborah to drive her down to Hurlingham.'

Biggles was momentarily aghast.

'You've *what?*' he asked incredulously. 'You sit there stuffing toast and marmalade and refuse to come on an adventure just because you've promised that young lady that you'll take her down to Hurlingham? What are you, Algy Lacey? Man or mouse?'

'But she'd be furious, Biggles,' said Algy in a tortured voice.

'Then brave her fury like a man. For God's sake, Algy, we won't be away for long. A week at the maximum, and absence makes the heart grow fonder.'

'Not with Deborah, old chap. Not with Deborah.'

When Ginger sent the telegram in Nisberg's name, he had not been prepared for quite as positive a reaction as it got from Biggles, but luckily he and Smyth were ready. The Cormorant was packed and fuelled, the documents in order, and by lunchtime they were in the air and flying at a steady 200 m.p.h. on the first leg of their journey south.

'Can't think how you managed it so quickly, dear old boy,' said Biggles breezily as he handled the controls. 'You and old Nobby here must have worked miracles to get us off on time. Anyone would think you planned the jolly trip yourselves.'

Ginger and Nobby Smyth were sitting in the rear two seats,

and at this Ginger felt an elbow nudge him in the ribs. Normally Ginger would have suffered from the pangs of conscience at the way he had deceived his friend, but he told himself that nobody enjoyed a practical joke more than Biggles, and knew quite well that once they got to Timbuctoo all would be forgiven. Already Biggles was looking happier than he had for months. His eyes were sparkling and he had that look of boyish concentration that he manifested only at the controls of a machine. Even Algy had recovered from the fit of sulks that followed a particularly stormy scene with Deborah when he announced the trip. The slightly hunted look about the eyes had gone already, and by the time they landed at Bordeaux the love-sick swain had been replaced by the Algy they had known of yore.

'Just like old times to be off like this again,' he chortled as he gunned the engines and the chocks were pulled away. 'Biggles, old lad, you were quite right to make me come. When I think of those poor devils in the desert, I wouldn't have forgiven myself if I'd left them to it simply to enjoy myself.'

The old Cormorant was flying beautifully, for all the world as if she too was bent upon a holiday. The sky was flecked with feather-like strands of cirrus clouds, the waters of the Bay of Biscay glittered in the summer sun, and soon the sunbaked landscape of Castile was steadily unrolling beneath them.

'What are our plans?' inquired Algy.

'We'll spend the night at Tangier' answered Biggles. 'It'd be madness to attempt to fly across the Sahara overnight, and anyhow I've sent Nisberg off a telegram telling him to expect us early tomorrow afternoon. We can only hope we'll be in time.'

'Not a great deal we can do if we're not, old scout,' replied Algy logically. Ginger thought that early afternoon would suit them very well, for he too had sent a telegram to Timbuctoo – to the manager of the *campement,* telling him to expect four English visitors, and to lay on a very special dinner for the evening.

Everyone enjoyed Tangier. They ate superbly in the Arab quarter of the city, booked in at the Rif Hotel, and visited a nightclub by the harbour where Algy was particularly taken by a belly-dancer rejoicing in the name of Fatima.

'Just look at that body, dear old chap,' he whispered noisily to Biggles. 'Sheer bliss on wheels. I really think you'd better let me order one more bottle of this terrible champagne.'

'Not on your life,' said Biggles sternly. 'Not even if they throw in Fatima as well. We've work to do tomorrow – and besides Algy, think of Deborah.'

'I do, old chap,' said Algy sadly. 'That's the trouble.'

Thanks to Biggles they were up at daybreak, and after breakfasting on rolls and steaming coffee at the airport they were away – this time with Ginger at the controls. For several hundred miles they followed the coast to avoid the mountains of the Anti-Atlas, then they struck inland to refuel at the French Foreign Legion outpost of Tindouf. Biggles took over then, and the flight continued almost due south, 1,000 miles across the waveless sea of the Sahara. Occasionally they saw a line of faint black dots against the endless yellow of the sand – a camel caravan making its way across the wilderness. But for almost all the flight, they saw nothing but the desert far below and the blazing sky above.

'Not being pessimistic, Biggles,' Algy asked, 'but what exactly *would* we do if we had a spot of bother here and had to land?'

'Not much you could do,' replied Biggles, grinning cheerfully. 'Apart from say your prayers and hope the Foreign Legion comes your way.'

But, thanks to Smyth's attention to the Cormorant's engines, the flight continued steadily until by three o'clock that afternoon the first faint sign of greenery appeared below. Shortly afterwards they saw the glint of distant water on the far horizon.

'The Niger River!' shouted Biggles excitedly.

'And that must be Timbuctoo!' said Algy as a minaret appeared. Soon they were right above the legendary city. From the air it looked exactly like an enormous ruin from the past, with row on row of now abandoned dwellings half swallowed by the sands of the encroaching desert. But in the centre of the city they could see newer buildings – the market-place the French had built, the barracks of the Foreign Legion, and several mosques with mud-brick towers rising like ant-hills over the crazy jumble of the flat-roofed houses. A mile or so away, as wide as the waters of an inland sea, flowed the majestic Niger River, one of the greatest rivers in the world, running for several hundred miles along the southern reaches of the desert.

'Somehow I think I'm going to like this place,' said Biggles with a grin as he brought the Cormorant in low over the dusty airstrip that did duty for an airport on the outskirts of the city.

Soon they were jolting in an ancient Renault truck through the dusty streets of Timbuctoo. The driver was a silent Frenchman with a squint.

'Seems to know who we are,' said Biggles. 'Nisberg must have told him. Wonder where on earth he is?'

'Probably out in the desert with the search-party,' Ginger suggested.

Biggles nodded. 'Devil of a job. Still, once we've cleaned ourselves up and had a spot to eat, we can join him. Wonder where this fellow's taking us?' He tried shouting to the driver over the racket of the engine, but the man's attention seemed to be entirely taken up with dodging the hordes of goats and small black children scampering between the houses.

'We'll soon be there, monsieur,' was all he would say. 'They're expecting you.'

'Well, thank the Lord for that,' said Biggles, as the long-suffering Renault gave a last despairing lurch, and skidded to a halt before a long, low, yellow-painted building with the French tricolour hanging limply from its flagpole in the scorching heat.

'*Messieurs*, the *campement!*' said the driver proudly, and from the entrance emerged an enormous negress in a gingham dress, lifting her massive arms in welcome.

'Major Bigglesworth?' she said, in perfect English. 'Welcome to our unworthy guest-house – and Happy Birthday!'

When Ginger finally explained the trick that he and Smyth had played, Biggles pretended to be angry – but not for long. Timbuctoo was not the place for that, and when he realised the trouble Ginger had gone too purely on his account he felt distinctly touched.

'Nobody's ever made much fuss of my birthday before you know, old scout, except in India, and that was years ago. Makes a fellow feel a bit appreciated. Really very kind.'

The *campement* was a splendid place – big, airy rooms, old-fashioned fans that circled from the ceilings, and a zinc-topped bar that could have come straight from a Parisian café on the Left Bank of the Seine. It was superbly stocked, and even boasted

Bollinger champagne – admittedly non-vintage – with which the friends immediately toasted Biggles' health.

'So you really mean we don't have to bother scouring the desert for our long-lost countrymen?' said Algy, with a happy grin across his freckled countenance. 'I must say, I'm deucedly relieved. Why don't we have another bottle? What do you say Biggles, you old codger?'

Biggles inclined his head. And so began the birthday party Biggles and his friends remembered all their lives. The lady in the gingham dress, whose name was Matatah, was officially the manageress, but she was also barmaid, cook and *confidante* for any foreigner who came to Timbuctoo. The boss-eyed driver of the Renault was her husband, and before her marriage she had been brought up by British missionaries in the Gambia – hence her perfect English. Since receiving Ginger's telegram, she had apparently been making special preparations for the party. In the courtyard of the *campement* there was already a great pile of wood stacked up in readiness to roast a sheep in Biggles' honour. But before all that there was time to wash, have another drink and see the city.

'Dreadful pity Deborah's not here,' said Algy, as he and Biggles gazed upon the ancient mosque of Sankore. 'She likes old ruins, you know.'

'Which is why she goes for you, old thing,' said Biggles with a laugh, 'But seriously, old chap, I think I've seen enough. Two mosques, the market-place, the ancient fort. Never have been all that keen on sight-seeing, come to think of it. On the other hand I wouldn't mind another drink. Dreadful thirst you know with all this sand and heat, and there's that lovely Bollinger back at the *campement*. How about making tracks?'

Algy nodded, and Ginger and Nobby Smyth were quite agreeable as well. Darkness had almost fallen, and Timbuctoo had suddenly become a place of mystery. Shepherds from the desert were already driving their flocks towards the city for the night. Blue-veiled Tuareg warriors rode past on silent camels. French Legionnaires, their duties over, marched past like extras from a film, and from the distance came the strange chant of the camel-drivers, welcoming the cool of evening.

Suddenly all the troubles and the tensions that had been afflicting Biggles and Co. for so long seemed far behind them, and at the *campement* Matatah had already started roasting the sheep in Biggles' honour. The air smelt wonderfully of wood-smoke and the scent of roasting meat, and soon the four friends were sitting on the terrace, drinking more champagne and watching the stars come out.

'You know,' said Biggles happily, 'it's really good to be alive.' He licked his fingers, burped appreciatively, and gazed at the sickle moon cleaving the desert sky. A dog howled in the distance, and the embers of the fire glowed faintly in the courtyard. Smyth had nodded off to sleep and Algy was distinctly drunk.

Ginger had not been over-happy with the meat. Like most sheep roasted in this way, it smelt far better than it tasted, and the hunks that Matatah had finally produced were either burned or under-cooked. But no one apart from Ginger seemed to notice, and there was also fish, local bread, figs, almond cakes and goat's cheese. At the last minute Ginger had remembered to produce the cake that he had brought from Curzon Street, and gradually the birthday feast had turned into a party as people wandered into the courtyard from the street and Biggles made them welcome.

'Never known anything quite like this, dear old chap,' said Biggles with a hazy smile. 'We must come here every year. Make it a sort of fixture on the bally calendar. Can't possibly begin to thank you enough for thinking of it, Ginger my old scout. Perhaps we should give those fellows over there a little more to drink.' He signalled happily to Matatah. More bottles were brought, and then her squint-eyed husband produced an ancient gramophone. The only records were French can-cans and regimental marches and they were very old and cracked, but the music added to the air of strange festivity – particularly when Algy started dancing tipsily with the enormous Madame Matatah.

'I hear it is your birthday,' said someone from the darkness suddenly addressing Biggles. 'Your health, monsieur, and my felicitations.'

Biggles peered up and saw a solid figure in the uniform of a Captain of the Foreign Legion standing, glass in hand, before him.

'Many thanks,' replied Biggles in near-perfect French. 'Most kind of you, I'm sure. Why don't you sit down and tell me about Timbuctoo. My name's James Bigglesworth.'

'And I, monsieur, am Capitaine Lecombe, French Foreign Legion, at your service.'

The Captain bowed, and Biggles offered him his hand – then poured him more champagne.

It was the sort of instant friendship that suddenly springs up in far-off places between unexpected individuals. The Captain was a vivid talker, and he spoke like a man who had been deprived too long of congenial human company. He also had a taste for good champagne and soon was telling Biggles of the extra-ordinary life he led – the loneliness of being always far from France, the toughness and dedication of his men, and the hazards of the tribesmen from the desert. He had many stories of the past – of the explorers who had died in Timbuctoo when it was still a lost forbidden city, and of the savage wars that he had fought.

'But it's quite peaceful now,' said Biggles gazing at the cheerful throng of people who had crammed into the courtyard, attracted by the music.

'Well, yes and no,' replied the Captain cautiously. 'In a place like this one never knows just when fresh trouble will flare up. Why, only yesterday there was a really dreadful murder here. Two men from the Bambara tribe were caught robbing a Yoruba trader in the market-place. They went berserk, and killed the poor old man and his wife, wounded a policeman, and escaped into the desert. In the morning I must be off early with a camel patrol to search for them. I'm not particularly looking forward to it as they'll have had thirty-six hours' start on us, and could be anywhere.'

'So how d'you find them?' Biggles asked.

'Oh, simply by hard work, monsieur. We know all the places where they might have gone – the water-holes and hiding places in the desert, and we take our time. We could be searching for those murderers for weeks.'

'Why don't you use an aeroplane?' asked Biggles logically.

'Why not indeed, monsieur? That would be marvellous, but in the Foreign Legion we have no aircraft. Men and camels are considered cheaper, and we get there in the end.'

'But that's ridiculous,' said Biggles, opening a fresh bottle of champagne. 'I have an aircraft here in Timbuctoo, and tomorrow morning, if you like, you can come with me and we'll track your murderers from the air. Now, a little more to drink before we wander off to bed. Your health, *monsieur le capitaine!*'

None of the friends remembered when the party ended, but the champagne finally ran out, the boss-eyed Frenchman wearied of winding up the gramophone, and the uninvited guests departed as swiftly as they had come. There were beds on the flat roof of the *campement*, and Algy seemed to think it would be fun to sleep beneath the stars, so Ginger and Madame Matatah helped him up the stairs and Biggles followed. (Smyth was left snoring gently in his chair upon the terrace.)

'Well,' hicupped Biggles, 'life certainly begins at thirty!' and he collapsed upon his bed. The next he knew, the dawn was breaking over the roofs of Timbuctoo, the muezzin was calling from the minaret, and Madame Matatah was shaking him by the shoulder.

'Major Bigglesworth,' she said. 'Major Bigglesworth. Captain Lecombe is here for you. He says that you are flying with him on a dawn patrol across the desert. Would you like some coffee?'

It was a miracle of mind over matter that Biggles managed to get up. His throat was dry, his head was splitting, and his eyelids felt as if they were glued together, but somehow he staggered to his feet, and tried waking up the rest of his companions. Here he was less successful.

'Duty calls, old boy! Rise and shine!' he croaked, shaking Ginger by the shoulder, but Ginger merely groaned and rolled away.

'Dawn patrol with the French Foreign Legion!' he said to Algy. 'Upsy-daisy!'

But all that Algy muttered in return was something unrepeatable.

'Oh well,' said Biggles shrugging his shoulders philosophically. 'These young fellows just can't hold their liquor. Coming Captain!' he shouted down. 'Just let me get my boots on and I'll be with you!'

The coffee was like nectar, and twenty minutes later the Cormorant, with Biggles and the Captain aboard, soared gracefully above the sleeping city, banked above the river, and sped towards the desert.

'I say, old boy, how're you feeling?' Ginger called to Algy some two hours later.

'Worse than I'd ever have imagined possible,' groaned a dishevelled Algy, rolling out of bed and gazing biliously towards the street below. 'Eyes full of hot ball-bearings, mouth like an emu's armpit. What on earth d'you think they put in that champagne, old thing?'

'Battery acid topped up with anti-freeze by the feel of it. Still, it was quite a party, and Biggles certainly enjoyed himself. Talking of which, where exactly is the old idiot? D'you think he could have rolled off the roof?'

'I shouldn't think so,' Algy answered, 'but perhaps you'd better have a look. He hasn't got a head for alcohol like ours. It's age, you know.'

He tottered to the parapet and peered below.

'No sign of him,' he shouted, 'but old Nobby Smyth's still snoring in a deck-chair on the terrace. Where on earth d'you think he is?'

'I seem to remember,' said Ginger frowning, 'that he tried to wake me in the middle of the night. Some nonsense about going on an early morning flight.'

'Now that you mention it, old boy, I have a hazy recollection of something of the sort myself. He must have been quite blotto, poor old fellow. Probably passed out downstairs. I'll toddle down in just a minute and inquire from Madam Whatsername. She'll probably have him under lock and key.'

But Madame Matatah was able to inform the friends of Biggles' whereabouts.

'You really mean he's on a man-hunt in the desert with that Captain from the Foreign Legion?' Algy asked incredulously. 'He's mad. Old age is really setting in.'

Once he was airborne, Biggles' head had cleared at once. As for the good Captain, either he had a stronger head than any of the friends, or else he was used to Madame Matatah's champagne, for he was looking distinctly spry and seemed to know exactly what he wanted.

'The first place I think that we should try,' he said, when Biggles asked his plans, 'is a small oasis sixty miles or so due north from here. It's called Yoraga, and the caravans stop there from time to time. There's a place where we can land, and we can soon see if there's any sign of the men we're after.'

'What happens if we find them?' Biggles asked, a trifle anxiously.

'*Pas de problème*, Major Bigglesworth,' replied the Captain with a quick smile. He tapped the enormous army automatic on his belt and added, 'They'll probably have calmed down by now, and shouldn't be any trouble. But if they are, then – pouff! We'll simply have to deal with them.'

Biggles was slightly shocked. Even in India he'd never come across quite such a casual attitude towards the natives, but, he reflected, the French had their own ways of doing things and lacked the benefit of the traditions of the British Empire.

It took some time to find Yoraga, but finally they did – a few straggly thorn trees and a brackish pool that barely justified the word 'oasis'. Thanks entirely to Biggles' skill they landed safely, but the Tuareg shepherds who had camped nearby had seen nothing of the men they sought. Nor had the tribesmen at two more spots they visited, but finally some Tuareg said that, yes, they had seen two men riding on a camel earlier that morning. They hadn't stopped or spoken to them, as they were Bambara, but they were heading north and their camel had seemed exhausted. Captain Lecombe thanked them, and the Tuareg, with their mysterious blue veils across their faces, inclined their heads, commended the two white men to Allah, and rode on.

By now it was several hours since Biggles and the Captain had left Timbuctoo, and the desert was a furnace. Petrol was getting low, and Biggles was distinctly anxious to return, but the Captain was excited by the news.

'Ah, Major Bigglesworth,' he said, 'we're on their trail and they can't be far away. Ten minutes in the aeroplane. Certainly no more.'

'Where could they be heading for?' asked Biggles. 'Surely it's suicide for them to go further into the Sahara?'

'It would be, Major,' said the Frenchman, 'but these villains clearly know what they're up to. There is a place not far from here called Wazzaba – a strange place in the middle of the desert. It used to be a salt-mine worked by slaves, but they left it long ago. I think it has water, and it would be a perfect place for criminals to hide until the hunt for them dies down. Perhaps we could see if there is any trace of them?'

'Is it far?' said Biggles. 'We're getting pretty low on petrol.'

'Ten minutes, Major Bigglesworth. Certainly no more.'

'O.K.' said Biggles, 'we'll go and have a look.'

But Captain Lecombe had an optimistic sense of distance, and the ten minutes that he said would bring them to Wazzaba passed without a sign of life or habitation in that glaring wilderness. Ten more minutes passed and Biggles started getting worried.

'How much further?'

'Two minutes. Just two minutes,' shouted the Captain excitedly. 'We're almost there.'

In fact, it was nearer twenty before they reached a spot where the desert changed into something like the surface of the moon, with rocks, craters and some ruined walls.

'Wazzaba,' said the Captain. 'Still no sign of them. Do you think that you can land?'

'No alternative, old chap,' said Biggles grimly. 'We're almost out of petrol.'

'You know, I'm getting worried, Algy.' Ginger said. 'It's not like Biggles to have been gone so long without a message, and I know the Cormorant had barely half a tank of fuel aboard.'

'Oh, he'll be all right,' said Algy, 'particularly with that Captain Johnnie to take care of him. Probably landed somewhere in the desert for a spot of lunch or something.'

'But there's nowhere in the desert for a spot of lunch,' said Ginger.

'There's bound to be, old man. Let's just have a drink and take things easy. Hair of the dog and all that sort of thing. Chin-chin!'

But Ginger was a worrier, and when they had finished lunch – braised kid, boiled artichoke and goats' milk cheese – he insisted on taking Algy through the heat of the early afternoon to inquire

at the French Legion Headquarters for news of Biggles and the
Cormorant. There was none, but the Duty Officer insisted there
was no need to worry. There were many places in the desert
where an aeroplane could land, and Captain Lecombe was an
officer of great experience.

'He'd better be,' said Ginger.

By late afternoon it was obvious that something had gone
wrong. Even the Adjutant at French Headquarters was
admitting it, saying he would alert the Legion's desert patrols,
and promising that if no news arrived next morning a full-scale
search would start.

'But what's the use of that?' said Ginger. 'They could have
flown several hundred miles, and it might take days to reach
them. In this heat they wouldn't stand a chance.'

'*Eh alors*, monsieur!' said the Adjutant. 'What else would you
have us do?'

'Can't you use an aircraft for the search?'

'An aircraft, monsieur? Here in Timbuctoo? You must be
joking. The only thing we have that flies is a dirigible belonging
to the Artillery.'

'A what?' asked Ginger.

'A dirigible. A cross between an airship and an ordinary
balloon. It has an engine, and it takes a crew of four. But it hasn't
flown for years, and no one knows how to use it.'

Ginger's ears pricked up at this.

'Where is this dirigible affair?' he asked.

'Oh, I'm not sure, monsieur. In one of the store-rooms I
imagine. I'd have to make inquiries.'

'Would you mind doing so at once?'

The Adjutant shrugged his shoulders.

'Certainly, monsieur, if you're interested, but don't expect too
much. As far as I remember, even the Artillery abandoned it.'

Ginger waited while the Adjutant telephoned, and finally a
small man in a corporal's uniform arrived, saluted, and asked
what he could do. His name was Dutoit, and he said, yes, he had
once worked on the dirigible and knew all about it. Could he
show it to the Englishman? Certainly. But he must warn the
Englishman that it was no longer serviceable.

'Don't worry about that,' said Ginger. 'Just let me see it.'

Half an hour later, Ginger was back at the *campement*.

'Well Algy, Nobby, I'm afraid that we have work to do.'

'Really, Ginger!' exclaimed Algy with a yawn. 'All this heat, and poor old Biggles lost in that flaming desert, and you talk of work! Have a heart!'

'But that's the whole point, Algy. I think I've hit upon a way of finding him – from the air.'

'You mean you've found an aircraft, Ginger? You're a blinking wizard.'

'No, Algy, not an aircraft – a balloon. I've just been looking at it. It's in a pretty good old mess, but I'm certain we could make it work. The envelope needs repairing and the engine will require all Nobby's genius to make it work, but there's several dozen cylinders of hydrogen, and they tell me it can cruise at thirty miles an hour.'

'Ginger, you're mad,' said Algy. 'Stark raving mad.'

Ginger flushed at this. 'Probably I am,' he said, 'but if you can think of any better way of finding Biggles, I for one would like to hear it.'

If anything, Ginger had been over-optimistic in his report on the balloon. Parts of the great silken envelope were badly ripped. Ants had attacked the wooden gondola, whilst the engine – a two hundred horse-power Peugeot water-cooled affair driving two separate propellers at the rear – seemed to be totally seized up.

'Well, old boy,' said Algy when he saw it, 'I suppose the jolly old dirigible *could* be restored – in about a month, with twenty fellows working on it. But even then I'm not sure I'd care to fly in it.'

Ginger nodded.

'Normally I'd agree with you entirely, but Algy, can't you see that it's our only way of ever finding Biggles now? If we don't get to him before tomorrow night, the old boy's had it.'

Ginger's enthusiasm was contagious, and as soon as word got round of what he wanted, he had all the volunteers he needed. An enormous drill-hall was turned into a makeshift workshop to repair the fifty-foot-long envelope of the balloon, and shifts of soldiers, under the supervision of the tiny Corporal Dutoit, laboured through the night. Others helped Ginger on the gondola, but the hardest work of all was Nobby Smyth's. With

Algy to help him he totally rebuilt the engine in the Legion's workshop. Few slept that night, but by dawn the work was almost done. The long grey envelope of the balloon was dragged into the open air. The guy-ropes were attached, the gondola put in position, and the slow work of inflating the balloon began.

It was a strange and moving sight as this ancient, all-but-forgotten balloon started to come to life. It grew before their eyes, gradually taking shape as the hydrogen hissed into it from the long black cylinders, and it was soon rising up and tugging at the guy-ropes in the morning breeze.

'How's that engine, Nobby?' Ginger shouted.

'Can't promise anything,' said Nobby Smyth, 'but I've done my best. I think she'll be O.K.'

'Good lad,' said Ginger. 'Now Algy, have we everything we need? Maps, compass, water, petrol, food?'

'Probably forgotten something absolutely vital,' Algy responded with a laugh, 'but I've done my best. At least it makes a change from aeroplanes. O.K. Nobby, start her up!'

From below, Nobby swung one of the propellers, the engine coughed and then roared to life. More hydrogen hissed into the balloon, the troops released the guy-ropes, and the old dirigible with Ginger and Algy aboard rose in the brilliant early morning sun and headed for the desert.

'Strange experience,' said Algy. 'Not all that sure I like it. Rather too peaceful to my way of thinking.'

'Oh, I don't know.' said Ginger, as he watched the last of Timbuctoo disappear behind them in the morning glare. 'I find it rather restful. Only hope that the old envelope holds. We had a dreadful job repairing it. You and Nobby seem to have excelled yourselves with the engine.'

This was true, for the Peugeot engine was now purring happily behind them, driving the two big propellers which carried the dirigible forward at a steady pace.

'Nobby really is a genius with engines,' said Algy. 'He practically rebuilt the thing from scratch. But tell me, Ginger, just what is the plan? Where could Biggles be?'

'Well,' replied Ginger, 'I spent some time last night with the Adjutant, working out the places where they might have landed.

There are several of them. There's a small oasis just north of here called Yoraga, and several other spots where the tribesmen camp. They could be at any of them, and there's the old salt-mine of Wazzaba right out in the desert ...'

Ginger passed Algy the map and together they began to work out their direction.

It was nearly noon, and Biggles was sheltering from the blistering Sahara sun in the dim interior of the mine-shaft – a narrow tunnel slanting down into the unwelcoming bowels of the desert.

'Idiot!' he kept saying to himself. 'Confounded idiot! To have let myself run out of petrol – and at my age too.'

He stared venomously across at Captain Lecombe – ever since the brandy and potato crisps had run out that morning, relations had been growing strained. There had been no sign of the murderers – nor, for that matter, of anything that moved, except for a number of large black bats which hung suspended from the tunnel roof and came alive at dusk.

'Extraordinarily stupid way to go!' said Biggles angrily. 'Stuck in a hole in this confounded desert!'

'Courage!' said Captain Lecombe. 'My comrades will arrive. They'll be searching for us with their camel patrols. They're bound to find us in the end.'

'It'll be the end all right,' said Biggles bitterly. 'I'm sick to death of this already. Where the heck is Algy?'

'Major Bigglesworth,' began the Legionnaire sternly, 'there is no point at all in getting yourself excited. Conserve your energies and be patient. Your friends can't possibly help you, for as I keep telling you, there are no aeroplanes in Timbuctoo. Just wait, and the camels of the Foreign Legion will rescue us.'

'It's another sort of camel that I want,' said Biggles.

'Please?' asked the Captain.

'A Camel is an aircraft that I used to fly in the war, and jolly good it was too,' said Biggles stiffly.

This made the Captain laugh. 'You had a flying camel, Major Bigglesworth? And I had a flying carpet!'

His laughter irritated Biggles and rather than submit to it, he rose and left the tunnel for the desert glare outside.

'Foreigners!' he muttered to himself. As he did so he heard a strange noise from the distance. It was not an aeroplane and couldn't be a car. For several minutes he was puzzled and stood scanning the horizon. Then, suddenly, he seemed to go berserk.

'Captain!' he yelled, 'Captain! Come and see! They've got a bally airship!'

'Pity to have to leave, old chap,' said Biggles with a rueful smile. 'I've started to get quite attached to Timbuctoo.'

'So have I,' said Algy. 'It rather grows upon a fellow, and I'll miss the old dirigible.'

It was two days after the rescue from the desert, and the Cormorant was serviced and refuelled for the return for England. Quite a crowd had turned up at the airstrip on the outskirts of Timbuctoo to see them off – Madame Matatah and her boss-eyed husband, half the French garrison, and many of the people who had turned up at Biggles' birthday party.

'No sign of your friend, Captain Lecombe,' said Ginger with a laugh.

'Can't say that I expected him,' replied Biggles. 'It was a dreadful loss of face for him when you two scallywags turned up to rescue us. And then, when it turned out that his precious murderers had escaped down the river after all, he felt an even bigger idiot.'

'Still, all the others seem to see the joke,' said Ginger, 'and the Adjutant appears delighted with us for repairing his dirigible. Corporal Dutoit has been promoted Sergeant to take charge of it. By the way, Algy, what was in that telegram that arrived for you this morning just before we left? Anything important?'

'It was personal, old boy,' replied Algy, pulling something of a face.

'Come, come,' said Biggles. 'We can't have any secrets from each other. What was it, Algy? Woman trouble?'

'Dammit, Biggles! How on earth d'you guess?'

'Ah-ah!' said Biggles. 'I know you rather better than you think. So what's happened?'

'It was from Deborah. She's left me for the tennis coach at Hurlingham.'

'Oh Algy,' Biggles said, 'I'm most dreadfully sorry. It's a tragedy, a real tragedy, isn't it Ginger?'

Ginger nodded and began to laugh.

'That's what comes of going off to Timbuctoo,' he said.

Algy began to laugh as well, as Biggles opened up the throttle and the Cormorant sped across the airstrip and began its climb into the early morning sky.

'Probably as well,' said Algy philosophically. 'You know I never really cared for tennis – and Deborah hated aeroplanes. I think that Timbuctoo has saved us both a lot of real unhappiness.'

7

The Great Race

The dining room of the Blazers' Club has seen Prime Ministers and potentates, press lords and Presidents, yet by a firm tradition of the Club all visitors, however eminent, are treated just like any ordinary guests. So there was no reason why James Bigglesworth should have realised on meeting Lord Elberton who on earth he was, not that it would have made much difference if he had. Biggles paid little heed to rank. He had a simple way of judging anyone he met – either the fellow was all right, or he wasn't. Lord Elberton seemed distinctly in the second category.

It was an evening late in 1934 and Colonel Raymond had taken Biggles off to dinner at his Club as something of a consolation prize for several very boring jobs he had recently performed for the British Secret Service. They sounded glamorous enough – a flight to Budapest to fetch Karminsky, the Hungarian cypher king, three weeks in Italy trying to discover the performance figures of the new Savoia-Marchetti long-range seaplane, a visit to a factory outside Paris where Duval, the great explosives expert, was rumoured to be manufacturing an aerial torpedo that had their Lordships at the Admiralty distinctly worried.

It suited Colonel Raymond to employ a freelance operator he could trust implicitly, yet disown if anything went wrong. And, thanks to no fault of Biggles', go wrong they had. Karminsky had changed his mind at the last minute and refused to come, the

Italian seaplane sank on its trials on Lake Garda, and the great Duval had blown up his factory and himself. As a perfectionist, Biggles found it difficult to cope with failure and these three setbacks in a row had depressed him terribly. Algy had done his best to cheer him up – as Algy always did – but Biggles remained firmly in the dumps, and it was the faithful Algy who had finally rung Colonel Raymond to suggest he have a word with him – hence the invitation out to dinner in the hallowed precincts of the Blazers' Club.

The dinner had been excellent as ever – the best smoked salmon this side of the Firth of Forth, a partridge slaughtered at Balmoral, claret from the cellars of a former President of France – and as the meal progressed, Biggles' spirits had undoubtedly improved.

'The trouble is, sir,' he confessed to Colonel Raymond, 'I really feel I'm getting soft.'

'Never heard such nonsense in my life,' replied the Colonel, jabbing at the Stilton with an eighteenth-century silver scoop, 'you and Lacey are the toughest pair of fliers it has been my privilege to meet.'

'That's very kind of you, sir. But the fact is that it's been years since the ending of the war. We've flown a lot, we've been around the world, and been delighted to perform the occasional odd job for you, but I feel that we require a challenge.'

Colonel Raymond gave an icy laugh.

'I'd have thought you'd had enough of them to last a lifetime, Bigglesworth my boy. But, if that's what you really want, I'll have to see what I can do.'

This was the point at which the small man sitting opposite them butted in. He was a gnome-like creature with a large head, hooded eyes, and a fringe of thin white hair around a naked cranium.

'That's what all the bored young idiots these days are saying. Challenges my foot! Why don't they get off their backsides and do a job of work for once?'

Biggles was just about to drink his port and, rather than embarrass Colonel Raymond, took no notice. But the small man opposite was clearly in no mood for giving up.

'It makes me sick, you know, to hear the way they talk. Molly-coddled lot. Never do anything for themselves. It's always other people who must look after them and pay for their mistakes. That's why the country's in the mess it's in.'

'At least they won the war for you,' said Biggles, doing his best to hide his mounting anger.

'That's what they always say. Pure self-pity, nothing else. This present generation loves feeling sorry for itself. They think the world owes them a living.'

'And what about your generation, if we're being personal, sir?' asked Biggles quietly. 'Weren't you the ones who landed us in the war, and then left us to do the fighting for you?'

'That's quite enough, Bigglesworth!' said Colonel Raymond quickly, and turning to the small man opposite, added, 'I suggest we change the subject, sir!'

'Blowed if I will,' the man retorted. 'I believe in saying what I think, and since your friend has chosen to insult me, I can only say that were I a younger man myself, I'd give him the answer he deserves.

'And if you were a younger man,' said Biggles evenly, 'I'd punch you on the nose.'

Colonel Raymond rose abruptly.

'Bigglesworth,' he said. 'I think it's time we left.'

'Phew!' said Biggles when they were safely in the ante-room. 'I'm sorry about that, sir, but there are some things a man can't take from anyone.'

'Quite so. All the same, it was a pity that they had to come from him. You know who he was, of course?'

Biggles shook his head.

'Elberton. Lord Elberton. They say he's the richest man in England.'

Algy had just returned from an evening with a Venezuelan divorcée at the 400 Club, and was in predictably high spirits when Biggles arrived back at the flat in Mount Street. The irrepressible Ginger Hebblethwaite was there as well, preparing a night-cap of his patent hot rum punch.

'Gorgeous little creature,' Algy was remarking. 'Says that she'd like a spin in the old kite. Any objections, Biggles, if we flip across to Paris for the weekend?'

'Do as you please,' said Biggles glumly.

'Steady on now,' Algy said, swinging his long legs off the battered sofa. 'What's up, old scout?'

'Oh nothing!' Biggles replied irritably, but Algy wasn't having that.

'Can't have this sort of thing. Trouble with that blasted bank manager of yours again? I'll skin his hide and use it to repair the Cormorant's fuselage.'

'Not such a bad idea,' replied Biggles, grinning now despite himself. 'No, it's not old money-bags this time. There was an oaf who picked on me tonight at the Blazers' Club with Colonel Raymond, and I rather lost my rag with him. Dashed embarrassing. I wish it hadn't happened.'

Algy smiled at this. 'Is that all? For a moment you really had me worried. Thought that we were just about to lose our precious overdraft. Who was this frightful bounder?'

'Somebody called Lord Elberton. Quite the most offensive man I've ever met.'

Algy's habitually placid countenance was suddenly aghast.

'Biggles, old man, you must be joking!'

'Not at all. A frightful hound.'

'But didn't you know about Elberton before?'

Biggles shook his head. 'What was there to know, except that I can't stand him?'

'Lord Elberton, dear boy, is a great pal of the Pater's, and we are relying on him to back us for our entry into the race to Singapore and back. Or rather, we were.'

'Great screaming seacows!' Biggles said limply. 'Somebody should have told me.'

The aerial race from London to Singapore and back was being billed as the most exciting race in history. It had been sponsored by a London paper, with a prize of £50,000, and already several entries had been made from Europe and America.

Biggles and Co. had been among the earliest to enter – partly for the fun of it, and partly too from sheer necessity. The rich days of the twenties were behind them. The Slump had come. Their life of high adventure had been marvellous, but for several years now it had failed to pay the bills. The occasional commissions Biggles got from Colonel Raymond were done from a sense of duty, not for cash, and but for Algy's now distinctly shrunken legacy, it is hard to see how Biggles and Co. could possibly have survived.

It was small wonder therefore that the prospect of the race had appeared as something of a chance of real salvation to them all. However, there were certain problems if they were to have any hope of winning. Most of them, as usual, involved money, or the lack of it. Apart from the inevitable expenses of entering the race – food, fuel, landing fees, and a hundred-and-one incidentals which the layman never thinks of – there was also the question of an aircraft. The Cormorant was ancient – and looked it. She had seen service now in every quarter of the globe, and was undoubtedly what Biggles called her when he was feeling pleased with life – 'a very fine old bus indeed'. But fine old buses don't win races, and the fact was that the Cormorant was obsolete and past her prime – hence Algy's efforts in the last few days to find a wealthy backer who would help finance a new machine.

Easier said than done. Backers that autumn were as rare as four-leafed clovers, and nothing but the direst desperation could have impelled Algy to discuss the matter with his father. For Lord Lacey had been growing more eccentric and more difficult with every year that passed. The failure of the critics to appreciate his life-work on the wild flowers of Sussex had embittered him, and he and Lady Lacey were both anxious now to get Algy to adopt a settled calling, find himself a suitable young bride, and act as was expected of the heir to a distinguished title. (Biggles' mother was still trying to persuade her son in the same direction, but with even less success.)

To Algy's considerable surprise, Lord Lacey had been more than helpful, and had actually introduced him to Lord Elberton during a family weekend at Lewes. For some reason the cantankerous old man had taken quite a shine to Algy, who had used all his charm and talked enthusiastically about the vital role of flying for the British Empire. Elberton, who owned the second largest aircraft factory in the land, had all but promised to entrust the company's hush-hush, long-range, twin-engined monoplane to Biggles and Co. for the race.

'All we can hope,' said Algy, 'is that the old boy fails to realise that Biggles and Co. has anything to do with the man who threatened to punch him on the nose at Blazers'.'

'He might,' said Biggles.

But he didn't. Next morning, scarcely was breakfast over, than the telephone was ringing in the hall.

'Someone wants you Biggles,' shouted Ginger. 'Sounds pretty urgent.'

'Can't a fellow finish *The Times* crossword puzzle in peace without being pestered by the blasted telephone?' Biggles grumbled, leaving an unfinished slice of toast and Coopers on his plate. 'Yes? Who is it?'

'Lord Elberton's secretary here. His Lordship asked me to convey his compliments to Major Bigglesworth and to say he'd like a word with him about the air race as soon as possible. Could you manage this afternoon?'

'Yes,' said Biggles. 'Yes, I can.'

Elberton House was just behind the Ritz, and Biggles had a final pink gin in the Rivoli Bar with Algy to keep his spirits up.

'Remember how you used to feel when faced with a pack of Halberstadts?' said Biggles as he drained his glass. 'Well, that's how I feel now – only rather worse.'

'Good luck, old scout!' said Algy. 'Do your best. You can't do more.'

'I'll try, old bean, but don't expect too much. I did threaten to punch the blighter on the nose.'

But when he was finally led in to meet the millionaire, no reference was made at first to their argument the night before. The little man looked more than ever like a gnome as he perched behind a vast desk with a view across the park.

'So, Major Bigglesworth,' he said, 'you are the friend of young Algy Lacey who wants to enter for the race to Singapore?'

Biggles nodded.

'And you wish to fly my aeroplane and have my full financial backing?'

Biggles felt tongue-tied and could only bring himself to nod again.

'I see.' The old man smiled to himself and peered at Biggles with extraordinarily sharp eyes. 'A bit unfortunate in the circumstances that you spoke to me the way you did last night.

No, don't apologise, it'll do no good. But tell me Bigglesworth – what would you do if you were sitting here in my position?'

'Rather a tough question, sir,' answered Biggles turning very red.

'It's meant to be.' He tapped reflectively against the desk, then lit a large cigar.

'If I remember rightly, Major Bigglesworth, you started our, er, conversation at the Club last night by saying that you'd like a challenge. Well, Major, I feel inclined to give you one.'

'That's very decent of you, sir,' said Biggles hurriedly.

'Now not so fast. Hear me out, young man. I said a challenge, and I mean exactly what I say. I'm quite prepared to stick to my part of the bargain, and back you both, on one condition.'

'Which is?' asked Biggles.

'That we have a little bet, just you and me. If you win, you and Lacey take everything – £50,000 prize money, and to make it more exciting, I'm prepared to double it.'

'But if we don't?'

'Ah-ah!' replied Lord Elberton, rubbing his bony hands together. 'I gather, Major, that you and Lacey are joint owners of a small company which you call Biggles and Co. Am I right?'

Biggles nodded, and Lord Elberton continued.

'Its assets, correct me if I'm wrong, include two aircraft, somewhat past their best, a Bentley motor-car, a lease on a flat in Mount Street, and a part share in a hangar down at Brooklands aerodrome.'

'Your Lordship is extremely well informed,' said Biggles, somewhat shaken by the old man's accuracy.

'A practice to which I owe what small success I've had in life,' replied the old man, smiling like a cheerful toad. 'Now, what I would suggest is this. Against my offer you would stake your company. Win the race and you get £100,000. Lose it, and I get Biggles and Co. What d'you say now, Major? At least I'm trying to make life just a bit more interesting for you.'

'Extremely kind of you, I'm sure,' said Biggles tactfully, 'but you must realise that I can't possibly take a decision like this on my own account. There's Algy Lacey to consider, and our old pal, Ginger Hebblethwaite – not to mention our mechanic, Smyth. They're all involved.'

'So much the better,' said the millionaire, who was grinning wickedly by now. 'Very well, then. I'm quite prepared to wait for your decision till tomorrow at noon. If I don't hear from you by then, the whole deal's off. Good day to you, Major Bigglesworth.'

'If pigs could fly,' mused Algy, 'I'd send a flock of them right over Elberton House, old chap.'

'Might improve the place no end,' replied Biggles, 'but since they don't, what *are* we going to do? I feel dashed bad about it all. It really is my fault.'

'Fiddlesticks!' exclaimed Algy. 'I'm beginning to wish you'd punched the old windbag on the nose and had done with it. It might have improved his manners. What's your opinion of his offer, Ginger?'

'Well,' said the Yorkshireman, frowning with concentration, 'I don't see what we've got to lose. If things go on as they've been going lately, Biggles and Co. will have ceased to exist a year from now anyway.'

'But what about this flat?' asked Biggles gloomily. 'If we don't win we'll be out on our collective ear. We'll lose our home – and poor old Algy's Bentley.'

'A risk we have to take,' said Algy cheerfully. 'I'm quite easy about it all, and I must say I agree with Ginger. We really haven't any choice. Besides, in a ghastly way, old Elberton's quite right, It is a challenge – and it will stop you getting bored.'

Two days later, all the personnel of Biggles and Co. were gathered on the tarmac of an aerodrome near Winchester, gazing excitedly at the sleek green monster which a group of Lord Elberton's mechanics had just wheeled out of his aircraft company's secret hangar.

'So that's the Swallow,' exclaimed Algy. 'Not so dusty. You must certainly hand it to old Elberton, he knows how to build aeroplanes, and no mistake, What's her speed, Biggles?'

'They're claiming something like 280 m.p.h. for her,' said Biggles cautiously. 'I'd like to test her for myself.'

'And range?'

'Two thousand miles between each refuelling stop. Again, that's what they claim.'

'Jehosaphat!' said Algy. 'You realise what that means, Biggles, if the claims are right? There's not an aircraft in the world to equal her. As long as we get to Singapore and back we'll keep the Bentley yet. When do we get a chance to fly her?'

'Any minute now. His Lordship wanted to be here in person when we tried her out. And unless I'm much mistaken, this is the unpleasant old gentleman now.'

As Biggles spoke an enormous black Rolls-Royce purred along the tarmac. It stopped, and Lord Elberton got out.

'Ah Bigglesworth! Lacey! Well, what d'you think of my latest toy?'

'Looks jolly good, sir,' Algy replied enthusiastically.

'Can we try her out?' asked Biggles briskly. 'We'd love a chance to see how she performs.'

'Of course, of course. But I've got news for you. The entries to the race are hotting up. I was lunching in the House of Lords with Lord Carbury, whose paper's running it, and he tells me more than twenty entries have now arrived. Some of them look like giving you a good run for your money – or rather, for mine.'

'Any news of who they are?' asked Biggles.

'Several from America, and half a dozen or so from France, including Lamartine who flies for Breguet. Doesn't he hold the record to Brazil and back?'

Biggles nodded. 'Splendid flier. Knew him in the war. We've got real opposition with him around. Any news from Germany?'

'Interesting that you ask. Carbury seemed a little vague about the Huns, but thinks the German government was backing someone flying a revolutionary aircraft built by the Heinkel Company. There are a lot of rumours about it, and the government is making it a matter of national prestige to win. Sure you don't want to back out while you've got the chance?'

'D'you think we're likely to, sir?' replied Biggles.

'Frankly, Major Bigglesworth, I don't'

'Not bad, eh?' shouted Biggles over the roar of the slipstream as he pulled the Swallow out of a power-dive and sent the machine hurtling across the aerodrome at fifty feet.

Algy's freckled face grinned back in boyish enthusiasm as he gave the thumbs up from the seat beside him. This was excitement such as neither had experienced since combat flying

in the war. The controls were perfect, and after the faithful
Cormorant, Biggles felt like a driver who had just exchanged an
old Ford for a racing car. He took the aircraft up to 14,000 feet
then opened up the throttle to the maximum. The dial on the
dashboard was quivering around 300 m.p.h. as the English
coastline disappeared behind them and the wave-flecked waters
of the English Channel beckoned them to France. The Swallow
seemed to fly herself, and Biggles would have cheerfully flown on
to Istanbul, but he knew that Elberton was waiting, and
reluctantly turned the Swallow's elegant nose for home and
brought her in to land with the sort of three-point landing he had
made his trademark.

'Well?' said Lord Elberton, grinning like a very old malicious
dwarf. 'And what's your verdict on my aeroplane now, Major
Bigglesworth?'

'Words fail me, sir, and that's a fact!' said Biggles, whose nerves
were still tingling with excitement.

'Come now, Major. Reticence is all very well, but I do expect a
clear report from my associates. Is the Swallow up to scratch?'

'I'd like to fly her round the world,' said Biggles.

'Just get her out to Singapore ahead of everybody else. That's
all I ask,' replied Lord Elberton.

The beginning of the race was still a week away, and Biggles and
Algy had last-minute preparations to complete, when disturbing
rumours reached them. The first was from America – a report in
the New York *Herald Tribune* that Charlie Bray, the stunt-man
from Milwaukee, had signed up with the Cessna Corporation to
fly their latest long-range aircraft in the race.

'Not *the* Charlie Bray?' exclaimed Algy with alarm. 'The man's
a flaming lunatic, and a frightful bounder. He's generally drunk.
When he gets in the cockpit, anything can happen.'

'Admittedly he's not a gent – but then, who is these days?' said
Biggles in reply. 'But Charlie's not a loser. When he flies he flies to
win, and with him at the controls of the latest Cessna we'll have
our work cut out, Algernon my boy.'

'Oh, we can cope with Charlie,' said the ever-optimistic
Ginger Hebblethwaite. 'It's the Huns who worry me. Do we

know yet who is piloting the Heinkel that Lord Elberton was so concerned about?'

Biggles shook his head.

'The old boy's been trying everything he knows to get the details of their team, but Berlin's suddenly clammed up. Not a dicky-bird,' Algy explained.

'Somehow I don't like that,' said Biggles. 'I never trust our sauerkraut-loving friends when they start getting secretive. I wonder just what they're concealing up their grimy sleeves?'

'We'll find out soon enough,' said Algy with a grin. 'We've licked them before and I'm quite confident that we can lick 'em now. Let's just concentrate on the Swallow. That's all that should concern us now.'

As it soon transpired, Algy spoke more accurately than he realised, for barely half an hour later, as the friends were relishing Mrs Symes's bacon, sausages and chips, the telephone pealed through the tiny flat.

'One day I'll throw that confounded instrument straight through the window!' grumbled Biggles. 'For Pete's sake answer it, Ginger, there's a good fellow. Oh, and Algy, easy with the tomato ketchup! That's all there is.'

Algy pulled a face, and Ginger dutifully went off to deal with the telephone. He was gone a long time and when he returned his face was grave.

'Ginger, my dear old chap, what is it?' ejaculated Biggles. 'You look as if you've seen the ghost of Christmas.'

'I only wish I had,' said Ginger. 'That was the Duty Officer from the airfield. Someone has sabotaged the Swallow.'

Less than five minutes later, the Bentley was thundering along the road to Winchester, with Algy at the wheel.

'You never know,' bawled Algy in his usual optimistic vein, 'it could easily be nothing very much. Once Smyth gets going on the damage, I'm sure he'll have the old bus shipshape in no time at all.'

'I wouldn't count on it,' shouted Biggles in reply. 'It sounded pretty bad to me. With only six days left before the race begins, it's really serious.'

'Let's wait and see,' said Ginger reasonably.

But as it turned out, Biggles was, as usual, right. As they reached the barbed-wire fence of the small airport, a fire-engine was just leaving, and a hideous stench of burning greeted them. By the Swallow's hangar, Smithson, the Duty Officer, greeted them, grim-faced with misery.

'How bad is it?' asked Biggles quickly.

Smithson shook his head.

'Go and see for yourselves. It couldn't be much worse.'

Biggles was the first inside the hangar.

'Well, Algy, dear old chap,' he muttered, 'It doesn't look as if we'll get to Southend – let alone to Singapore.'

'You're sure you know who it was?' inquired Lord Elberton.

Colonel Raymond nodded bitterly. 'No doubt at all. The chaps in Special Branch have traced him to the German Embassy – a secretary attached to their trade delegation. Blighter by the name of Krueger. Been on our files for years. Several people have identified him as being near the airport on the night the fire occurred.'

'So why don't you arrest him, man!' exclaimed his Lordship with a vehemence that Biggles recognised at once.

'Lord Elberton,' replied the Colonel wearily, 'you know as well as I do why I can't. There's not a scrap of proof that would stand up in court, and anyhow, the wretched fellow's covered by diplomatic privilege. If we tried to arrest him we'd have the Foreign Office on us like a ton of bricks. No, I'm sorry gentlemen – there's nothing we can do.'

'But this is preposterous! Preposterous!' shouted Lord Elberton. 'What do you blighters at New Scotland Yard imagine that we pay you for?'

The Colonel shrugged his shoulders, but made no reply, and it was Biggles now who butted in.

'One question, sir. Have you discovered why the Huns wanted to destroy the Swallow? I mean, it is a little strange to take so big a risk over a single aeroplane.'

Colonel Raymond looked up sharply. 'Good question, Bigglesworth. Something I've been asking myself ever since I heard the news. I sent out a query to our fellow in Berlin about it. His reply might interest you. He thinks that someone rather high up in the German government is determined that their entry in the Singapore air race will win at any cost.'

'You mean as a matter of national prestige?' asked Biggles.

'No, rather more than that. It's almost as if it had become a personal affair.'

'And did your man find out who was behind all this?'

'No. No, he didn't.'

'Then he should have done.' barked Elberton.

'Not a great deal we could do about it if he had,' replied the Colonel logically.

'Well, I'm not satisfied,' said Elberton. 'Not satisfied at all, and I intend to raise the question in the House of Lords. Good God, man, do you realise how much that aeroplane of mine cost? The time and talent that have gone into it? And now to have to scratch it from the race like this! The whole thing is a damned disgrace.'

'Now, steady on, sir,' interjected Biggles. 'I don't think you're being fair to Colonel Raymond. And who said anything about scratching from the race?'

'Well, obviously we've got to, man. There's no alternative. The Swallow's ruined.'

'Then so are we my Lord. You seem to be forgetting that we have a little bet.'

'Oh, come now Major. Surely you don't think that I'd insist on that, given the circumstances? I may be a hard man, but I like to think I'm fair.'

'Lord Elberton,' said Biggles gravely, 'I was brought up to believe a bargain is a bargain and a bet's a bet. I've never been defeated by a German yet, and I don't intend to be defeated now. As far as I'm concerned, the bet's still on. All I would ask of you is help from all your people down at Winchester to rebuild the Swallow.'

'You'll never do it, Major Bigglesworth. There are only six days left before the race begins. The thing's impossible.'

Biggles smiled coolly. 'That's another thing that I was taught when I was a boy in India. When you decide to do a thing there's no such word as "impossible".'

For Biggles and Co., the race to Singapore began that morning – a desperate race against the clock to get the Swallow rebuilt in time. The flat at Mount Street was vacated, and Biggles, Algy

and Ginger Hebblethwaite moved into the hangar at Winchester. For the next six days it was their home and their
headquarters.

At first sight, the damage to the Swallow seemed appalling –
the fuselage was gutted by the fire, the tail destroyed and the
undercarriage had collapsed.

'You really think we'll get to Singapore in this, old chap?' said
Algy with a hollow laugh. 'You must be joking!'

But Nobby Smyth was not so pessimistic.

'Well, sir,' he said to Biggles, 'there were times in France when
we had to deal with worse than this. Remember when von
Richthofen brewed up the hangars and the workshops at
Maranique with incendiary bombs? We still got the Squadron in
the air. At least the Swallow's engines are all right, and the
cockpit and forward section are more or less untouched. I can't
promise miracles, but at least we'll have a go.'

And have a go they did. For the next four days the labour went
on round the clock, with shifts of workers from the factory slaving
through the night. Biggles and Algy joined them, whilst Ginger
served as Smyth's assistant. The noise at times was deafening, and
no one had much sleep. But gradually, like a phoenix rising from
the ashes, the Swallow was reborn. The race was due to start on
Saturday. By Wednesday night the tail and fuselage had been
rebuilt and the hangar reeked with the fumes of dope and
varnish. By Thursday morning, the entire body of the aircraft
was raised from its trestles and the rebuilt undercarriage put in
place. On Thursday night no one slept as the final checks were
made and the wiring and controls meticulously installed. And
then on Friday morning, just as dawn was breaking, the doors of
the great hangar were drawn back, and a cheer rose from the
weary men inside as the Swallow cautiously emerged to face the
world outside.

'This calls for a little celebration,' exclaimed Algy.

But Biggles, hollow-eyed with tiredness, said, 'No, old lad.
We've just been making up lost time. We've still a lot to do before
we celebrate.'

Normally the testing of a brand-new aeroplane takes weeks.
Algy and Biggles did the whole thing in a day. Just after
breakfast-time the Swallow's twin Rolls-Royce engines started
up, the chocks were pulled away, and taxiing trials began. By

lunchtime she was in the air. Whilst Biggles and Algy grabbed a hurried snack, adjustments were completed, and they were soon back in the cockpit for yet further trials, which went on till dusk made further flying dangerous.

'Well, what d'you think of her?' asked Ginger.

Biggles shrugged his shoulders.

'Well,' he said, 'I could be happier, but she'll have to do. At least she flies and Smyth will be working flat out on her all tonight. We can't do any more.'

'But what about you and Algy?' Ginger asked, solicitously. 'You're both done in before you start.'

'Oh, we're all right,' said Biggles gamely. 'We were brought up on lack of sleep.'

'That's nonsense, and you know it,' replied Ginger. 'The pair of you will crack up long before you get to Singapore if you go on like this. Why don't you and Algy drive across to Croydon straight away in the Bentley, have a good dinner there, and spend the night in the hotel. I'll fly the Swallow over first thing tomorrow morning. That way at least you'll both have had a good night's sleep before the race begins.'

Biggles bit his lip, then said, 'Good notion, Ginger. Thanks. We'll do exactly as you say. But just one thing – go easy with the Swallow when you fly her over. If you prang the old crate now, I'll not forgive you.'

It was a fine September morning, and it could have been a gala Saturday at Croydon Airport as the entries for the biggest race in history started to assemble on the tarmac under the shadow of the squat tower of the airport hotel. Most of the planes had flown in the day before, and when Algy and Biggles strolled down from the hotel breakfast room, they started sizing up the opposition. The mechanics were already scurrying like ants around the aircraft, making last-minute checks and adjustments. Take-off was billed for ten o'clock, and already there was a touch of frenzy in the air. Lamartine, the famous Frenchman, seemed to be having hysterics as his mechanic changed his sparking plugs. Charlie Bray's big white Cessna monoplane was being wheeled out from its hangar, and Watanabe, the bespectacled Japanese air-ace, was grinning like a cheerful frog as he posed for photographs beside his biplane with the rising sun painted on the tail.

'What news of the Huns?' muttered Algy to Biggles as they passed among the crowd of journalists and fans. 'Doesn't appear to be a sign of them.'

'Probably suffering from a guilty conscience – or simply scared of a touch of their own medicine,' replied Biggles grimly. 'From what I hear they're keeping their aircraft under wraps until the last minute, just to make sure nothing can go wrong. It's in that hangar over there, with a gang of specially imported German thugs to keep the nosey parkers off the premises. Pity we didn't do the same, old thing.'

Algy nodded. 'Any news of the crew?'

'Under wraps as well. Old Elberton has done his best to get their names, but even he has failed. There's something very fishy going on, old trout. Not that I'm particularly concerned. All that worries me now is the Swallow. She should be here by now. What d'you think old Ginger's playing at?'

'He'll be all right,' said Algy, glancing at the big clock on the hotel tower. 'We've still got fifty minutes. I've arranged for last-minute refuelling. Hallo, what's this?'

The doors of the German hangar were opening, and a hush fell on the crowd as they caught their first glimpse of the gleaming aeroplane within.

'Ho-ho!' said Algy, 'so that's what all the fuss has been about. Looks pretty powerful. Twin-engined, swept-back wings. Must be a special version of the Heinkel bomber we've been hearing so much about. Dirty dealings apart, it looks as if we'll have our work cut out.'

As he spoke, the German aeroplane was towed across the tarmac and swung into position for the start.

'Very pretty piece of hardware,' murmured Biggles. 'Where the heck is Ginger? P'raps we'd better get ourselves togged up and ready while we're waiting.'

When they had changed into their flying suits (with just a touch of superstition, Biggles had brought along his ancient Sidcot suit) the stewards were already announcing the departure draw. To avoid the danger of the aircraft taking off together, it was decided they would leave at five-minute intervals, and Lord Carbury's curvaceous daughter had the honour of drawing the pilots' numbers from one of her father's old top hats. It was a chance for the press photographers to take their final pictures, and the competitors were soon lining up along the tarmac for the draw.

'Hi-yah, Biggs, you ole palookah,' shouted the fresh-faced Charlie Bray. 'Where's your aeroplane? Wanna borrow mine?'

'I wouldn't risk it, Charlie. Not if you had anything to do with it. No, our old crate is on its way. She'll soon be here. Incidentally, Charlie, any sign of our friends from Deutschland?'

The American shook his rumpled head. 'Perhaps that plane of theirs doesn't need a pilot.'

'I'm not so sure if this isn't the answer to the mystery now,' said Algy.

A large Mercedes from the German Embassy had driven out from the front of the hotel, and as it sped towards them they could see two men in flying gear sitting behind the chauffeur. Suddenly Algy shouted with amazement.

'Biggles! By the Kaiser's cami-knickers, do you see who it is?'

The car drew up near the table where Lord Carbury's daughter stood smiling, with her father's topper in her hands, and a leather-clad figure descended and saluted. There was an unmistakeable scar that ran from his hair-line to the angle of his jaw.

'I should have known,' hissed Biggles. 'Von Stalhein!'

There was no time however now for useless speculation. The draw had started and one of the earliest to have his name chosen from the hat was Charlie Bray.

'Yippee!' he shouted, giving Lord Carbury's startled daughter a resounding kiss.

Lamartine, the Frenchman, was another of the lucky early leavers. Several unknowns followed, and then Biggles heard the name he hated more than any other in the world.

'Number sixteen, Hauptmann Erich von Stalhein of Germany, with his co-pilot, Herr Ludwig Ingelbacher.'

'Wonder who Ingelbacher is when he's at home?' whispered Algy.

'Shh!' said Biggles as the draw continued.

'Followed by Major James Bigglesworth of Great Britain and his co-pilot, Captain the Honourable Algernon Lacey.'

'He'll have us flying right behind him,' muttered Algy.

'Not for long, old boy,' said Biggles. 'Not if I have anything to do with it. Some people think the war stopped with the Armistice. Where the flaming heck is Ginger?'

'Don't worry, Biggles. He'll get here on time if I know Ginger. Now, this looks interesting. Count Frankenstein is about to pay us his respects!'

With the completion of the draw, the pilots were dispersing to their aircraft to await the beginning of the race, but von Stalhein and Herr Ingelbacher were advancing towards them. The Hauptmann clicked his heels and bowed with elaborate Teutonic courtesy.

'Ach, Major Bigglesworth! We meet again.'

Biggles gave the Prussian the iciest of nods.

'A pleasure to be up against a real enemy,' replied Biggles. 'But von Stalhein, I never realised that you could fly. I thought sabotage was more your speciality.'

A flash of hatred blazed for a moment in the Junker's eyes, but he replied with studied self-control. 'That was wartime and the war is over, Major Bigglesworth. Now with the peace this old dog has, as you British say, learned new tricks. But where is your aircraft, Major? Fifteen minutes now to starting time. You're running things a little close.'

'Precision timing, von Stalhein,' replied Biggles airily. 'We had a spot of trouble with some friends of yours who should have known better. but that's been dealt with now. Unless I'm much mistaken this is our aircraft now, warmed up and ready for the race.'

Even as he spoke the graceful silhouette of the Swallow skimmed across the boundary of the airfield, flashed past the hangars and with perfect airmanship landed and came taxiing towards them.

'I expect that we'll be seeing more of one another, von Stalhein,' said Biggles. 'Now if you'll excuse me, there is work to do.'

Beneath his apparent calm, Biggles was furious with Ginger for the delay, but as the hapless Yorkshireman explained, there had been trouble with the starboard engine and he and the mechanics had been up all night replacing it.

'Get her refuelled fast,' said Biggles. 'Everything else O.K.?'

Ginger nodded. 'We've done our best with her, and Smyth deserves a medal if anybody does.'

'Good man,' said Biggles. 'I'll remember to bring one back for him from Singapore. Ready, Algy? Looks as if the show is just about to start.'

But there was one final interruption. As the stewards checked the line-up for the start, a big Rolls-Royce came screeching up and a tiny figure with a large bald head got out.

'Holy mackerel!' Algy groaned. 'Old Elberton himself. What does the old trouble-maker want? He could have waited till we're in the air.'

'Ah, Major Bigglesworth, Captain Lacey! Glad that I'm in time,' piped the ancient millionaire. 'Just thought I'd come to wish you both good luck. Trumper and I have been to Fortnums and we've a little something just to keep your spirits up en route.' As he spoke, his bull-like chauffeur brought a massive hamper from the boot of the car and humped it over to the Swallow.

'Think you'll have room for it?' he queried.

'I should just say so, sir,' answered Biggles. 'Even if it means dumping Algy. Terribly decent of you, sir, and much appreciated.'

His Lordship raised his hand.

'Please, Bigglesworth, don't thank me. Makes me feel uncomfortable. And don't forget, that bet of ours still stands.'

'We won't forget,' said Biggles, with a grin.

'Well, how's she going, Biggles?' Algy inquired as the coast of England disappeared behind them in the morning haze.

'Like a dream, old boy. I never thought we'd make it, but by gosh, it's all been worth it.'

The plane was flying like the thoroughbred she was and Biggles was in his element at last. The double cockpit was cramped – particularly with Lord Elberton's hamper between the seats – but the two friends could take turns at the controls, and they had already overhauled several of the slower entrants in the race. Algy was navigating and according to their plans the first stop would be Athens, in eight hours' time.

'Any sign of von Stalhein?' Algy asked.

Biggles shook his head. 'That Heinkel is the only plane that really worries me. She could be a bit faster than we are, Algy. Still, for that matter, so is Charlie's Cessna. But I can't believe they've got the range that we have.'

'Nor the experience, old bean. Von Stalhein's not a real flier and the true test will come once we get over Asia Minor on the next leg to Karachi. That's what will really sort out the men from the boys.'

A slow smile spread over Biggles' still boyish countenance. 'Revenge will be very sweet,' he said.

The Swallow was flying on a straight line to Athens, and in perfect autumn weather they saw northern France and the Black Forest float beneath their wings. By mid-afternoon Biggles was already gaining height to approach the Dolomites, and it would soon be time for Algy to take over.

'How's about some grub, old bean?' he inquired.

'Algy, my dear chap, gluttony will be your downfall,' he replied. 'Still, if you must, you must. There are some raisins and potato crisps underneath your seat, but go easy with them, there's a good fellow.'

'Potato crisps be blowed,' said Algy mutinously. 'What about his Lordship's hamper?'

'Algy, you know your self-indulgence never ceases to amaze me. This is supposed to be a record-breaking flight, not a gourmet tour. Still if you must, you must . . .'

The first shadows of the Mediterranean dusk were shrouding Athens in a purple haze as they came in to land. The Parthenon was on its little hill, the street lights twinkling far below and a crowd had gathered at the airport.

'Quite a reception committee by the look of it, old scout,' said Biggles cheerfully, but then a note of horrified amazement crept into his voice.

'Good grief!' he said. 'The blighter's already here before us.'

As he pointed to the tarmac, Algy could see the object of his consternation – von Stalhein's Heinkel was at the far end of the runway like a huge grey shark.

Algy whistled softly through his teeth.

'Just how the heck d'you think he managed it?' he asked. 'I never thought he had the range to beat us.'

'Must have done, old fruit,' said Biggles philosophically. 'But never say die, Algy lad. It's quite a stretch from here to Singapore and a lot can happen on the way.'

Under the rules of the competition, and to avoid the danger of fatigue and night flying, the competitors were to spend the night at Athens, before flying on at daybreak to Karachi. But before going off to their hotel, Biggles and Algy spent some time watching the mechanics working on their aircraft and picking up the news of their competitors. Several, it seemed, had scratched already, and all the others, lacking the Swallow's range, had been forced to stop en route to refuel. But Charlie Bray's Cessna was not far behind them, and while they talked to the mechanics his powerful single-engined aircraft roared in to land, closely followed by Solario, the Italian ace.

'Hi folks! How's tricks?' bawled the shambling American as he swung down from the cockpit. 'Boy, could I use a drink! You joining me?'

'You bet,' said Algy. 'How did you get on?'

'Not bad, not bad. That poor damned Frenchman Lamar-something copped it in the Alps. Tried drilling Mont Blanc with his propellor. Mont Blanc won.'

'Good Heavens! Is he dead?'

'Probably. There was a dreadful mess on the mountainside. But say, how did that Kraut get here before you?'

'That's what we'd like to know,' said Biggles.

Later that evening over dinner in the Hôtel Grande Bretagne the mystery of von Stalhein's record speed to Athens cropped up again. Von Stalhein and his bullet-headed co-pilot were already celebrating with a number of their countrymen at a far table when Algy, Biggles, Charlie Bray and the British Consul entered. The Consul, an egg-like man called Owen, had once been in the Marines and had already responded to a request from Biggles for an all-night guard on the Swallow.

'Rather too many accidents have happened,' as he put it. 'Don't want one of von Stalhein's merry men starting an accidental bonfire underneath the Swallow.'

'Quite,' said the Consul diplomatically, and later in the meal he suddenly remarked, 'Oh, by the way Bigglesworth. How much petrol will you be carrying tomorrow to get you to Karachi?'

'Nearly 2,000 gallons,' Biggles answered. 'Why?'

'Something very odd about von Stalhein's plane. She uses less than half that.'

'But that's impossible,' said Biggles. 'As far as I can see, she's powered with standard B.M.W. aero-engines. If anything, they're more powerful than ours. You must be wrong – mustn't he, Charlie?'

'Sure,' said the American. 'My crate's single-engined. Even so, I had to stop in Rome to refuel. You've got it wrong, buster.'

'Not at all,' said Owen. 'The Shell manager here's a friend of mine, and he was puzzled too. When the Heinkel was refuelled she had 900 gallons, which was all her tanks would take.'

'And yet we know von Stalhein plans to fly non-stop to Karachi,' interjected Algy. 'What's the blighter up to, Biggles?'

'Why don't you go and ask him?' replied Biggles, glancing pointedly across the room to where the Germans had begun to sing their wartime drinking songs. Von Stalhein was sitting back, his monocle in place, gazing at Biggles with a cold smile on his lips.

'Somehow I don't think he'd tell me,' Algy answered.

Next morning, just as dawn was breaking, the fliers were assembled at the airport waiting to be off. The time-keepers were in place, and von Stalhein's Heinkel, with the twenty-minute start that it had won the day before, was first to leave. Then it was the Swallow's turn – and for several anxious moments it seemed as if the starboard motor would refuse to start. But finally it fired, coughed, then roared to life, and the great plane, weighed down with its massive load of fuel, swept up to greet the rising sun and headed for the sea.

This time the two friends flew with a grim determination quite different from their cheerfulness the day before. Both knew quite well that if the Germans managed to repeat their previous performance, they had no chance of winning now. But this was something neither would admit, and Biggles was intent on urging every ounce of power from the Swallow's engines as they sped above the coast of southern Turkey. Soon they had reached the coast of Syria, and half-an-hour later, somewhere past the city of Aleppo, they picked up the line of the Euphrates which they followed down towards Baghdad. They had a tail wind here, but as they knew only too well, von Stalhein would be sharing their advantage.

'You realise,' said Algy, 'that if what Owen said last night is true, that blasted Heinkel should be landing at Baghdad for fuel. It will take half an hour at least, and we'll still beat them to Karachi.'

'I wouldn't count on it,' said Biggles. 'But keep your eyes skinned as we fly across Baghdad. If von Stalhein is refuelling, he'll still be there.'

But there was no sign at all of the Heinkel on the dusty runway at Baghdad.

'You see, old lad,' said Biggles, trying to disguise the hopelessness he felt, 'the blasted bird has flown.'

'But how?' said Algy furiously. 'I just don't get it, Biggles. Unless that plane of his has learned to fly on lighter fuel, it's just not possible.'

Biggles shook his head. 'Von Stalhein's up to something, Algy. I don't know what it is, but I know von Stalhein and I wouldn't trust him any further than I could throw Lord Elberton's Rolls-Royce. Obviously he has staked everything on winning this confounded race.'

'Like us, old boy.'

'Except in his case I imagine that the German government's involved as well – along with the prestige of their air force and von Stalhein's whole political career. Algy, old scout, we're going to find out exactly what that tricky Prussian's up to. I don't mind being beaten fairly, but I'm dashed if I'll be cheated – and particularly by von Stalhein.'

It was a gruelling flight across the Persian desert, and there were dust storms in Baluchistan that made it necessary to fly at 18,000 feet and switch to oxygen. The great plane bucketed and twitched like a leaf in a December gale, but the two friends knew their job and slap on time the gleaming waters of the Arabian Sea appeared. By five o'clock the Swallow was beginning its approach run to Karachi. Biggles was at the controls with Algy navigating, and as they swept across the airport, Algy shouted, 'Biggles, my dear old boy, I think we've beaten them. There's not a sign of them.'

'Perhaps the dust storms caught them – but I wouldn't count on it. At all events we're equal with them now,' said Biggles happily.

'Perhaps those dust storms forced them down,' said Algy brightly. 'I don't know about that fellow Ingelbacher, but von Stalhein's not the most experienced of pilots. Dreadful pity if they've crashed, eh Biggles?'

But he spoke too soon, for shortly after the Swallow landed, and long before the two friends had finished supervising the refuelling and routine maintenance of the engines for the following day's long haul over India and the Bay of Bengal to Singapore, there was a roar of engines from the west, and von Stalhein's Heinkel was soon coming in to land. Algy glanced at his watch.

'Twenty-eight minutes behind us Biggles. That means we're neck and neck. Everything depends on tomorrow.'

They watched the two Germans climb down from the cockpit and Biggles could not resist shouting out to them.

'Bit slow today, von Stalhein! What went wrong?'

'Ach!' growled von Stalhein, glaring at the friends with evident disbelief. 'How did you get through those storms? They carried us off course, but tomorrow we will show you Englishmen.'

'Perhaps you will, von Stalhein, and perhaps you won't. But tell me one thing. How does that aeroplane of yours consume so little fuel?'

Von Stalhein was evidently tired, for he made no effort to conceal his anger at the question.

'What are you suggesting, Major?' he replied.

'Nothing at all,' said Biggles innocently. 'But I'd like to know how you managed to get here using less than half the fuel we needed.'

Von Stalhein glared at him, then curled his lips into a derisive smile.

'As you should know, Major Bigglesworth, our German scientists are the finest in the world, and that aeroplane of yours is out of date already. Not even you, Major Bigglesworth, can possibly defeat the power of Germany.'

'We'll see about that tomorrow,' replied Biggles steadily.

Von Stalhein clicked his heels, '*Jawohl*,' he said.

'Dashed pity about poor old Charlie Bray,' said Algy, over dinner at the Karachi Club that night, 'but absolutely typical. Just fancy trying to fly underneath a dust-storm with a single engine!'

'Original as ever, dear old Charlie, but at least he's safe, judging by the reports. Probably come rocking up here on a dromedary in a fortnight's time. None of the other entrants seems to have got much further than Baghdad. So that leaves only two of us, old fruit. Britain against the Huns. Quite like old times!'

Biggles grinned in keen anticipation at the thought of the final battle he and Algy would be waging next day in the skies of Asia. It was a private duel with von Stalhein, a battle for the survival of Biggles and Co., and now it was something more. The honour of the Empire was at stake.

Biggles glanced around the Club at the portraits of the kings and governors and viceroys that adorned the walls. Now he was back in India he felt the magic of this strange land of his birth.

'You know, old chap,' he said as he finished the last mouthful of a delicious Chundra chicken curry, 'it makes a fellow proud to be carrying the flag for all of this.'

Algy nodded as he crumbled a chapatti. 'I know exactly how you feel. But to be practical, old scout, just how do we propose to ditch that blinking Hun? It's obvious there's dirty work afoot, but it's also obvious, to me at any rate, that von Stalhein's Heinkel is faster than the Swallow. And we still haven't discovered how the blighter's flying all that way without refuelling.'

'Perhaps he's right,' mused Biggles. 'Perhaps those German scientists have devised a way of halving fuel consumption. Always have been crafty devils.'

'Poppycock!' exploded Algy. 'There's something nasty in the woodshed, Biggles, and unless we find out what it is, I fear Lord Elberton will soon be riding in the poor old Bentley.'

According to the official stewards, the Swallow was some fifteen minutes ahead of its competitor, and so accordingly next morning the two friends were the first to leave Karachi. Biggles was smiling now, and Algy recognised his mood from those far-off days in Squadron 266 when they were really up against it. An enormous orange-coloured sun was blazing up from the horizon. A pie-dog started howling, then the boundless silence of the early morning shattered as the Swallow's engines roared in unison.

Biggles raised his gloved hand to the watching stewards, and then in a hurricane of dust the Swallow was away on the last and crucial stage of its flight to Singapore.

Soon they were over the tobacco-coloured heartland of the great sub-continent – Ahmadabad and Baroda disappeared behind them in that clear-cut morning light. Then came the great Narbada River and the mountains of Satpura.

'You know,' said Biggles pensively, 'when I was a kid in India I used to dream of flying just like this. It's hard to believe that it's come true.'

'I know,' said Algy. 'It seems like yesterday. Strange things, aeroplanes. Once you've really caught the bug you're hooked for life. Perhaps von Stalhein feels the same, but somehow I doubt it.'

'Talking of whom,' said Biggles, 'we must begin to keep our eyes skinned now. He may be managing to overhaul us.' But by midday, when they reached the eastern Ghats and prepared for the long haul east across the monsoon-swept Bay of Bengal, they had seen nothing in the sky except the lonely kite-birds floating lazily below them. They crossed the coast above the town of Vishakhapatnam, then changed course slightly to avoid a typhoon that had been reported sweeping up from southern India. As they did so, Algy gave a shout, and pointed far below.

'Do my eyes deceive me, Biggles?' he exclaimed.

'A flying-boat!' said Biggles. 'What on earth's it doing here? What is it?'

Algy snatched a pair of powerful binoculars from the rack above their heads and gazed at the far-off aeroplane.

'Looks like a big one, Biggles. Holy smoke, old boy! It's one of those latest Dornier jobs we read about in *Flight Magazine*. Built in Bremen – still officially on the German secret list.'

As Algy said this, Biggles' eyes hardened into points of steel.

'I think, old scout, we may have stumbled on von Stalhein's little secret after all. With any luck that Hun down there hasn't spotted us and we have the advantage of the sun behind us. We're going up, old boy. I want to see what happens.'

The throb of the Swallow's engines rose an octave as he opened up the throttle and eased back the joy-stick.

'Make sure you keep that Dornier in sight,' he shouted gleefully. 'That's all I ask.'

By now the Dornier was several miles away, but Algy's eagle eyes could see it circling a spot in the ocean.

'What the heck's the blighter doing?' he muttered to himself. 'There's nothing in the sea. Biggles, old chap, we're wasting time.'

'Hang on,' said Biggles. 'We'll give it a few more minutes.'

'If you say so,' grumbled Algy. Then suddenly he gave a whoop. 'Look, Biggles. There! By all that's holy, it's that blasted Heinkel! And the Dornier is coming up to meet it.'

As he watched through the binoculars he could see the unmistakeable swept-back wings of von Stalhein's aircraft far below. The flying-boat was soon above it and for a moment it appeared as if the two planes would collide. But they flew together and a second later, Algy saw something snaking down from the flying-boat towards the Heinkel.

'Biggles, just take a look at this,' he shouted, thrusting the binoculars towards him. 'What's going on?'

As Algy held the Swallow on its course, Biggles began studying the scene below him with a practised eye.

'Ho-ho!' he said, with sudden satisfaction. 'I think we have the answer now to the secret of that Hun's success. You know what they're doing, Algy? They're refuelling in mid-air. Very nifty. Alan Cobham's been experimenting with it, of course, and our German friends have evidently picked up the idea. So much for those magic engines of von Stalhein's Heinkel.'

'But it's against all the rules. He'll be disqualified.'

'But how d'we prove it, Algy lad? Here in the middle of the ocean we've got no witnesses. That's what's so devilishly clever.'

'We could photograph it.'

'But we haven't got a camera. No, old chap, there's only one thing for it. Action stations, Algy. Here we go!'

As he said this, Biggles swung the Swallow round, and with the engines screaming, hurled her down as he used to dive his Sopwith Camel out of the sun onto a pack of unsuspecting Halberstadts below. It was a dizzying descent, but Biggles' ancient skill had not deserted him. Down, down they went, with the bright blue ocean rushing up to meet them. The German planes were straight ahead by now and in that one brief moment Algy glimpsed the terrified expression on the pilot's face. Even Algy was certain they must crash, but Biggles had complete control. This was the sort of knife-edge flying he had learned in combats on the Western Front, and just as collision seemed inevitable, he pulled the Swallow to one side and flipped its wings so that it passed between the two big German aircraft. At the same time, there was a resounding thud as the leading edge of the Swallow's off-side wing sliced through the fuel pipe connecting the big flying-boat with von Stalhein's Heinkel. Algy glanced back in time to see the petrol spewing from the severed pipe into the sea below. A slow grin spread across his features.

'Nice flying, maestro! Very nice indeed! I'd give a lot to see von Stalhein's face right now.'

'A pleasure I can do without,' said Biggles happily. 'And now, full-speed ahead for Singapore. With any luck we'll be in time for dinner.'

Ten days later there was a gala night at the Savoy Hotel, with Biggles and Algy, as outright winners of the London to Singapore air race, the guests of honour.

'This is the part that I could do without, old bean,' said Biggles as he struggled with his boiled shirt and white bow-tie. 'Any idea where Mrs Symes has put my medals?'

'She was cleaning them. She said they needed it,' said Ginger.

'Lot of nonsense, all this carry-on,' grumbled Biggles. 'Anyone would think we're on the music-hall. Algy, for cripe's sake, deal with the confounded journalists.'

'Then, who'll accept the cheque?' asked Algy with a laugh.

'I will,' said Biggles firmly. 'Ah well, chaps, into the lion's den!' he added as all four members of Biggles and Co. crammed themselves into Algy's Bentley, and headed for the hotel.

In fact, the evening was a great success, and when the speeches and toasts were over, and Biggles had his cheque for £50,000 safely in his pocket, Lord Elberton appeared, his bald head gleaming like a billiard ball beneath the chandeliers.

'Ah, Major Bigglesworth,' he said, 'time we settled up. What was the figure we agreed on?'

'One hundred thousand pounds, my Lord,' said Biggles coolly.

'Oh, so it was,' replied Lord Elberton, taking his cheque book from his pocket with a grin. 'Pretty easy money, I should say. By all accounts it was a fairly uneventful flight.'

'A piece of cake,' said Biggles, pocketing the cheque.

8

The Fuehrer's Lady

'I don't care how good-looking the wretched woman is,' said Biggles furiously. 'She's been married twice already. She's a German and a Nazi Party member. Algy should have more sense than have anything to do with her, let alone be photographed in public with the silly cow!'

He hurled his copy of *The Tatler* angrily across the room, narrowly missing Ginger in the process.

'Oh, come now Biggles!' replied Ginger soothingly as he retrieved the tattered journal from the fireplace. 'You know Algy well enough to realise that such considerations don't come into it. He's an incurable romantic, and Frau von Sternberg's very much his type – blonde, blue-eyed, dominating. Rather reminds me of the girl he was in love with years ago, the tennis-player, Deborah something-or-other.'

'But she was relatively harmless,' replied Biggles sharply. 'This one isn't. She's right in with all the leading Huns from the Fuehrer down – or up. Her ex-husband is a pal of Goering's, Ribbentrop's some sort of relative, and ever since she made that record-breaking flight to Buenos Aires the German propaganda experts have been using her as one of the Nazi Party's top attractions. Before he knows what's hit him, our Algy will be caught up with all that merry gang as well.'

'Now that's not fair,' said Ginger. 'He's not that stupid.'

'Isn't he?' fumed Biggles. 'Listen Ginger, I've known that

cousin of mine since he was in short grey trousers, and women have always been his downfall.'

'But Biggles, Algy's thirty-eight next birthday, and you really must allow him a little private life. Just because we're a pair of crusty old bachelors ourselves, it doesn't follow Algy has to live a life of total chastity. If he wants a bit of fun, good luck to him, I say.'

'That's not the point, Ginger, and you know it. Last week he was off flying with her in some confounded air display at Munich. Now there's a picture of him with the wretched woman at the German Embassy. If things go on like this, he'll soon be staying as a weekend guest at Berchtesgaden.'

'Well, if he does, he does,' said Ginger wearily. 'It's Algy's business and I do suggest that you stay out of it.'

'Rubbish!' snorted Biggles. 'It's our business. Algy's one of us, and the next thing you know people will be thinking that we've all gone over to the Germans. I'm going to tell him exactly what I think!'

'Well, if you must, you must,' said Ginger, opening a new tin of his favourite St Bruno Flake, 'but I would still advise against it.'

During the three years since Biggles and Algy made their name by their spectacular success in the London to Singapore air race, fortune had seemed to smile upon them both. The £100,000 that their win had earned them had been carefully invested on behalf of Biggles and Co., and this had given them the capital they needed for their adventures to continue. They had flown in Africa and revisited their favourite haunts in the Pacific. They had been to South America again, and also had some time in southern India – but although the adventures had continued, there had been a subtle change in the friends' attitude to life. Biggles summed it up in one of his favourite phrases at the time – 'Enjoy it while you can, for none of this is going to last.' He knew that war was on its way, and that when it came precious little of the life they loved could possibly endure.

They had lived the good life to the full and done their best to ignore the storm clouds gathering over Europe. In 1936 Biggles and Algy both narrowly avoided real involvement in the Spanish Civil War, after Franco's bombers sank the cruise ship in which

they were holidaying in the Mediterranean. (Biggles had had a
troublesome recurrence of his old malaria and the cruise had
been on doctor's orders.) But even then, they studiously avoided
taking sides in what they felt to be a purely Spanish matter. Had
anybody questioned Biggles on his politics, he would have said he
was a King and Empire man – and changed the subject. But he
had one unchanging and unchangeable belief or prejudice, call it
what you will: profound distrust of Germany. 'The Germans are
either at your feet, or at your throat,' he used to say, and for this
reason his one hero in contemporary politics was the arch-enemy
of appeasement, Winston Churchill. Almost all the remainder of
his country's politicians he summed up as 'ninnies, Reds or
traitors'. Because of his passionate affair with Frau von
Sternberg, Algy was almost in the third category himself.

One might have thought that Algy, who knew his cousin better
than anyone alive, would have understood this. He still
worshipped Biggles, and had always gone to almost any lengths
to keep him happy. In the past, a quizzical expression on his
cousin's face followed by a simple verdict such as 'not quite our
sort, old chap' had been enough to seal the fate of any luckless
maiden who failed to pass the test of Biggles' scrutiny, but
Irmgard Ulrike von Sternberg had been different. Algy had met
the lady at the Hendon Air Display. She was already famous for
her record-breaking flights around the world, and had been
sponsored by the German government to fly her massive Junkers
monoplane across to Britain for the show. Everyone was
intrigued to see this German Amazon. The press had made a fuss
of her and it was thought quite natural to introduce her to the
famous British long-distance flier, Captain the Honourable
Algernon Lacey. Algy fell in love with her at once.

It was hard to tell how she felt in return. She was obviously
flattered to discover this distinguished, aristocratic British flier so
totally in love with her. Algy courted her with everything he
could – flowers, chocolates, evenings at Ciro's and afternoons at
Henley. She was also clearly most impressed by Algy as a flier.
She was a very cool professional herself, and they had countless
subjects for discussion if they tired of love – undercarriages, pay-
loads, altimeters, fuel tanks – the list was endless. She got on well
with Algy's parents, and gave herself with slightly clinical
abandon after a vegetarian dinner at the Dorchester. (She had

the smooth, hard-muscled body of an athlete, and exclaimed 'my flier' at the crucial moment, which had Algy somewhat puzzled.)

But there was something calculating and uncomfortably inhuman about the lady – at least in the eyes of others. Ginger had christened her 'the lady with ice-cube eyes' and everyone could see exactly what he meant – everyone, that is, except Algy. He had flown with her, holidayed with her, been several times to Germany with her, and seemed to grow more fond of her with every day that passed.

Biggles could certainly have been more tactful when he delivered his ultimatum to Algy. A quiet corner of the Royal Aero Club and a fatherly word over a whisky and soda might well have done the trick. Instead, they had what rapidly turned into a most fearful row. Biggles and Ginger had breezed innocently enough into what Biggles called his 'favourite watering hole' at the Café Royal when he had noticed Algy at the bar with the glamorous Frau von Sternberg. He was about to turn away when Algy spotted him and called him over.

Until this point, Biggles had carefully avoided meeting the famous German flier, but now there was no evading her – especially with Algy looking rather pink and anxious in the background.

'Biggles! Ginger!' he exclaimed. 'You must meet Irmgard. Irmgard, these are the best two chums a fellow ever had, my cousin Biggles, and the famous Ginger Hebblethwaite.'

Biggles thrust out his hand, but instead of shaking it, Frau von Sternberg raised her own in stiff salute and said, 'Heil Hitler!'

'Oh – er – yes!' replied Biggles, momentarily at a loss for words.

'What's your poison, Biggles?' asked Algy nervously. (Normally he would not have dreamt of asking Biggles what he wanted, knowing that he always drank a couple of pink gins at this time of the evening.)

'Oh, the usual, Algy, if it's all the same to you,' said Biggles, looking uncomfortably towards the ice-cold female presence opposite.

'And how are you enjoying England, Frau von Sternberg?' he inquired.

'Not greatly,' she replied.

'A pity. And why not?' asked Biggles.

'Here in this country there is not sufficient discipline,' she said. 'It is quite different in Germany. We would not tolerate the sort of nonsense that I see in Britain – sloppiness everywhere, and no respect for authority. And then there is this so-called democracy of yours.'

'Oh?' said Biggles. 'And what's wrong with that? It generally seems to work.'

'But how can you say that, Major, when it allows a criminal like this man Winston Churchill to criticise my country? In Germany he would be in prison.'

'Would he now' said Biggles evenly. 'I think perhaps too many people are in prison in Germany.'

'Are you criticising my country, Major?' she hissed, with a steely glitter in her eyes.

'Frau von Sternberg, you began this conversation by criticising mine. But perhaps we should keep off politics. What about this aeroplane of yours?'

'Yes,' said Algy eagerly, 'tell Biggles about this flight we plan to do together. It'll be fantastic.'

'Algernon,' she cut in quickly, 'our plans are not to be discussed, any more than my aircraft is, with enemies of my country. Major Bigglesworth, good day to you. Algernon, I shall be back at my hotel.'

With this she grabbed her handbag, glared at Biggles, and was gone – leaving consternation and the scent of Chanel No. 5 behind her.

'Phew, I'm sorry, old chap,' murmured Algy, 'but you shouldn't have picked on her like that. She's very sensitive, you know.'

'Sensitive?' roared Biggles. 'She's as sensitive as an anti-aircraft gun! And as for me picking on her, you heard the way she started off on Winston. I didn't even say a word against her Corporal Schickelgruber.'

'Now Biggles!' interjected Algy.

'Don't "now Biggles" me, my lad!' expostulated Biggles, thumping his fist upon the bar. 'You need to come to your senses, my good fellow! Maybe she's wonderful in bed. I wouldn't know, thank God, but that's no earthly reason for betraying Britain.'

By now, everybody in the bar was listening agog. Biggles was white with rage, and a crimson flush had spread over Algy's countenance. There was a pause, then Algy picked up his Martini, glared at Biggles, and threw it in his face.

'How dare you!' he exclaimed.

'All right,' said Ginger for the umpteenth time. 'So it *was* the wretched woman's fault, but what is done is done, old chap, and no amount of blaming her is going to fetch him back.'

'But I don't want him back!' exploded Biggles. 'I wouldn't speak to him if he came and begged my pardon on his bended knees. All that worries me is the thought of Algy going off to Germany for good. He's such a silly ass. And in that woman's hands ...'

'There you go again!' said Ginger, as he discreetly edged the Gordons out of Biggles' reach. 'Just forget her. Algy will tire of her in time – he always does. Or else she'll be the one who gives him the old heave-ho! Either way, it'll all work out and Algy will finally be back, none the worse for wear.'

It was two days since that fateful evening at the Café Royal, and a lot had happened. Algy had failed to return to Mount Street, and inquiries from Ginger had elicited the fact that he had now mmoved in with Frau von Sternberg at the Dorchester Hotel. The gossip columnists had instantly latched on to the rumpus – and the details of the row lost little in the telling in the morning papers. This had been followed by an interview with Algy in *The Times* (strongly pro-German in those days), in which he had calmly said that he intended settling in Germany, marrying the Frau von Sternberg as soon as her divorce was settled, and flying with her in her future record-breaking bids.

'So this means the end of the old partnership with Major Bigglesworth?' *The Times* man inquired.

'Afraid it does,' said Algy stoically. 'But it's perhaps as well. Some partnerships can last too long, and jealousies and antagonisms can develop. I have immense respect for Major Bigglesworth, and always will, but I'm sure it's best for all concerned ...'

The Times man tried to contact Biggles, but Biggles cursed him down the telephone (not recommended when dealing with the press) and Algy's version of the story hit the headlines. Later that same day, Algy rang Ginger, asking him to pack up his belongings for him, and by the evening Algy had moved out of the little flat which he and the friends had shared through thick and thin for nearly twenty years. Biggles and Co. had broken up.

At first the break-up seemed to make little difference. Biggles and Ginger still kept their aircraft down at Brooklands, Smyth still serviced them, and they even had a holiday together early that summer on the Norfolk Broads, where Biggles found he rather enjoyed sailing, in a leisurely sort of way. He drank somewhat more than usual, but otherwise life continued as before. Algy was never mentioned.

From time to time there were reports of Algy in the foreign pages of the press. He hadn't married but was plainly still as close as ever to the Frau von Sternberg. That summer they had piloted the Junkers to New York, breaking the record for the transatlantic crossing, and had returned to a full-scale hero's welcome in Berlin. Algy was subsequently photographed with Goering and several leading German politicians. Later he toured Germany, visiting German Air Force installations, and helping the Frau von Sternberg in her lectures and her meetings with the members of the German aircraft industry.

Ginger discussed it all with Nobby Smyth.

'Can't understand it, Nobby,' he complained. 'It simply isn't like old Algy. Must be that confounded woman.'

Nobby Smyth agreed. 'Weak as water, poor old Algy, where women are concerned,' he added sagely.

'Still,' continued Ginger, 'I blame Biggles for what happened. Always has been too possessive over Algy, and it was stupid of him going off the handle as he did. Finesse is what you must have where women are concerned.'

'Absolutely, Ginger,' Nobby Smyth agreed. 'That's how I run my married life. What I like to call the subtle approach. Always works with women. But tell me, Ginger, how's Biggles really taking all this latest news from Germany? Isn't he upset?'

'More than I've ever known him to be,' he replied. 'Of course he keeps it bottled up, his sort always does. But in a way I don't think he'll ever quite recover from it. He doesn't only feel that Algy's let him down, he thinks he has betrayed his country.'

'I always say that pheasant is absurdly over-rated, don't you agree, James?' asked Colonel Raymond, scanning the evening offering at the Blazers' Club. (Some time a year or two before, Biggles had been elevated from 'Bigglesworth' to 'James' in the Colonel's personal vocabulary. Biggles, however, still continued to address the older man as 'sir'.)

'Dry, fairly tasteless,' the Colonel went on. 'A boring fowl, fit for nothing but the casserole. I recommend the partridge. Shot, incidentally, on the estate of your old friend, Elberton. They should be rather good.'

'That sounds marvellous,' said Biggles, surrendering the choice of food as usual to the Colonel. 'How is the old boy, incidentally?'

'Unbearable as ever,' said the Colonel with a somewhat toothy grin. 'He was in the other night, and inquiring after you. Seems that he has a brand-new version of the Swallow being developed for the R.A.F. Terribly hush-hush, of course, so keep it to yourself, but it could be just the bomber the Air Force needs. He seems to be wanting you to test-fly the thing for him sometime, so I expect he'll be in touch with you. You've been warned.'

'Thanks very much for telling me, sir,' said Biggles with a wry smile. 'Perhaps I should become a test-pilot and have done with it. A short life, but a cheerful one.'

'Oh, I don't know about that, my boy. With this war in the offing, I think we can find you something a bit more interesting than that, if it's still excitement that you're after. Now, how about some smoked trout to begin with – or why don't we push the boat out and have caviar? A year or two from now and caviar will only be a memory.'

Biggles knew from long experience with Colonel Raymond that a sumptuous meal at the Blazers' Club invariably preceded some assignment with the British Secret Service and, as a rule, the better the food, the worse the task that followed. So, when the caviar arrived, Biggles was on his guard. But Colonel Raymond was in a mellow mood that night. He talked about the salmon fishing in the Highlands, the shooting on the Surrey-Hampshire borders and the hunting with the Quorn. He reminisced about their time in France and spoke discreetly – but disparagingly – of his colleagues at New Scotland Yard. In short, he spent a good three-quarters of that most delicious meal beating about the bush, and it was not until the *marrons glacés* had appeared that he finally inquired, 'Oh, and by the way James, heard anything of Algy Lacey lately?'

'No,' said Biggles without looking up. 'And I'm not sure I want to.'

'Oh, it's like that is it?' replied the Colonel, chewing solemnly and trying to decide between the Cockburns and the Courvoisier.

'Well, don't you feel the same, sir?' answered Biggles sternly. 'You knew him almost as well as I did, and I still can't quite believe that Algy, of all people, has gone over to the Huns.'

Colonel Raymond looked up quickly.

'That's what you honestly believe?' he asked.

'Well, what else can a fellow think? First there's this wretched von Sternberg woman, then he goes flying for the Junkers company and now I hear he's living in Berlin. Surely there's only one word one can use about a rotter who does that. Algy's a traitor to his class and to his country.'

There was a pregnant silence as Biggles uttered these cruel words, and for a while the Colonel seemed to be examining the surface of the table as if uncertain what reply to make. Finally, he screwed his monocle in place and glared around the dining room to make sure nobody was listening.

'James,' he said at last, putting on that cold, impersonal voice he always used for matters of the utmost secrecy. 'There's something that I have to tell you about Lacey. Previously, I insisted that for his sake, you, like everybody else, would have to be kept firmly in the dark, and he agreed – reluctantly – but he agreed. Algy Lacey is no traitor. On the contrary, he's one of the bravest men I know.'

'You mean he was,' said Biggles bitterly.

'I mean he is. Today. At this very moment. Everything that happened, James, was done on my express instructions – from the very moment he was introduced to that appalling woman, to the day he left with her for Germany.'

Biggles looked slightly stunned at this.

'But that's impossible,' he said. 'What about that row we had at the Café Royal? He even flung a full Martini in my face, you know!'

The Colonel smiled and nodded to himself. 'That was my suggestion, I'm afraid. One of my finer strokes, I thought. Two of my chaps were just behind you at the time to make sure nothing could go wrong, and I took great care the papers got the story.'

'You did *what?*' said Biggles angrily. 'Really, sir, I don't know what you're playing at – or why – but there are limits. And I'd say that getting a chap like Algy to insult his oldest pal in a place like the Café Royal goes beyond the bounds of civilised behaviour.'

The old spy master smiled like an embarrassed greyhound.

'James, my dear boy,' he said. 'Calm down, calm down. Your attitude to Algy does you credit, but we live in an unpleasant world, you know. A dashed unpleasant world. At times I feel like you and think I'll chuck it in, but someone has to do the dirty work, and so much is at stake that some of us must compromise. Algy saw the point at once.'

'What point, sir? I still don't understand,' said Biggles, mastering his emotions sufficiently to pour himself a glass of port.

'That the von Sternberg creature was an invaluable potential source of information on the latest air developments in Germany, of course. For some time now, the R.A.F. at Farnborough has been desperate to find out more about that Junkers monoplane she flies. That's how it all began. As soon as Algy met her at the Hendon Air Display, I saw the possibilities, but it isn't often that one gets quite the reaction that eventually occurred. Of course, she has a fearful reputation. She's what we used to call a regular man-eater, don't you know?'

'And you fed my old pal Algy to her, sir? Is that what you're trying to tell me?'

Colonel Raymond nodded. 'Rather afraid it is. Not that Algy was all that averse to being eaten. Rather enjoyed himself by all accounts – at any rate at first. What was it he said? "Not often that one does this sort of thing for King and Country." Rather good, what?'

Biggles frowned. 'I find it all exceedingly distasteful, sir. I know that sometimes you use women for this sort of thing, but dash it all, they're different. You've exploited Algy just as if he was some Mata Hari.'

'Oh, come now James, you mustn't be old fashioned. You'd be surprised at what goes on these days, and Algy Lacey has turned out to be a first-rate operator. Taken to it like a horse to water.'

'I thought it was a duck' said Biggles drily.

'Is it? Well, call him what you like, but the point is that since he's gone to Germany, we have been receiving quite incredible reports from him – news of the latest German aircraft, airport layouts, their defensive plans from air attacks, even seems to have had a chat with that fat fellow, what's his name?'

'Goering,' said Biggles tersely. 'I flew against him once in France. He was rather good. That was before he put on weight.'

He downed the remainder of his Cockburns, and rose to leave. 'Well, thank you, sir, for a delicious dinner. And thanks too for telling me the truth about poor old Algy. I see now that I've misjudged him and that we can still be friends. That means a lot to me.'

'Sit down, sit down,' said Colonel Raymond with just a hint of irritation in his voice. 'Pour yourself another glass of port and listen carefully. I haven't told you this simply to make you feel better over Algy, though I'm naturally delighted that you do.'

'Why then, sir?' asked Biggles, feeling suddenly uneasy.

Colonel Raymond gazed at him appraisingly through shrewd grey eyes.

'James,' he said at last, 'there's something that I think that you should know. Algy Lacey is in frightful danger, if the reports that I've received are true.'

Biggles felt his mouth go dry, despite the port.

'Danger, sir?' he hissed.

Colonel Raymond nodded. 'It's been suggested that his messages are being intercepted. I wouldn't know, but what really worries me to death is the report that our man in Berlin filed this morning. You know who has suddenly appeared upon the scene?'

'No. No idea,' said Biggles.

'An old friend of yours. Hauptmann Erich von Stalhein.'

Biggles clenched his fists beneath the table.

'But that's not possible,' he said. 'Von Stalhein's been in disgrace ever since we made a fool of him in the Singapore air race. Besides, he was never in the Nazi Party. Himmler hated him.'

The Colonel shrugged his shoulders.

'That's as maybe, James,' he said, 'but we mustn't fool ourselves. He always has been a cunning devil and I know he's vowed revenge on you and Algy after the Singapore affair. For a while he was in a concentration camp, but suddenly he's right

back in the middle of Berlin. Three nights ago he was dining at
the Adlon with Goebbels himself, and he has several powerful
allies in German Military Intelligence. Worst of all, he seems to
have been taking an unhealthy interest in Algy. It may be pure
coincidence of course, but he was in the audience when Algy and
the von Sternberg woman lectured the German High Command
the other day.'

'Are you sure?' asked Biggles.

The Colonel cracked his bony hands.

'The source was unimpeachable,' he said.

'Then why on earth not order Algy back at once? Once they
can prove that he's a British spy, there's absolutely no hope left
for him.'

'You've no need to remind me of that, James,' replied the
Colonel sharply. 'But that's not the point. With von Stalhein in
the picture, I daren't make a move. Algy is obviously being
shadowed night and day, and any move that I make will betray
him. He'd never escape from Germany alive.'

'What's to be done then, sir?' asked Biggles.

'Precisely the question I've been racking my brains to answer
for the last few hours. I've hit upon a plan. It's hideously risky,
but with the right man and just a little luck it ought to work.'

'Wonderful!' said Biggles, brightening at once. 'I knew that
you would find a way. But who's this chap you need?'

'You,' replied Colonel Raymond.

Biggles had never been inside the German Embassy before and
he could only hope that his expression would not betray his
feelings – particularly when faced with a full-length portrait of
Herr Hitler in the second secretary's office. It had all proved
surprisingly easy – the phone-call to von Wittelsbach, the
German Air Attaché, the meeting they had had beside the
Thames at Wapping, and now this summons to meet Kornfeldt
at the Embassy. He had heard about Kornfeldt in the past.
Theoretically, he was an ordinary diplomat, but as Colonel
Raymond had already warned him, he was the top representative of the German Secret Service based in Britain. He was a
close associate of Himmler and had probably more power than

any other German at the Embassy – even including Herr von Ribbentrop, the Ambassador. So Biggles was quite curious to see this man on whom so much depended.

Von Wittelsbach had met him at the door and was there to introduce him to his master, and Wittelsbach was clearly nervous. Biggles had got on well with him. He was a tall Bavarian and a former combat flier who had been attached to von Kirtner's 'circus' during the last phase of the war. Biggles had fought against him in the skies of France, and sensed instantly that camaraderie which unites airmen of all nations who have risked death in the cockpit. He was a brave man and a skilful flier, but it was obvious that he had the jitters about facing Kornfeldt.

But, when Kornfeldt finally appeared, Biggles was surprised. Instead of the ogre he expected, he saw a plump, ingratiating little man with pince-nez and a clammy handshake. Biggles noticed that his finger-nails were bitten to the quick. Tea was served. Polite conversation followed about English weather, the boat race and the Royal Family, and it was Biggles who finally brought up the subject he had come about.

'There's this new aircraft that Lord Elberton's company's developing from the Swallow prototype, you know. Von Wittelsbach and I have been discussing it.'

'Ah yes,' said Kornfeldt, nodding amiably. 'Lord Elberton, a splendid man! How is his Lordship?'

'Fine,' said Biggles. 'We're on the best of terms. And as I was saying, this new plane of his is probably the most effective bomber of our time. Extraordinary range, enormous pay-load – a revolutionary warplane in every sense.'

'Ah,' said Kornfeldt once again.

'Well, knowing Lord Elberton as I do, I have been asked to test-fly the aircraft for the company. There'll be no problem. As you know, I've flown the prototype before, and I'm quite looking forward to the job. But I'm in something of a quandary, Herr Kornfeldt.'

'A quandary?' asked the German softly, and for just a moment Biggles caught a flash of keen intelligence behind the spectacles.

Biggles nodded, and paused to search for words before continuing. 'Can I speak quite frankly to you, Herr Kornfeldt?'

The German smiled encouragingly and spread his hands, as if to show that he had nothing in the world to hide.

'Please, Major Bigglesworth,' he said. 'I like to feel that we are friends.'

'Well, it's about my old pal, Algy Lacey. He's my cousin and associate and, well, I've known him all my life. We're very close.'

The German nodded and lit a small cigar. 'I know a little already about Captain Lacey, Major Bigglesworth.'

'I rather thought you might,' said Biggles evenly. 'It's probably not news to you that he's been very foolish.'

'Over the Frau von Sternberg? Young men like Captain Lacey are often foolish where women are concerned, and she is very beautiful. Also a strong-willed lady. So?'

'That's not the point I'm getting at, Herr Kornfeldt,' Biggles answered. 'Algy has been a frightful ass, and has allowed himself to get involved with the British Secret Service.'

The German blew a thoughtful cloud of pale Havana smoke, then added softly.

'That too I knew. A very dangerous game to play these days in Germany.'

'Exactly, sir. That's what I told him, but he insisted on going through with it. And now I hear he has to pay the price. Von Stalhein's after him – and I know von Stalhein well enough to understand exactly what that means, Herr Kornfeldt.'

'You're very well informed, Major Bigglesworth, but why tell me all this? What can I do? I am a humble diplomat.'

'Perhaps,' said Biggles, 'but the point is this. I will do anything for Algy, absolutely anything, and if his so-called friends in the British Secret Service won't help him, then I feel it's up to me.'

'And how would you propose to do that, Major Bigglesworth?'

'By doing a deal with you – a private deal. Herr Kornfeldt, I am prepared to exchange the secrets of Lord Elberton's new bomber for my friend.'

'I see,' said Kornfeldt, sounding as if Biggles had just proposed a quiet game of bridge. 'And how would this be done?'

'Well, it would not be all that difficult for me. I'm trusted by Lord Elberton and know his staff. I know a lot about the plane already, and within a few days I can have all the details you would want.'

'And how would you get them to us – just supposing we agreed?' purred Kornfeldt.

'That's what I've been wondering myself,' said Biggles. 'I

don't trust von Stalhein any more than he trusts me. We'd obviously have to meet on neutral ground. I suggest Strasbourg – it's in France but close enough to the German frontier. I can be there in three days' time. There's a hotel called the Maison Rouge in the Place Kléber. I must deal with von Stalhein personally. I will be there next Thursday evening with detailed plans of the aircraft. In return, von Stalhein must bring Algy Lacey with him. Is that understood, Herr Kornfeldt?'

The plump German smiled his pudgy smile. 'I can see certain obvious objections to your plan, but I will make sure that your message is passed on, Major Bigglesworth. I promise you will hear from us. And now, another cup of tea before you go?'

The Maison Rouge is probably the best hotel in a city that is renowned for good hotels, and, in any other circumstances, Biggles would have thoroughly enjoyed the chance of staying there. He had flown to Strasbourg late that afternoon in the old Cormorant. The ancient aeroplane was fast becoming something of a museum piece, but thanks to Smyth's tender care it was still in splendid nick and Biggles saw it as an old and valued friend, and loved to fly it. It also had the great advantage of attracting less attention than any of the newer aircraft Colonel Raymond had suggested.

Since visiting the German Embassy, Biggles had carefully prepared himself for his meeting with von Stalhein. A dossier of plausible, but utterly misleading, documents on the new bomber had been concocted by John Prizeman, the celebrated forger, whose work had baffled half the banks in Europe in its time, and who was now a trusted employee of Colonel Raymond's, with his own extraordinary department at New Scotland Yard. Biggles had also been to Elberton's secret airfield in the Cambridgeshire fens and flown the bomber several times himself. (He was enthusiastic, but found time to make some critical suggestions on the cockpit layout which were, in fact, incorporated into production models of the plane.) Finally, he had been to Wapping once again to meet von Wittelsbach, who told him tersely that the deal was on and that von Stalhein had agreed to contact him at Strasbourg some time on Thursday evening at the

Maison Rouge. That was all he knew – but it was enough for him
if it meant that Algy could be saved.

Biggles always had pretended to despise the role of a spy, but it
was one that suited him. He was always at his best in times of
crisis and loved a duel of wits. And so, despite his genuine concern
for Algy, he was looking forward now with keen anticipation to
his encounter with von Stalhein.

At the hotel – a very grand establishment dripping with
chandeliers and flunkeys – he booked in, in the name agreed
upon with von Wittelsbach, Conrad Peterson, a Swedish dealer
in oriental carpets, checked his room, and settled down to wait. It
was an unenviable situation, for as he knew quite well, von
Stalhein had the advantage of being the one to make contact first.
But Biggles wasn't frightened of him, and thought he knew him
well enough to understand the workings of his cold Teutonic
mind.

So he played the part of Conrad Peterson, sat for an hour in the
bar, drank a stein of Strasbourg beer, and then went in to dinner
on his own. The dining room was nearly empty and he was
beginning to feel uneasy, for there was no sign of the Prussian –
and still less of Algy. Von Stalhein should have come by now.
Something was going on, and he hated the idea that the life of his
old chum had now become the pawn in whatever game of wits
von Stalhein chose to play. But there was nothing he could do,
except wait until von Stalhein finally decided to reveal himself.

He had to force himself to eat, and as he did so, he reminded
himself that forcible feeding was something of a speciality of the
city. A sudden sense of sympathy for those unfortunate
Strasbourg geese put him off ordering pâté de foie gras – or any of
the other gastronomic pleasures of this well-fed city – and he
contented himself with consommé and chicken Maryland. Both
were equally disgusting. So was the music being played by a trio
to beguile the diners as they ate. Biggles was no music-lover and
the *Tales from the Vienna Woods* grated on his nerves.

He looked around him at his fellow diners, but there was no
sign of von Stalhein – a group of jolly businessmen at the next
table, a pair of lovers near the orchestra, and a fat old dowager
near the cash desk stuffing herself with cream cakes with
appalling gluttony. Biggles felt angry and on edge, for something
had obviously gone awry, and as he knew only too well, if his

mission failed, his chance of ever seeing Algy alive again was slim indeed.

He drank his coffee, gave the waiter the number of his room, and rose to go. As he did so, he noticed the old woman rise as well and shuffle towards him leaning on a stick. Her bloated face was rouged and powdered, and her bright red hair made her appear particularly grotesque. But as she passed, she smiled at him and said, 'Herr Conrad Peterson? I think you have something for me.'

Biggles stared at her – and suddenly saw something familiar about the eyes.

'Von Stalhein!' he cried. 'By all that's holy, what on earth . . .?'

'Just walk straight on,' said the old woman. 'I'll be behind you. And no tricks please. I have a gun concealed in my dress and if you try anything I'll blow your head off.'

'So,' said von Stalhein when they were safely seated in Biggles' room on the second floor of the hotel, 'you thought that I would bring your foolish friend Lacey here with me? Really, Major Bigglesworth, I would have credited you with more intelligence than that.'

'So where is Algy then?' asked Biggles, with a tightening of the muscles of his throat.

'Safely in Berlin and still enjoying life with Frau von Sternberg. Naturally, my agents keep him under full surveillance, but he doesn't know it. I will deal with him when it suits me, but just for the moment I'm content to leave him where he is. And now to business, Major Bigglesworth. But first, if you'll excuse me, I'll remove this wig. It's rather hot.'

In any other circumstances Biggles would have laughed at the sight that now revealed itself – the fat, old-woman's body crowned with the Junker's close-cropped head and the duelling scar just visible through the make-up on his cheeks. But the hatred in von Stalhein's eyes wasn't funny. Nor was the Mauser automatic in his bejewelled hands.

'Where are the documents you promised, Major?' barked von Stalhein.

'Find them yourself,' said Biggles, trying to stall for time.

'I will – if you compel me to,' replied the Prussian, saying which he pressed the bell for service. Almost instantly the door behind him opened and a man with the face and shoulders of an all-in-wrestler entered and clicked his heels.

'Ja, Herr Hauptmann?' he inquired in the accent of a Hamburg docker. 'You rang for me?'

Von Stalhein nodded. 'Yes, Gustav. Search this, er, gentleman for me. Make sure he isn't armed, then scour the room for documents. He's probably concealed them somewhere very obvious.'

There was no point in struggling, and Biggles felt the brutal hands of von Stalhein's bodyguard searching him.

'He's unarmed, Herr Hauptmann,' the man said. Von Stalhein nodded. 'Excellent. And now the papers. Where are they Major?'

'I was promised Algy Lacey, and thought you'd keep your word. I see I was mistaken.'

'Ach!' growled von Stalhein. 'You English really are absurd, with your ideas of what you are pleased to call "the decent thing". When will you learn that life is not a game, Herr Bigglesworth?'

Biggles treated this remark with the contempt that it deserved, and watched as Gustav methodically searched the room. Things were working out exactly as he had planned, and he smiled to himself when Gustav found the documents where he had hidden them – taped behind a picture over the bed.

'A little obvious, Major Bigglesworth,' von Stalhein said, a glint of satisfaction in his eyes. 'I would have expected something just a little cleverer. Well, there is nothing else that need detain us in this boring city. Is the car ready, Gustav?'

'Yes, Herr Hauptmann.'

'Then we will go downstairs together now, Herr Bigglesworth. You will pay your bill and explain that you have been called away on business. And, please, no nonsense. I would hate to have to shoot you now.'

Gustav picked up Biggles' suitcase, and the Junker paused a moment by the mirror to replace his wig.

'Where are we going then?' asked Biggles brusquely.

'Why, to Berlin of course. Where do you think? You wished to

see your Captain Lacey and you shall. And since your aircraft's
here, I think we'll use it.'

As Biggles brought the Cormorant in to land at Tempelhoff, his
mind was racing. He had been certain all along that von Stalhein
would attempt to trick him, and he had risen to the bait. As for
the next move, all would depend upon von Stalhein's behaviour
now. Biggles had no clear plan of action, but he was confident
that he could cope with anything that lay ahead. There were
times in life when one quite simply had to take a chance and use
one's wits and courage to defeat the enemy. Once he had seen
ancient Algy he could work things out from there.

   So, with von Stalhein's automatic in his ribs, he checked the
airport landing lights with steady expertise and brought the old
Cormorant in to a copybook three-pointer.

   'Nice flying, Major Bigglesworth,' said von Stalhein suavely.
'A pity that you don't fly for our German Luftwaffe. We could
use pilots of your calibre.'

   During the flight, von Stalhein had changed out of his disguise,
and was now the Prussian with the bullet head and ramrod back
that Biggles remembered from the past. He barked an order, and
Biggles felt himself being bundled from the cockpit by the burly
Gustav, and checked an impulse to crack the fellow firmly on the
jaw.

   'Take him away Gustav,' snarled von Stalhein. 'I'll see him
later.'

   It was a tiny cell where Biggles found himself. There was a
hard-backed chair but nothing else, and the lights were on
permanently. He had no idea where he was – the windows of the
big Mercedes that had driven him from the airport had been
carefully blacked out – and he would have given almost anything
for a cigarette. But there was no chance of that, for all his
possessions had been taken. Nor could he sleep. Instead he sat,
and racked his brains and waited for the dawn. It took an age to
come, but even when it did it brought him no relief. Finally, the
door was opened and a dumb-faced guard thrust a tray of gruel
and watery coffee at him, but when Biggles tried to shout at him,
he turned and simply slammed the door. There was nothing for it
but to wait.

The hours ticked by, and hunger mingled with anxiety, but Biggles knew enough to realise the game his enemies were playing. To stop himself from going mad, he forced himself to play all sorts of mental games – working out a detailed order for a squadron to attack a target on the Western Front, going through each working part of a Bentley rotary aero-engine, making a mental journey from the flat in Mount Street to his stockbroker in Lombard Street and back. It helped to pass the time and finally, in what he guessed to be the middle of the afternoon, the cell door opened once again and Biggles found himself confronted with a figure from the past.

'Good God,' he gasped. 'Marie!'

In the years since he had seen her, she had put on weight, but otherwise was little different from golden-headed temptress who had been his mistress in his youth. She was dressed severely – knee-boots, dark tweed skirt and jacket, white silk jabot at her throat – but this merely served to emphasise her beauty.

'Biggles!' she said, and flashed a sad but utterly entrancing smile. 'And so the Fates have brought us back together. I always knew they would, but what a pity that it has to be like this.'

'Whose fault is that?' asked Biggles bitterly.

'I know, my dear,' she sighed, 'but there was nothing I could do. I had my duty to perform – and you had yours.'

'But did you have to leave me for von Stalhein, of all people?'

'Ah Biggles,' she said softly, 'I can see you're still as innocent as ever. How little you can understand the workings of the human heart. I have had many men, but there are only two that I ever truly loved – you and von Stalhein.'

'But why?' gasped Biggles. 'I don't understand. The man's a swine, and completely ruthless ...'

'Perhaps that is what appeals to me,' she said, and laid a gentle hand on Biggles' arm. 'Try not to judge me, Biggles, please!'

Biggles pushed her hand away.

'What are you doing here anyhow?' he asked angrily. 'He must have sent you. He could have spared me that at least.'

'But Biggles, please be reasonable,' she said. 'I'm here to help you. No one else will and I had to beg him for this interview.'

'But what do you want?' said Biggles. 'I made a deal with von Stalhein and he's broken it. I risked everything I had to secure Algy Lacey's safety – and I end up here like any common criminal. How can you possibly expect me to co-operate with somebody like that?'

'Biggles,' she said, and now a sharper note had crept into her voice, 'you must be fair with me as well. We know what you were up to. Kornfeldt in London is no fool. He's had you followed, and he tells us of your meetings with that creature, Colonel Raymond. Also, my love, our experts have been studying those so-called plans you brought us of the secret aeroplane.' She shook her head. 'Really, Biggles, really! And you accuse von Stalhein of dishonesty!'

'But surely you never thought that I could possibly betray my country?' Biggles muttered.

'No, of course not, Biggles. That's why I never believed any of this nonsense from the start. But both you and your friend Algy are in most frightful danger. Thanks to Kornfeldt, the Gestapo are now all set to arrest Algy, and the Gestapo aren't like us. I truly shudder to think what will happen to him. Whatever else von Stalhein is, he's not a torturer or a cold-blooded murderer, but once they have Algy they will come for you as well. We have no power to stop them.'

'So we're really in the soup,' said Biggles, trying to disguise the cold fear in his heart. 'Not much that anyone can do about it.'

'Probably not,' said Marie, with a tremor in her voice, 'but I can't stand and watch you dragged off to the torture-chamber. Whatever else I've done, I couldn't live with that on my conscience.'

'Don't be stupid,' Biggles said.' We asked for it, and if we've come unstuck it's our own silly fault.'

'No Biggles,' she said firmly, 'there is a chance, a slim one, but if you're man enough to take it, you and Algy could still escape. Now listen carefully . . .'

'Herr Bigglesworth, wake up! Wake up Herr Bigglesworth! It's time to go!'

From where he was lying on the hard floor of the little cell, Biggles had seen the cell-door open and Gustav enter. Through veiled lids he watched the ape-like creature shambling towards him, but he made no move – except to tighten his grip upon the automatic which Marie had given him.

'Wake up, Herr Bigglesworth,' shouted Gustav, and Biggles smelled his sour breath as he bent down to shake him by the shoulder. Still Biggles made no move. The gun was hidden by his body, and he held it firmly by the barrel. The German swore and struck him hard across the face. But Biggles bit his lip and still lay doggo. The German swore again and, just as he leant forward to pull Biggles to his feet, Biggles came alive. He judged his moment perfectly, uncoiling like a steel spring and catching the unwary German just behind the ear with the gun butt. All Biggles' force was in that blow – and Gustav gave a feeble groan, subsiding to the floor like a burst balloon.

Biggles left his gaoler in the cell, locking the door behind him with his keys, and thanks to Marie's instructions he had no trouble finding his way out of the building. There was a tense moment when he had to pass the Duty Sergeant at the entrance desk, but Biggles' luck was in. He nodded to the man, said 'thank you very much' in German – and the man saluted. Biggles had no difficulty finding the big Mercedes which had brought him from the airport. It was exactly where Marie had said – parked behind the building – and the official number-plate gave him instant precedence as he accelerated through the evening rush-hour into the centre of Berlin. At the end of the Unter den Linden was the Hotel Adlon, where he parked the car and hurried in.

Luckily the place was crowded owing to a Nazi Party function being held there, and the foyer of the huge hotel was crammed with the Party members and their monstrous wives. It was not a pretty sight, but it diverted the attention of the S.S. men who were supposed to be keeping watch on Algy's suite on the second floor. Marie had given him the number of the room, and Biggles' German accent was quite adequate to get him past the lift-boy. He knocked, and Frau von Sternberg opened the door in person.

'*Mein Gott,* Herr Bigglesworth!' she cried, and tried to slam the door on him. But Biggles' foot was firmly in the doorway, and he was in no mood to be polite.

'Where's Algy? he cried, pushing past her.

'Herr Bigglesworth, this is an outrage!' she exclaimed. But Biggles grabbed her rudely by the shoulders.

'Shut up!' he said, and glanced around the empty room. 'Tell me where Algy is, or I'll break your neck!'

It was probably the one time in her life that the Frau von Sternberg had been spoken to like this and it produced results.

'He's in the bath,' she croaked.

'Algy!' bawled Biggles. 'Open up, old lad. It's Biggles! Don't mind me, but bath-time's over, dear old chap. We've got to go.'

The bathroom door was opened instantly, revealing Algy dripping wet and naked as the day that he was born.

'Biggles!' he exclaimed, 'by all that's good and holy, what are you doing here?'

'Rescuing you, you blasted idiot. What do you think? Come on!'

'Well, give a chap a minute to get dressed,' said Algy plaintively.

'No time for that,' said Biggles. 'The Gestapo's after you and will be turning up at any minute. Here, bung this on, old boy!'

As he said this, Biggles threw his friend a towelling dressing-gown, and seized him by the arm.

'Quick, say goodbye to your girl-friend, Algy! We're off!'

Once again, luck was on Biggles' side. The ill-assorted pair hoofed it along the corridor and down the service stairs to the street below, where a huge Mercedes with a swastika flying from the bonnet was decanting an enormous figure in a pale blue uniform outside the hotel, and thus attracting everyone's attention.

'Crikey!' Algy said. Goering himself!'

'And he couldn't have come here at a better moment. Here, Algy, we're parked round the corner.' With this, the two chums sprinted for the car, and in seconds were away, and roaring down the road to Tempelhoff.

The dear old Cormorant was waiting faithfully where Biggles had left it just the night before, and thanks to the official car, nobody stopped them when they drove onto the tarmac.

Biggles leapt out first, with Algy, still in his skimpy dressing-gown, not far behind. There was a guard who tried to remonstrate with them, but a swift uppercut soon put an end to his objections, and in a moment both the chums were in the cockpit.

'Contact!' cried Biggles as the engines fired.

'Contact it is!' echoed Algy happily, as with a deep, full-throated roar the Cormorant's engines surged with power and the graceful aeroplane swept down the runway and up into the air above Berlin.

'Time to head for home, old fruit,' said Biggles with a twinkle in his eye. 'I think we've had enough of Germany, and Mrs Symes has your old room prepared for you in Mount Street.'

'Biggles,' said Algy feelingly, 'you know that you're the best pal a fellow ever had. I feel that there's an awful lot I should explain.'

Biggles cut him short with a grin. 'Don't worry, Algy. I'm only glad we've got you back. I expect Colonel Raymond will be wanting to see you, but the explanations can come later. If you look in the rear locker, you'll find an old overcoat of mine. Perhaps you ought to put it on, if only to avoid embarrassing the Customs men.'

9

Second Time Round

'Well, old chap,' said Biggles wearily to Algy. 'That about wraps it up. Miserable business, but it can't be helped. I never realised quite how much rubbish we'd accumulated during the years we've been together. Are you absolutely sure you don't want these old flying boots?'

'Absolutely,' replied Algy with a grin. 'Give them to Mrs Symes. One of her nephews might be able to find a use for them. What are you doing with our remaining stock of booze? 'Locking it away in the cupboard in my den,' said Biggles, 'and I'll keep the key, my lad.'

'I rather thought you would,' replied his cousin.

It was November 1939, and for all the chums' attempts at cheerfulness, it had been a most depressing day, as they closed up the flat at Mount Street. Mrs Symes was staying on for the duration of the war, but Biggles and Algy thought it best to pack away their valuables and personal effects until it was over – whenever that might be – and the effort had been like the ending of a chapter of their lives. Also, it emphasised the break-up of the old alliance that had started in the far-off days of Biggles and Co. Now that the war had started, Algy, as Flight Lieutenant, had been officially posted to a night-fighter squadron 'somewhere in southern England', as it was officially described. Pilot Officer Ginger Hebblethwaite was flying Spitfires from Biggin Hill, and

Biggles, to his chagrin, had been classified too old for active-service flying.

'But I'm only forty, for Pete's sake!' he had exploded to the Postings Officer when the news came through. 'What are you going to do with me? Shove me in an old folks' home?'

'Of course not, Squadron Leader,' the officer replied as diplomatically as possible, 'but with your experience you're far too valuable to waste in a Front Line squadron. You have been posted as Chief Instructor to No. 18 Flying School as Hazledon in Berkshire.'

'Berkshire? A flaming training school! Good grief, man, what d'you think I am?' raged Biggles. 'It's a confounded insult. I'll be seeing somebody about this, I can tell you!'

But although he saw a lot of people – from Air Chief Marshals to the Under Secretary for Air himself – the posting stood, and Biggles had reluctantly accepted it.

'Old age, with a vengeance, dear old chap!' he said ruefully to Algy, as he packed his bag, and Mrs Symes announced the arrival of his taxi to the station. 'Well, this is it, old scout. Drop us a postcard if you've got a moment – and mind how you go on those night-time operations, particularly with the W.A.A.F.s. You won't have Biggles to look after you.'

'And you look after yourself as well,' said Algy, doing his best to fight down the emotion that he felt. 'As soon as I can get a drop of petrol, I'll be up to see you.'

'Good lad, Algy. Do your best,' said Biggles. 'I'll miss you. Oh, and if by any chance you happen to bump into old Raymond, would you kick him firmly in the pants from me?'

'You bet I will,' replied Algy bitterly. 'Just give me the chance.'

The resentment of the two cousins against their former chief was all too understandable. They hadn't in the least begrudged him his success in landing an impressive job at the Air Ministry when war broke out, nor his promotion to the rank of Air Commodore. As they knew quite well, no one was better fitted for the post of Deputy Director of Air Intelligence than that wily old policeman. And when he had called upon the chums for one of the most suicidal early operations in the war during that September, they had responded with an eagerness that did them credit.

This was the extraordinary affair of Bergen Ait, the secret base the British had prepared on a tiny island in the middle of the Baltic. In his book, *Biggles in the Baltic,* Captain Johns has told the story of this operation in which Biggles, Algy and Ginger Hebblethwaite mounted a series of extraordinary missions from the rock against the German forces based at Kiel. They had succeeded beyond all expectations. Indeed, on their return to London, Raymond had nonchalantly informed them that he had thought that he had been sending them to certain death. He had thanked them in his usual, somewhat grudging manner – and that had been the last any of the chums had seen or heard of him.

Of course, they were used to such behaviour from the past. 'Gratitude is not exactly Raymond's middle name,' said Biggles ruefully, but what had riled them all had been the way that Raymond had subsequently disowned them – or so it seemed. It was the period of the so-called 'Phoney War' when nothing much was happening, but the Air Commodore had totally refused to get involved in Biggles' efforts to avoid his posting to his training school. He even refused to see him, and when Biggles fired off an indignant letter on the subject, it was returned with an icy comment from some Whitehall whipper-snapper. Biggles had been beside himself with fury and even the pacific Ginger was indignant. But there was nothing anyone could so, and the dreams the chums had had of fighting the war together faded.

So it was that the historic year of 1940 began with Biggles safely tucked away in the obscurity of his training school in Berkshire. Truth to tell, he rather liked the work and got on well with the eighteen-year-old trainee pilots it was his job to teach. It was the first contact he had had with the new generation of wartime fliers and there was much about them to appeal to him. Indeed, they took him back to his own youth when he had learned his trade as a combat flier on the Western Front, almost a quarter of a century before. The planes had changed but not the pilots, and he recognised much of the Biggles spirit in these new warriors of the air – the same longing for adventure, the same desire to prove themselves against the enemy, and the same scorn for the rigmarole and red-tape of service discipline.

They, in their turn, respected him and soon regarded him not only as a first-rate instructor – which he was – but also as a 'character'. The Commanding Officer – a peacetime regular called Wing Commander Boakes – treated him with caution, and most evenings in the Mess would end with Biggles chatting informally to an admiring circle of young trainee pilots who plainly relished all his stories of the past. The Adjutant, a stickler for protocol, disliked the way they called him 'Biggles' to his face, but his objections went unheeded.

'As long as they learn their job, they can call me what they like,' said Biggles breezily, when he misguidedly raised the subject. 'Besides, I've always answered to the name of Biggles, so I don't see why I have to change because I'm back in uniform.' The Adjutant muttered about 'due respect for rank'. Biggles countered with something that sounded dangerously like 'Poppycock!' And that was that.

Although Biggles liked his job, and even quite enjoyed piloting the yellow-painted Master trainers which he flew, he still secretly resented being what he called 'nothing more than a confounded school-master' as the war proceeded – and the news that he received from his old chums nourished his discontent. Ginger, now a Pilot Officer, wrote enthusiastically about the Spitfire. 'A real thoroughbred' he called it, adding that he'd never known the real joy of flying before. Biggles had also met Algy on several occasions back in London, but these meetings weren't a great success, for Algy too was thoroughly enjoying life with his night-fighter squadron, and although he tried to be as tactful as possible, nothing could save Biggles from the feeling that in contrast with his cousin he was missing out.

'Rubbish, my dear old chap!' expostulated Algy after one of Biggles' periodic moans about being relegated to the scrap-heap. 'Once things start hotting-up, you'll get your chance. Just mark my words, they'll soon be knocking on your door.'

'With all these bright young men about?' replied Biggles wryly, nodding towards the group of young R.A.F. men drinking at the bar of the little club in Curzon Street that they frequented. 'They're the ones they need now. Not old crocks like me.'

But Algy spoke truer than he realised.

It was a few weeks after Biggles' meeting with Algy, and spring had almost come to Berkshire. Biggles was busy with his latest intake of trainees, and mildly irritated to receive a summons to report to the C.O.

'Confound the man!' he muttered to himself. 'Another of his niggling complaints. I expect the Adjutant's moaning on again that I'm improperly dressed.' (There had been quite a tussle just a few weeks earlier when it was discovered Biggles wasn't wearing the medal ribbons he was entitled to.) But, when Biggles entered the Wing Commander's office, he was surprised to find the C.O. in an effusive, not to say respectful, mood.

'Bigglesworth, my dear chap, what have you been up to?' he asked affably.

'Up to, sir?' replied Biggles guardedly. 'Nothing very much, worse luck.'

'Oh, come now,' said the Wing Commander. 'I've just had the Air Ministry on the line about you. Top priority. They want you there at once.'

'But why?' asked Biggles.

'Didn't say. Terribly hush-hush and all that sort of thing. You'd better take your kit and go immediately.'

'You mean I'm leaving the training school, sir?' replied Biggles.

'Sounds like it I'm afraid, old boy. We'll be sad to see you go. I've arranged transport for you in twenty minutes' time.' He held out his hand. 'Goodbye, Bigglesworth. Good luck, and thanks for all you've done.'

Biggles was always mystified by the workings of the official mind, and felt rather like an erring schoolboy summoned by the head as he entered the gloomy portals of Whitehall. He was evidently expected. The Flight Sergeant at the reception desk looked up quickly as he gave his name, and without more ado conducted him along a corridor and up some stairs, then halted by an impressive office door and knocked. Someone shouted 'Enter!' from within, and as Biggles strode into the office he was greeted by a figure from the past. There behind the desk, with the same old steely presence, despite the resplendent trappings of Air Commodore, sat the man whom Biggles had previously known as 'Colonel' Raymond. And from the beginning of the interview, it was the same old story. Biggles began by doing his best to show resentment at the way Raymond had exploited then neglected him, and gave a distinctly curt reply to the Air Commodore's over-hearty greeting.

Raymond asked him how he was.

'As well as can be expected, sir, all thing considered,' answered Biggles coldly.

There was a pregnant pause as the Air Commodore sized up the jaunty figure in the somewhat battered uniform who stood before him.

'I was wondering,' he said finally, 'if you felt up to a particularly demanding job of work.'

Biggles attempted to look nonchalant, but there was an excited gleam in his eyes that could not be suppressed.

'I like to feel I'll always do my duty, sir,' said Biggles stiffly.

'Good man, James,' said Raymond quickly. 'I knew we could count on you. The point is that over the last few months there's been a lot of argey-bargey here about the way to tackle the sort of unconventional assignments we've done together in the past. I won't go into all the arguments, but as you can imagine there've been an awful lot of them. If hot air could win the war we'd be in Berlin by now. But the truth is, we've had some frightful cock-ups since your little mission to the Baltic, and the other morning at the meeting of the Joint Chiefs of Staff, your name came up.'

'My name?' asked Biggles unbelievingly.

'Now don't get swollen-headed, James, but I should tell you that it was Churchill himself who mentioned you. There's not a great deal that escapes the old man, I can tell you, and when they were all discussing how to avoid such washouts in the future, the great man said, " What about that fellow Bigglesworth? Did a dashed fine job in the Baltic. Why not put him in charge?" '

'He said *that?*' said Biggles, feeling as if he'd suddenly been told he'd won the Irish Sweep Stake. Raymond nodded.

'His very words. And I need hardly add that when a man like Churchill says that sort of thing, it's tantamount to an order. So, James my lad, congratulations! It looks as if you've earned yourself a Squadron of your own.'

It was an historic moment, and Biggles found it hard to credit that everything he'd dreamed of had suddenly come true – the promise of adventure, his own command at last, and the chance to fight the common foe. But, thrilled as he was, he wisely kept his head, and made the most of his advantage.

'What about aircraft, sir?' he asked at once.

'Well, James, we'll have to see,' the Air Commodore replied, scratching his head a trifle furtively. 'It naturally depends on what's available.'

'I don't see why,' said Biggles firmly. 'If the Squadron's important enough for Churchill to take an interest in it, it can have nothing but the best. Spitfires or nothing, sir.'

The Air Commodore made a note on his jotting pad and nodded somewhat wearily.

'Anything else?' he asked.

'Yes, sir. Personnel.'

Raymond gave his toothy smile.

'I rather thought we'd come to that,' he said. 'I suppose you want the same old gang. Biggles and Co. rides again, eh what? Very well, James. I'll see what I can do. Lacey and Hebblethwaite should certainly present no problem, but what the remainder of the Squadron?'

'Well, sir,' said Biggles, 'you know I'm not a snob, but in a show like this everything depends on having the right sort of chap. One bad hat can dish the whole caboosh. It's rather like a family.'

Raymond nodded.

'I take your point, James. Very well, you'll have the final say on who's selected. It'll be up to you. But just one word of warning, James. From now on you're in the limelight, and a good deal of my personal reputation will depend on you. Don't let me down.'

'Have I ever, sir?' said Biggles in reply.

The next few days must count among the busiest in Biggles' life – interviews with senior officers, rows with supplies departments, letters to be sent to ordnance depots, and invoices dictated by the dozen. The rigmarole of building up a first-rank squadron in a hurry was enough to frighten off the most methodical of men – and Biggles was not particularly methodical. Indeed, administration – or 'admin' as he disparagingly referred to it – had never been his strongest suit.

'Confounded bumph!' he used to rage when faced with the mountain of pro-formas that his job entailed. Luckily, he soon had Ginger Hebblethwaite to help him. Biggles secured his promotion from Pilot Officer to Flight Lieutenant, and his sturdy Yorkshire common sense did much to guarantee the orderly procedure of the Squadron, leaving Biggles to get on with what he was best at – finding the men he needed and inspiring them with that indefinable *esprit de corps* which is the hallmark of a first-rate squadron.

It was here that his time with No. 18 Flying School stood him in good stead, and he had the pick of several of the star pupils he had taught – young fellows like the inimitable 'Tug' Carrington, Henry Harcourt and the appropriately nicknamed 'Ferocity' Ferris, the former scrum-half of the London-Welsh.

Algy was soon seconded to assist him – and automatically put in charge of the all important 'A' Flight of the Special Duty Squadron. It was Algy who suggested several candidates of his own – Flying Officer 'Taffy' Hughes, the dour but dependable Flight Lieutenant Angus Mackail who was given 'C' Flight, and the rumbustious American, 'Tex' O'Hara, once the star of an American flying circus and now a volunteer with the R.A.F. But there still remained one vital post to fill – a flight lieutenant to take charge of 'B' Flight. Several names came up – and all were summarily rejected. Biggles turned one man down because he wore a 'Windsor knot' to his tie – 'always the sign of a bounder!' was his only comment, and Algy reluctantly agreed. Another highly recommended chap said 'Pardon' twice, and referred to his wife as 'the little woman'.

'Out of the question, I'm afraid,' said Biggles.

'Quite,' agreed Algy.

'But who the devil can we find? It shouldn't be too difficult. You'd think that somewhere in the R.A.F. we could discover a flight lieutenant who was our sort of chap?' lamented Biggles.

'Well,' replied Algy cautiously, 'actually there is a fellow that I've had in mind. Codger by the name of Lissie, Bertie Lissie – rather a mate of mine.'

'Lissie?' said Biggles thoughtfully. 'That rather rings a bell. Didn't he drive a Riley down at Brooklands in the good old days?'

'Right first time, old fruit. Only one snag about him, I'm afraid. He's a member of the House of Lords.'

'Is he?' said Biggles. 'I never realised. Well, we can't hold that against him, can we? After all, old thing, once your old man croaks, you'll be there yourself. We'd better have a look at him.'

At first sight Biggles didn't take to Bertie Lissie – and nor, to tell the truth, did Bertie take to Biggles. Algy had introduced them at a little place he used in Maddox Street, the Whizz-Bang Club, and Biggles was distinctly stuffy from the start. The Whizz-Bang wasn't Biggles' sort of place. 'Too many fast young men and loose young women!' was his verdict on it later, and he bridled visibly when an abundant blonde called Myra addressed him as 'my hero', and asked him for a drink.

'Later my dear!' said Algy, doing his best to pour the proverbial oil on troubled waters. 'We're looking for his Lordship. Any sign of him? He said he'd meet us here.'

'D'you mean old Burlington Bertie?' she replied, giggling, so she thought, seductively. 'I think he's in the bar as usual. Why don't you have a look?'

Algy thanked her and led Biggles to the room beyond where, stretched out in a battered old arm-chair, lay a recumbent figure in the uniform of an R.A.F. Flight Lieutenant, apparently asleep. Algy shook the figure by its shoulder.

'Wakey, wakey, Bertie!' he exclaimed – at which the figure stretched a pair of extraordinarily long legs, yawned, screwed a monocle in place, and gazed at the world with evident disfavour.

'For Cripe's sake, Algy, can't you let a fellow be? I've not had breakfast.'

'Can't help that,' said Algy heartily. 'There's someone here to meet you. My old chum, Biggles.'

Bertie stretched out a languid palm which Biggles shook with obvious reserve and refused the offer of a drink. To start with, all the conversation, what there was of it, was made by Algy. Biggles made disapproving noises as his cousin rambled on about various characters he'd never met. Finally, Biggles felt he'd had enough and mentioned combat flying. At this, a transformation seemed to come over the recumbent peer.

'Best plane in the world, the Spitfire,' he announced quietly.

'You've flown one then?' asked Biggles with an air of disbelief.

Lissie nodded. 'Actually I test-flew the prototype last year, and I've been flying 'em ever since. Haven't had much chance as yet to try it out against a German Messerschmitt, but had a crack at one in France a few weeks back.'

'What happened?' Biggles asked, all prejudice forgotten now.

'Out-manoeuvred the blighter every time, but he got away, drat him. I had a spot of engine trouble, but I've been working on it and it won't happen next time.'

For the remainder of the afternoon, Biggles, Algy and Bertie Lissie talked about the Spitfire – its range, its fire-power, its strengths and weaknesses. There seemed nothing about the aircraft Bertie Lissie didn't know, and by the time the three of them strolled off for an early dinner at the Carlton Grill, the final vacancy in the Special Duty Squadron had been filled.

That epoch-making spring of 1940 soon proved to be a time of furious activity for Biggles' squadron – No. 666 as it was officially designated now. At first they were based at Tangmere and it was there that Biggles did the preliminary work of what he described as 'licking them into shape'. This included aerobatics, close formation flying, and days of intensive practice in techniques of combat flying. For while 666 was specially designed to take on any unusual assignments going, Biggles was also anxious to make it the crack Spitfire squadron in the R.A.F. He was a splendid leader and was inspired by the memory of the way that Major Mullen had built up his Sopwith Camel Squadron during those hard-fought months in France in 1917. Algy, of course, proved an invaluable second-in-command, and Bertie Lissie – oddities apart – soon showed himself to be an exceptional pilot, flying his aircraft with the dash and flair with which he had driven his racing cars before the war.

But there was little time for 666 to practise now. At the beginning of May they were in France as the German *Blitzkrieg* swept through undefended Holland and Belgium. They were fighting in the air as Calais fell, and during that fine May weather were in the thick of things as the German armies rumbled on through France. For a few days they were based at Amiens, and when it was threatened they were ordered back to Tangmere. It was from there that Biggles led them through the heroic days of the great evacuation from Dunkirk.

These were the days when the untried fliers in the Squadron proved themselves, whilst for Biggles, this ceaseless flying round the clock was like a repetition of his toughest days on the Western Front – lack of sleep, continual battles with the enemy, and wondering which members of the little Squadron would fail to return. But the personnel of 666 appeared to live a charmed existence. The only casualty was 'Tex' O'Hara.

With the Dunkirk evacuation at its height, the Squadron was doing its bit to keep the Luftwaffe from the beaches, and Algy saw O'Hara's Spitfire set upon by a pair of Messerschmitts which had been machine-gunning the queues of troops waiting to embark. Tex took them both on, single-handed. This was against Biggles' orders, for he insisted all along that the flights must always stick together – and 'Tex' had paid the price. The last Algy saw of his aircraft was a trail of thick black smoke heading to the sea. That night, the Squadron drank to 'Tex's' memory – but two days later he turned up again at Tangmere, his left arm in a sling, but otherwise not much the worse for wear.

'Sorry Biggles,' he exclaimed, as he reported back for duty. 'Tried to be a bit too clever. Should have remembered what you told me. Guess I'm darned lucky to be here to tell the tale.'

'What happened to you, then?' asked Biggles, trying to hide the relief he felt.

'I fixed one of them, but the other one got on my tail and that was that. Some joker on a fishing boat pulled me out of the drink, and here I am!' He grinned. 'They always say it takes a helluva lot to kill a Texan.'

'Good lad,' said Biggles, who couldn't help admiring his spirit. 'Get yourself patched up. How long before you think that you can fly again with that arm of yours?'

'Tomorrow, if it's all the same with you,' said Tex. And at dawn next morning, as the Special Duty Squadron took off to battle in the skies above the Channel, Tex was back amongst them.

Biggles came through these weeks of battle splendidly. This was the life that he was born for. Fighting was in his blood, and much as he'd enjoyed the soft life and adventures of his years of peace, he loved the challenge of the dedicated combat pilot – the knowledge that his life depended on his skill within the cockpit, the deadly game he played among the clouds, and the final head-on confrontation with another human being set to kill him. Perhaps his reactions were a little slower now than in his youth, but if they were he didn't notice. It seemed that as a pilot he was in his prime – a tougher, more experienced and determined flier than he had ever been – and danger, far from ageing him, had made him younger, as it always did.

During this period he had heard nothing from the Air Commodore, and had had little time to think about him either, so that it came as a surprise when he returned from a patrol that second week of June to find the familiar figure sitting in the Mess. He was looking thinner and more lined than when Biggles saw him last, and responded wearily to Biggles' greeting.

'Good to see you James. I hear you're flourishing. Excellent reports about your Squadron. Very proud of you, my boy.'

'We've done our best,' replied Biggles modestly, giving that slightly nervous laugh with which he habitually responded to unexpected praise.

'What are you drinking, sir?'

'The usual Scotch and soda, if it's all the same to you.'

Biggles joined him, and as the two men drank, Raymond shook his head.

'These are tough times, James, you know.'

Biggles nodded.

'No need to tell me that, sir. But the French could still hold out as they did last time.'

'I doubt it. No, we're really up against it. Churchill's in Paris at the moment, trying to put some backbone into their confounded government, but they're a miserable crowd. Not a real man among 'em. No, James, I don't give much for his chances. The French are caving in. A week or two, and I wouldn't be surprised if the Huns don't occupy the whole of Europe. That's why I'm here, James.'

'Really, sir?' said Biggles, who knew that Raymond wasn't one for social visits.

'Rather a tricky job of work I've got for you, I'm afraid.'

Biggles nodded. 'That's what I'm here for, sir,' he said.

'Quite. Ever heard of a character called Clairvaux, James?'

'The aircraft designer? Yes, of course. Met him a few years back when he was trying to get the Schneider trophy with that monoplane of his. Can't say I took to him.'

'No, nor did I, but that's neither here nor there. Fact is, the blighter's been developing the plane since then and from the reports we've had it's pretty revolutionary. Something to do with superchargers for the engine. Double-Dutch to me, but our boffins say they'd give their eye teeth for a look at it.'

'You mean they haven't seen it?' asked Biggles. 'But I thought the French were meant to be our allies?'

'Some of them are, James. Others aren't, and that includes friend Clairvaux. The Schneider business soured him and he's consistently refused to work with us. I won't say the man's a traitor, but he's resisted all our efforts to persuade him to disgorge his secrets. He's sitting tight. The French government's got other things to think about, and in a day or two it'll be too late anyhow – the Germans will have reached him.'

'Where is he then?' asked Biggles quickly.

'Just outside Saumur, along the River Loire. Village called Andrey. He's got a factory there with its own small airfield. According to Intelligence reports, the aircraft's there, and so is Monsieur Clairvaux. I want them both.'

'That shouldn't be too difficult to arrange,' said Biggles thoughtfully.

'In theory, no,' the Air Commodore replied, 'but I must warn you that it could be trickier than it appears. Clairvaux himself could well prove difficult, and no one seems to know how near the Germans are. The Front's collapsing and the Huns are anxious to get hold of Clairvaux too.'

'We'd better get a move on, then,' said Biggles.

It says a lot for Raymond's influence, as well as for the keenness of the Special Duty Squadron, that the operation went as smoothly as it did. Few of the Squadron had much sleep that night. Plans were discussed, maps studied, and shortly after midnight a twin-engined Wellington touched down at Tangmere. As dawn was breaking, it took off again and headed south, with Biggles and Algy at the controls. Both knew the dangers of the flight, for the Germans had swept over northern France, and their aircraft

could control the skies ahead of them. Raymond at first suggested
the whole Squadron as an escort, but Biggles had vetoed this.

'Too risky, sir, and certain to attract attention. Frankly, I'd
rather that we took them by surprise as we used to in the good old
days. South to the Bay of Biscay, then follow the Loire, flying as
low as possible.'

Algy had backed him up in this, and as the twin-engined
bomber came in from the sea and followed the river towards its
destination, it was at little more than roof-top height. It was
exciting flying, calling for perfect judgment.

'Nice flying, Biggles!' shouted Algy, as they seemed to skim a
bridge by inches. Biggles grinned happily in reply.

'Not such a bad old crate, is she Algy? How're the others?'

Algy glanced back at Ginger and Tex O'Hara, who were
strapped into the rear crew-seats of the aircraft, and gave them
the thumbs-up sign in greeting.

'Ginger's looking worried, Biggles. Perhaps for his sake you'd
better take her up a little higher. You're not flying Spitfires any
more.'

'Right you are!' said Biggles, easing back the controls and
sending the Wellington up to a few hundred feet.

'That better, Ginger?' he called out.

'Thanks, Biggles,' Ginger answered. 'This height's a little
easier on my nerves.'

From here it was possible to see the signs of French defeat. It
was another perfect summer day, and many of the roads were
crammed with the cars and carts of fleeing refugees. A village
beyond Nantes was burning and further on they saw two German
tanks.

'Just hope we're going to be in time,' shouted Algy grimly, and
as he spoke there came the rattle of machine-gun fire and the
Wellington lurched sickeningly. Algy glimpsed the grey and
green fuselage of a Messerschmitt diving past them, and Biggles
struggled with the controls. For several moments it was touch and
go. A church tower seemed to loom ahead of them and Algy
never knew how Biggles missed it, but then the Wellington came
zooming up, and banked sharply to the left as the German plane
came diving back for the kill. The Wellington was not
constructed for this sort of flying, for Biggles was treating it like a
fighter-plane. Few pilots would have got away with it, but by

that sixth sense he had developed in a lifetime's flying, he saved the heavy plane from stalling, and spun it round so that 'Tug' Carrington, in the Wellington's rear gun-turret, was presented with a perfect target. Tug did his deadly work with cold precision, and his twin Vickers guns went barking out their tracer-fire as the German flashed across his sights. At such short range the German had no chance, and Algy glimpsed the Messerschmitt disintegrating in mid-air.

'Nice shooting, Tug!' said Biggles quietly across the intercom. 'Any sign of any more about?'

'Seems to have been on his own, Biggles,' Tug replied.

'Well, keep your eyes skinned from now on. We can only hope he didn't radio our position back to Base before we got him.'

The Wellington was soon back on course, and their luck held out. Saumur appeared, and a few minutes later Algy was saying, 'Well, it looks as if we've made it, Biggles. The airfield's slap ahead. I wonder what we're going to find?'

Biggles brought the Wellington in to a perfect landing, and taxied up the tarmac to a hangar and a group of buildings. After the action of the previous few minutes it was a strangely peaceful scene, and the whole place seemed deserted. He switched off the engines and, unbuckling his safety belt, turned round to give his crew their orders.

'Algy, old lad, you'll stay where you are, and so will Tug. I want to be prepared for instant take-off in the event of trouble. The rest of you come with me. We'd better get a move on if we're going to get this Monsieur Clairvaux and his plane before the Huns arrive.'

Biggles was the first one out, gun in hand. The others followed, and as they entered the hangar Biggles whistled softly beneath his breath.

'Crikey, Ginger! What d'you think of that? Really worth coming for!'

There in the centre of the hangar, sleek as some enormous silver bird, stood a low-wing fighter plane.

'So Raymond was right as usual,' replied Ginger. 'Clairvaux had finished it after all. It's ready to be flown. I wonder where the blighter is.'

'Probably hopped it,' answered Biggles. 'Can't say I blame him. Give us a hand up. I'm going to have a look inside the cockpit.'

But, just as Biggles pulled back the canopy, a voice rang out.

'Stay where you are – and gentlemen, please drop your guns!'

Framed in the hangar entrance stood a slender figure in a field-grey uniform. Just behind him were four other men with sub-machine-guns, German paratroopers. Biggles could see at once that he and his comrades had no chance.

'Drop it, Tex!' he shouted, seeing the headstrong Texan was about to start a gun-fight that could only have ended in disaster.

'O.K. Biggles,' Tex replied, dropping his Smith and Wesson on the floor and raising his hands towards the German. Ginger did likewise.

'Very wise of you' remarked the German officer in perfect English, as one of his men retrieved the guns. 'Into the office, please! The man you came to fetch is there as well. I'm afraid that we arrived before you.'

There were several Frenchmen in the little office, guarded by another German, and among them Biggles recognised Clairvaux, who greeted him with a bitter smile.

'So the British did come after all, but just a little late, as usual.'

Biggles could have said a lot – but wisely held his tongue.

'We did out best,' he said.

'Enough of this!' barked the German. 'I am afraid that you will have to wait awhile until our glorious German Army comes to occupy this part of France. It won't take long, but in the meantime, no tricks please. My men will keep you under guard.'

He barked an order, and two of the paratroopers entered the office and herded Biggles, Tex and Ginger up against the wall. They were allowed to sit and smoke, but nothing else.

'Wonder what on earth old Algy's up to?' muttered Biggles out of the corner of his mouth. 'He must have realised by now that something's up.'

'Silence!' shouted one of the Germans, pointing his machine-gun threateningly at Biggles.

But, as if in answer to the query, there was the sudden unmistakable roar of the Wellington's engines from outside, followed by the brisk bark of machine-gun fire. The roar grew to a crescendo and, seconds later, Biggles saw the bomber as it flashed past the office window and its noise receded. He smiled at Ginger. Algy, at any rate, had got away.

After that the hours dragged. The guard was changed. At around two o'clock coffee was brought in, but nothing else, and Biggles kept wondering how much longer it would be before the full force of the enemy arrived. Obviously not long. From where he was sitting he could clearly see the far end of the runway, but nothing stirred and he was getting very stiff. Then one of the Germans shouted excitedly, 'Transport planes! They've come!' and Biggles saw the silhouette of two three-engined Junkers 52s circling the airport and coming in to land. Ginger had seen them too, and shrugged his shoulders in a gesture of weary resignation. It would not be long now before they would all be on their way to Germany, to spend the rest of the war inside a German prison camp. So much for their efforts to secure the Frenchman and his secret aircraft. A pathetic ending for their precious Special Duty Squadron!

But even as Biggles pondered this gloomy future, he heard another German shouting, 'Spitfire! Spitfire!' Then he saw them too – six Spitfires in immaculate formation sweeping across that clear blue sky, closely followed by a Wellington. Algy and his comrades had returned.

The German aircraft didn't stand a chance, and were soon plummeting in flames. Seconds later, the Spitfires were coming in to land and the German guards were rushing out to meet them. In the confusion, Biggles, Tex and Ginger dodged out of the office and back into the hangar just in time to see the battle on the runway as a dozen Royal Marine commandos leapt from the Wellington and stormed towards them.

It was a grim encounter while it lasted, with the Germans firing from the shelter of the airport buildings. The German officer went down in a hail of bullets, and then it was suddenly all over and a figure with a Sten gun was standing in the hangar entrance.

'Anyone at home?' it called.

And Biggles answered, 'Algy! My dear old chap, am I glad to see you!'

'Better get a move on, Biggles,' Algy said laconically. 'There's half the blinking German Army up the road by the look of things. We can't stay long. What're we going to do about the plane?'

'What do you think, my lad?' said Biggles quickly. 'I'm flying it. You'd better see to the Frenchman. He's in the office at the back.'

Clairvaux and his colleagues made no objection now to coming back to England. He even seemed pleased at the idea that his plane would come as well.

'Better the British than the Boche!' he answered when Biggles explained their plans. Luckily the plane was fuelled and ready. The hangar doors were pulled right back and, seconds later, Biggles was taxiing across the runway where he joined the waiting Spitfires of his Squadron. He recognised the unmistakeable features of Flight Lieutenant Lissie in the leading plane and raised his hand to him in thankful greeting. Bertie waved back, and then with Biggles in the lead the planes took off and headed home to England, leaving Andrey and its airfield to the Germans.

The fall of France a few days later started the period when Britain stood alone. For Biggles and 666 Special Duty Squadron, this meant that they were now committed to the Front Line in the battle for survival. There was a note of thanks from Raymond for their mission and, unofficially, Biggles heard that the irritable Monsieur Clairvaux had been persuaded to put his talents at the full disposal of the Allies, and that the British scientists were more than grateful for his aircraft with its revolutionary engine.

But once the Luftwaffe launched its mass attacks against the south of England from its fields in France, 666 became a normal fighter squadron and special missions all but ceased. The only one that did crop up occurred when Biggles had to go back to Amiens to pick up an important top French scientist who, like Clairvaux, was badly needed back in Britain. It was a straightforward enough affair – in theory – and not unlike the sort of work Biggles had done behind the enemy Lines in 1918. He was flying a Lysander – a heavy, rather gentlemanly plane after the Spitfire – which could almost land on half-a-crown, making it ideal for operations of this sort. He went by night.

Raymond's liaison had been excellent this time, and Biggles had no problem landing on a torch-lit field outside the town. Then came inevitable delays. The French Resistance group who met him kept assuring him their man was on his way, but it proved a good three hours before he finally drove up, apologetic and explaining that the Boche patrols had held him up. Dawn was already breaking before Biggles got away, and he knew that in the heavy old Lysander he was a sitting duck for any enemy patrol that spotted him. He did the one thing possible – hedge-hopping all the way back to the coast, then trusting fervently to luck that the enemy would have other things to occupy their minds than a solitary Lysander – and, for once, they had.

For by now, the Battle of Britain had begun in earnest, and from dawn to dusk Reichsmarshal Goering's Dorniers and Heinkels were sailing in formation through the summer sky, guarded by attendant packs of Messerschmitts. And from dawn to dusk, Squadron 666, along with the other fighter squadrons along that hard-pressed shore, flew up to give them battle.

Their day began when their batmen pulled them from their beds at 4.30 a.m. for 'dawn readiness', and Biggles was surprised that it was always Bertie Lissie, that fervent enemy of early mornings, who was invariably in his Spitfire first. Their routine was always much the same. Biggles was fanatical about the vital need for height superiority – another lesson he had learned the hard way years before – and once the Controller ordered take-off, they would fly upwards in formation to a height of 20,000 feet, then wait for battle.

They rarely waited long. At this height they would be on oxygen, and as soon as someone in the Squadron spotted the enemy below, he would report across his radio to Biggles, who in turn would give the order 'Tally-ho!'. Then, all nine Spitfires would sweep down on the formation like avenging angels. By now they had worked out the best routine for dealing with them. The Messerschmitt was vulnerable from behind and when attacked, the German pilots would usually attempt a half roll before diving vertically to get away, but the Spitfires would be after them, and soon the sky above the Channel would be witnessing ferocious dogfights as Biggles and his Squadron battled for the kill.

Then, it was back to Base for breakfast – usually baked beans and fried eggs in the Mess – and when the aircraft had been checked, refuelled and their guns re-loaded, 666 would once again take off to await the next wave of enemy attack.

The Squadron had its losses. Early that August, Taffy Hughes ignored Biggles' constant warning – 'beware the Hun in the sun' – and while taking on a Dornier was caught from behind by a yellow-nosed Messerschmitt. Ginger reported later that the last he saw of him was a black trail plunging to the sea. Bertie's plane went down in flames just two days later, but he managed to get out, and his parachute was spotted by the Deal lifeboat. He lost his monocle and got very wet, but was in the air again at six next morning. Biggles nearly copped it too, for by the end of August he was getting slightly 'battle-happy', and was beginning to take risks he would have normally avoided. This may partially have been the effect of age, and it was around this time that the Wing M.O. had tried to 'ground' him, saying that his nerves would soon be shot to pieces. Biggles avoided this, of course – he always did – but Algy began to get worried about him now, and it was Algy who ultimately saved his life.

They had been up twice that morning, and the Squadron had already taken on a massed formation of the enemy. All had gone well for several minutes as the Spitfires did their deadly work. They had had several kills and, more importantly, the German bombers had been forced to break formation, and several were already heading back for France. This was the point at which the Spitfires would normally break off their attack and return to Base as well, but suddenly across his radio Algy heard Biggles' voice. He can't have realised he was transmitting, for he was swearing furiously to himself, and then he started shouting that he'd 'seen the Hun that got old Taffy' and was after him. Then the radio went dead.

Algy was out of ammunition but he immediately began to search the skies for Biggles. There was no sign of him. The German planes had disappeared, and Algy could see Tex and Ginger just below him heading back towards the English coast. Algy climbed higher. Still no sign of Biggles, so he kicked the rudder-bar and, climbing higher still, he made for France. It was a perfect August morning, and from this height he could see for miles – the glittering azure of the Channel, the twin white cliffs of Calais and Dover on each horizon, and a destroyer far beneath him like a child's toy as it made for Portsmouth. But although he scanned the skies, there was no sign of aircraft now. At this point, Algy had to take a chance. He knew the Messerschmitts had come either from Belgium or from northern France. He wasn't certain which, but plumped for France and finally spotted what he sought. Far below him, just to the north of Calais, he saw a pack of half a dozen Messerschmitts encircling one lone aeroplane – a Spitfire.

There was a deadly duel in progress and he could see already that the British plane was trapped. From the way it was performing, he knew the pilot must be Biggles, but the odds against the plane were far too great. One of the Messerschmitts went down in flames, but even as Biggles dived past it, two other Messerschmitts were climbing high above him for the kill.

'O.K., you blighters, here I come!' Algy muttered through clenched teeth, and shoving the stick hard forward, aimed his aircraft in a power-dive straight for the leading Messerschmitt. He cursed himself for being out of ammunition, but was counting on diverting the attack to give his chum the chance to get away. Down, down he went and practically blacked out. Then, over his radio, he heard one of the German pilots shouting, '*Achtung, Achtung,* Spitfire!' It was a brave attempt, and had his guns been loaded Algy could have finished both Messerschmitts at once. As it was, the leading aircraft took evasive action, rolled and dived away, but the one behind it kept straight on for Biggles, and as Algy pulled out of his dive and banked, he saw behind him in his cockpit mirror deadly tracer-fire raking Biggles' Spitfire from the rear.

Algy was powerless, and saw the Spitfire's wing come off, smoke start to billow from its engine, and the fuselage twist in the beginning of a spin. He saw it all as if it was happening in slow-motion, and he told himself that Biggles must be dead. But then a miracle occurred. Just as the first flames were licking from the engine, the Spitfire's canopy slid back, a figure tumbled out and, seconds later, Algy glimpsed the white fleck of an opening parachute. It mushroomed out with Biggles dangling on the end of it, kicking his legs to straighten out the cords.

They were over flat green farmland, and Biggles hadn't all that far to fall, but even so, one of the Messerschmitts showed signs of coming back to deal with him – until Algy flipped his wings to warn him off.

'No you don't, my lad!' said Algy softly to himself, making a tight turn round his cousin as he drifted down. He saw Biggles wave – though whether in greeting or farewell, he wasn't sure. Then he was down in the middle of a field, the long line of the parachute spewed out behind him. Algy still buzzed protectively overhead and for a moment wondered what to do, but coming down the road beyond the field was something that made his mind up for him – an open German Army lorry with half-a-dozen field-grey soldiers in the back. There was no question now of leaving Biggles to their tender mercy. Instead, he banked the Spitfire, flattened out above a line of trees, and landed barely ten yards from where Biggles stood.

'Taxi!' shouted Biggles, raising a gloved hand and grinning ruefully at Algy.

'Hurry up, you idiot!' yelled Algy, above the roar of his Rolls-Royce Merlin engine. 'The Huns have got a welcoming party down the road. Hop in, unless you want to spend the rest of the war behind barbed wire.'

Biggles required no second bidding, especially with German rifle-fire now zinging round his head. It was a horribly tight squeeze inside the cockpit, but even before he'd shut the canopy, Algy had gunned the engine and released the brakes, and the overloaded Spitfire was trundling across the meadow. It missed the line of trees by inches and minutes later was above the waters of the English Channel.

'Sorry, Algy,' mumbled Biggles. 'I was a blithering idiot. Simply lost my rag. Should've known better. Thanks for fetching me, old scout!'

'Don't mention it, old boy' said Algy. 'It was a pleasure. Just the same, go easy, eh? Committing suicide won't get poor old Taffy back.'

Luckily for Biggles – and for 666 – things were easing up, for by late September 'the Few' had won the battle of the skies and the great German onslaught slackened. That autumn, Biggles took a few days' leave, and even started up a brief affair with a blonde called Pam, who worked in an officers' club in Kensington. Algy and Ginger took a proprietorial interest in the romance and had both done their level best to encourage it – on the grounds that 'the old boy's been taking life too seriously and needs taking out of himself'. They had discussed this several times, and it was Algy who finally suggested Pam, and had made the original introduction. She was an ancient flame of his, a gentle, rather jolly creature in her early thirties, with a well-developed bosom and a flat in Eaton Square. Biggles seemed extremely taken with her, but when his leave was over and Algy asked him how it had all gone, he shook his head.

'No go, old fruit. It simply wasn't on.'

'Why on earth not?' responded Algy, mouth agape.

'Algy, I'd rather not talk about it,' said Biggles stiffly.

'Oh come now Biggles, for Pete's sake!' answered Algy. 'We've known each other long enough, and we're not exactly school-girls. What went wrong?'

'She's married, Algy. That's what's wrong.'

Algy laughed with evident relief.

'Good Heavens, Biggles! Is that all it was? But I thought you knew! For a moment I imagined it was something really serious.'

'But it was serious,' said Biggles levelly. 'Dashed serious. For me at any rate. You see, I asked Pamela to marry me. I felt I ought to, after what had happened. That's how I found out. And now, if you'll excuse me, we will change the subject.'

Later that evening Algy discussed it all with Ginger.

'Dreadful pity,' Algy said. 'She was exactly what he needed. Quite an affectionate little thing and a husband in the Navy. She would have been ideal.'

But Ginger shook his head.

'Algy, when will you realise that Biggles isn't a cad like you where women are concerned? He's a romantic. He respects them.'

Algy nodded.

'Yes, I suppose you're right. Poor old Biggles. What a helluva thing to be. But what a good thing dear old Pam *was* married.'

Luckily for Biggles, aircraft really took the place of women in his life and he had little time to brood. During that winter 666 was mainly occupied with night-time flying – trying to meet the German Blitz on London – and then, in the spring of 1941, there were a number of demanding operations on behalf of Air Intelligence. During one of these – described by Captain Johns in his book *Biggles Fails to Return* – Biggles was actually given up for lost after the failure of a mission to the Italian-occupied territory of the south of France to rescue the celebrated 'Princess X' whose father, a noted anti-fascist, was being blackmailed, before he was finally killed, with threats against his daughter. For several weeks Biggles was given up for dead, and this was the one occasion when Algy took command of 666. Biggles reappeared on this occasion in North Africa, having made good his escape in a commandeered Italian flying boat.

It was shortly after this that Biggles met the only woman who could match his reputation in the air – the extraordinary Joan Worralson, or 'Worrals of the W.A.A.F.' as she was known to her admirers. The assiduous Captain Johns saw fit to chronicle a few of her adventures, but once again discretion – and quite simple fear of rousing Biggles' ire for what he would have termed the author's 'blasted scandal-mongering' – made him fight shy of giving any details of her friendship with our hero. Algy, who knew her rather well, always insisted that 'she was absolutely made for Biggles', and regretted that things turned out as they did. But the more one learns about this flying Amazon, the more one understands why Biggles acted as he did.

'Dashed fine flier,' he replied once when I mentioned her to him. 'But tough, and not what one would call a cosy sort of girl. Not very womanly, you know.' Confirmed male chauvinist that he was, Biggles liked 'cosy' women, and was not attracted by young women who attempted to usurp the male role. But despite this, he was undoubtedly impressed by his first sight of Miss Joan Worralson – and may well have 'led her on' in the months that followed.

He had been on the tarmac, waiting for delivery of replacement Spitfires which had been promised some days earlier from the central pool. The condition of the Squadron's aircraft had been worrying him and he had had a number of furious exchanges with the Air Ministry upon the subject. He had demanded three new aircraft – which were promised faithfully. But all that finally turned up was one solitary Spitfire, and no sooner had it landed than Biggles stormed across to vent his wrath upon the pilot.

According to Algy, there was 'something of a shindig' as Biggles fumed away at 'those confounded nincompoops in the Air Ministry', and ordered the pilot to return to the central pool and say that he wanted his three planes or nothing. The pilot stayed very cool throughout all this, and seemed quite unaffected by Biggles' wrath and highly coloured language.

'Would you please put your refusal to accept this aircraft in writing, and any other observations that you care to make.'

'Observations! What the blazes do you mean by observations?' thundered Biggles. 'I want those three confounded Spitfires I was promised. You can tell that to those flaming nitwits who sent you. And while you're about it, man, I think you should get yourself a haircut.' For Biggles had seen a thick black curl escaping from the side of the pilot's flying helmet.

At this the pilot turned and grinned, then quietly replied, 'I'll tell my hairdresser, sir.'

'Hairdresser!' choked Biggles. 'What the blazes . . .?'

For the helmet was suddenly removed, and the Spitfire pilot stood revealed as an attractive young brunette.

'Flight Officer Worralson of Transport Command at your service, Squadron Leader,' she replied. 'Most people call me Worrals.'

'Good heavens, so you're Worrals. I've heard all about you. You must excuse my language, but one gets a bit frustrated at a time like this,' answered Biggles, somewhat sheepishly. 'You must come over to the Mess and have a drink.'

And so the friendship started, for Worrals stayed to lunch, was introduced to all the members of the Squadron, and that same afternoon Biggles insisted on ferrying her back to Transport Command headquarters in the twin-engined 'Oxford' aircraft which the squadron used for flying V.I.P.s. Thanks to Worrals, 666 did get the rest of the replacement Spitfires which had been promised. She flew them over personally next day. During the weeks that followed there were more occasions for her to visit Tangmere, so much so that Algy was soon making quite a joke about it all.

'It's that Worrals girl again,' he'd say to Biggles with a wink. 'You'd better watch out or you'll have her applying to join the Squadron. I wonder which of us she fancies?'

'Really, Algy,' Biggles said. 'That's no way to speak about an officer and a lady. She just does her job – and jolly well she does it too.'

'Well, you should know old chap, if anybody does.'

'Now, look here Algy,' snorted Biggles. 'I find this sort of innuendo coarse and tasteless in the extreme. Good heavens, man, Worrals is young enough to be my daughter!'

'Exactly Biggles. She obviously sees you as a father figure. You know what young girls are.'

But Biggles clearly didn't know what young girls were – at any rate, not young girls like the determined Worrals of the W.A.A.F. – and despite a lot of somewhat heavy humour in the Mess, it rather looked as if Biggles had finally been hooked. He would have said, of course, that it was all extremely innocent – brief expeditions through the Sussex lanes in Worrals' red MG, a chaste dinner at the Dorchester followed by an equally chaste film in Leicester Square, a spot of dual flying down at Tangmere in which Biggles' admiration for the young girl's flying skill increased. They talked a lot – or rather, Biggles talked a lot, with Worrals wide-eyed and adoring as he went through his well-tried repertoire of flying stories from the past. He even kissed her – once. It was the most fatherly of kisses, in the deserted ante-room at the end of a squadron dance. (The station band was playing 'Auld Lang Syne' and Biggles was briefly overcome.) It might have led to other things, but a few days later the call to action intervened, and Worrals was permanently displaced by a shadowy figure out of Biggles' past.

It all began when Squadron 666 was suddenly involved in a desperate operation against the German U-boat base at St Nazaire. Thus had begun as an attempt by Air Commodore Raymond to work with the French Resistance. Because of his near-perfect French and his proven skill at working 'in the field', as Raymond put it, Biggles had had the task of parachuting into Brittany to liaise with the local French Resistance group and plan a joint attack by a British bomber force and Free French saboteurs.

The beginning of the plan worked admirably. Biggles was dropped outside the town, picked up by the French and spent several days disguised as a French dockyard worker living in the town. During this time, the whole attack was planned down to the last detail – timing, the explosive charges to be planted by the French inside the U-boat pens, and the targets to be dealt with by the British bombers. Biggles was looked after by a French couple he knew as 'Madeleine' and 'Gaston', and he admired them greatly for their coolness, their hatred of *les sales Boches*, and the skill with which they did their work. It was thanks to them that everything went smoothly on the night that Algy came to fetch him – flying the same Lysander Biggles used at Amiens. The attack was fixed for three days later.

It was a near disaster. The British bombers flew in from the sea to meet some of the toughest opposition of the war. Biggles, who flew with them, had never seen so many Messerschmitts in the air at once, and fifteen of the bombers failed to return. None of them did appreciable damage to the U-boat pens – nor, as it turned out, did the saboteurs. Biggles discovered later that the whole Resistance group had been arrested by the Germans on the very morning of the attack.

Biggles had always taken failure badly, and had the miserable duty of attending the 'inquest' on the operation at the Air Ministry a few days later. An Air Vice Marshal was in charge, and while no actual blame was laid on Biggles, there was a lot of criticism of the rôle of Air Intelligence.

'What were your fellows doing, Raymond?' thundered the Air Vice Marshal bitterly. 'The opposition must have known what we were up to from the start. They set a trap and we flew slap-bang into it.'

Raymond nodded, stony-faced.

'I've no excuse sir. There must have been a leak. These things happen.'

'Well they shouldn't. We've lost sixty of our finest men, and all for nothing. I insist upon a full inquiry.'

'You shall have it, sir,' said Raymond grimly.

As Biggles left the inquest, he was button-holed by Raymond. 'Just a minute, James. We've something to discuss.' With sinking heart, Biggles followed his old chief towards his sanctum.

'I'm sorry, sir,' said Biggles, as he met that steely gaze across the familiar desk. But Raymond brushed his apologies aside.

'No time for that, James. War by its nature is a risky business and mistakes occur. The only thing to do is profit by them. I didn't mention it just now, but I think I've found out what went wrong.'

'You have, sir? How?'

'From one of our agents who has just returned from France. Got back by the skin of his teeth himself, and what he had to say makes the whole dog's breakfast pretty clear, to me at any rate. No James, we have one man and one alone to blame for what occurred. An old friend of yours.'

'A friend of mine, sir? Just tell me who the swine is and I'll kill him with my own bare hands.'

'Not such a bad idea,' replied Raymond thoughtfully. 'Though I imagine you'd have quite a job. It was von Stalhein, James. It seems he's back in his old job at the head of German field security in France. He's working from the *Abwehr* headquarters in Paris, but now I hear that he was in St Nazaire for several weeks before the raid. Somehow he'd penetrated the Resistance network and we played straight into his hands. He must have known about you all along. I must admit I thought it pretty fishy at the time that everything appeared so easy for you. I should have realised. That man's a devil, James. The most dangerous brain we're up against.'

'Isn't it time we dealt with him for good and all?' said Biggles, trying to disguise the fury in his heart.

Raymond nodded.

'Yes James. I think you're right.'

Biggles was absent from the Squadron for the next few weeks, and there was much idle speculation about what he could be up to, for at this point not even Algy was in the secret. Officially, Biggles was in London having treatment for his back.

'Touch of the old trouble, Algy,' he explained. 'The medics seem to think I need an overhaul.'

In fact, he was at a certain house in Middlesex which specialised in what was known as 'the Secret War'. There were cryptographers, saboteurs, experts in unarmed combat, and agents recently returned from France. But most of Biggles' time was spent in the small department specialising in counter-intelligence, studying everything on record about one elusive individual – Erich von Stalhein. Many of the facts he knew already, but there was much that was completely new to him, particularly concerning the Prussian's rise to influence and power since the Occupation. It was apparently von Stalhein who had played a vital part in building up the notorious 'Fifth Column' of traitors inside France who had contributed so much to their country's swift defeat, and now he was using all his fox-like cunning to destroy the French Resistance. Estimates varied on the damage he had inflicted on the Allied cause. Some reports claimed he was responsible for arresting more than two hundred Allied agents, and it was clear that the St Nazaire disaster was only one of the successes of the Prussian super-spy.

There was much information on his private life as well, including quite recent photographs taken by agents using long-range cameras, and despite himself, Biggles could not help admiring his enemy as he studied them. One showed von Stalhein in his black Mercedes, driving through the Paris streets, and there were others taken of him leaving his office on the Rue de Rivoli. He was as slim, as ramrod straight as ever, and the grim countenance with the crossed duelling scars had barely changed since Biggles had first clapped eyes on it, more than twenty years before. During that time he had become the evil genius who haunted Biggles' life, the man who seemed to symbolise the enemy.

There were some other pictures too, which instantly caught Biggles' eye. These showed a more relaxed von Stalhein, taken in the garden of the villa where he was living outside Paris. He was sitting in a deckchair, reading, and in one of these photographs there was the blurred image of a woman standing just behind him. It was impossible to see her face, but the body was the one female figure Biggles would recognise until the day he died. It belonged unmistakably to Marie Janis.

Biggles didn't mention this to anyone – not even to the Air Commodore himself when he arrived a few days later for a final action conference with the top brass of British counter-intelligence.

'Well, James,' he said breezily, 'I trust you've done your stuff, and got it all worked out?' The blighter's got a lot to answer for, and destroying him will be the equivalent of wiping out an Infantry Division for the damage it will do the enemy.'

'That's one way of looking at it, sir. I prefer to think about the men I flew with into St Nazaire. Someone should avenge them.'

'Quite,' said Raymond.

A few days later Biggles was back in France. The way he went was practically routine – a night-time drop by parachute into a field near Fontainebleau, a waiting group of French Resistance men to meet him, then shelter in a 'safe house' on the outskirts of the town. Biggles was disguised as a typical French working man, down to his grimy overalls and stubble on his chin, and his documents would have fooled the French Sûreté itself. But from the moment he arrived, he was treated with considerable respect, for news had somehow filtered through of why he was in France.

'You're a brave man, *mon vieux*' remarked his host, 'and you're going to have your work cut out to get von Stalhein. Don't think we haven't tried already, but he's as slippery as they come, and we have to be a little careful. The Boches have started shooting hostages when any of their men are killed, and we don't want innocent people shot unless it's absolutely necessary.'

Biggles nodded.

'They've explained all that to me in England, and none of you will be involved.'

'Who's going to do it then?' the Frenchman asked.

'The R.A.F.,' said Biggles softly. 'To be precise, the chaps in my Special Duty Squadron. I've already briefed them personally, and they've been practising for weeks. The boys won't miss their target, and none of you French will be involved.'

The Frenchman looked relieved at this.

'What do you want, monsieur?' he asked. 'How can we help you?'

'Quite simple,' answered Biggles quickly. 'I need a vantage point from where I can watch von Stalhein's villa. I need to know his movements – when he arrives and when he leaves. I have a small transmitter with which I can signal back to my boys in England. They can be here in half an hour, but we must be absolutely sure von Stalhein's in the villa when they arrive. We've one chance – and one chance only.'

A look of quiet satisfaction spread across the Frenchman's face at this.

'Monsieur, I'll guarantee you get it,' he replied.

The next few days reminded Biggles of the tiger shooting he had seen in India as a boy. There was the same long wait, the same desperate need for patience, and endless false alarms and bungled chances as he waited for his prey. His hosts had been extraordinarily efficient. The very morning after his arrival he had been taken in a baker's van which stopped outside a big suburban house in a leafy street in Neuilly, and the door was opened by an ancient female housekeeper in black. She asked no questions, but had conducted him upstairs to the attic. There, she had pointed to a dusty little window, and when Biggles peered through it he saw exactly what 'he needed – a clear view of von Stalhein's villa at the far end of the street. Biggles' long wait had started.

He had all he needed – binoculars, his small transmitter, and a book to while away the hours when nothing happened. There was a camp bed there, and regularly, three times a day, the old woman brought him food. No one else bothered him, and when he tried to talk to her she never answered. The first evening he was there he saw von Stalhein. The big Mercedes had arrived outside the villa just after six o'clock, driven by a uniformed chauffeur who descended from the car, unlocked the big iron gates, then drove right up to the door beyond. The front door opened, and as von Stalhein entered, Biggles had seen the dim shape of a woman welcoming him. He couldn't see her features clearly, but he knew it was Marie, and an hour later, when the car returned, he saw her properly. She was in a bright green dress and his heart turned over as he glimpsed through his binoculars that flawless profile. She was alone. The chauffeur had saluted, opened the rear door of the car for her, and they had driven off.

This was the moment when Biggles should have acted, for von Stalhein was alone inside the villa now – the perfect target. But something made him hesitate. Perhaps it was the feeling that his luck was too good to be true and that he needed more time to make absolutely certain. It was a mistake. Around ten o'clock the car returned, Marie descended, the villa gates were shut, and Biggles spent a sleepless night, knowing that the man he hated and the woman he still loved were lying in each others' arms behind the shuttered windows of the white house opposite.

The next three days were hell. Until he had actually seen Marie, Biggles had barely given her a thought. He knew she was with von Stalhein, and had honestly believed that he was completely cured of his ancient love for her. If it was necessary for

her to die along with von Stalhein, so much the better. It would
even serve her right. But now he had seen her, Biggles knew that
this was inconceivable. Marie remained what she had always
been – the one love of his life. Not even jealousy and bitter hatred
for von Stalhein could make it possible to do anything to hurt her.

So, Biggles waited on – consumed with jealousy and anger, and
at the same time dreading having to make the call to London that
would destroy von Stalhein – and put Marie in dreadful danger.
By now, he had decided that the only thing to do was wait until
he knew for sure that Marie had left the house with von Stalhein
safely in it. But suddenly this seemed impossible. At eight o'clock
each morning the car arrived to take von Stalhein to his office,
and at seven he would return. The second evening they went out
together – and returned together. And so this maddening routine
went on throughout the week. Several times he saw her in the
garden, and once when she went out walking with a dog and
passed beneath his window, Biggles was seized by a mad urge to
rush down and speak to her again. Ten minutes later she walked
back, and Biggles watched her hungrily. How beautiful she was –
tall, confident, the blonde hair flecked with grey, the loveliness
that he had known from her girlhood now at its full maturity. The
dog had stopped outside his house. For a moment she looked up,
and Biggles could have sworn that she had seen him watching
her. Then she walked on, called the dog and the villa gates
clanged shut behind her.

Finally, the chance that he was waiting for arrived. It had been
a long hot summer day and the unventilated attic had been
stifling. He had seen von Stalhein leave as usual in the morning,
but since then there had been no sign of life from the villa. Then,
around six o'clock, the Mercedes had returned – earlier than
usual. Von Stalhein had got out and entered the house, but the
Mercedes waited, and ten minutes later Biggles saw Marie come
out alone, enter the car and drive away. The moment he had
waited for had come at last. The tiger was safely in the trap. All
that was needed was the signal to destroy him.

Biggles was trembling as he took the small transmitter from its
case and set it up. It was a simple operation. All he had to do was
press a switch to send a signal on a pre-arranged frequency to the
monitoring experts back in Britain. Once this was done, the
deadly operation would be set in motion as the take-off order

flashed from Intelligence Headquarters to Squadron 666 at Tangmere. He took one last look at the villa. Nothing stirred. The iron gates were shut, the street still empty in the heat of early evening. Biggles put his finger on the switch, and pressed it, hard.

He glanced at his watch – 6.13 p.m. It had been calculated that the aircraft would take roughly thirty minutes' flying time from Tangmere. Allowing for inevitable delays in take-off, it could take just a little longer. Certainly by seven it should all be over – mission accomplished, and the dead of St Nazaire finally avenged. Biggles waited, praying now for one thing only – that von Stalhein stayed exactly where he was.

Those next thirty minutes were the longest and cruellest half hour of Biggles' life. Soon he was pacing round the attic.

'Come on Algy, come on Ginger! Get a move on! For Cripe's sake, get it over with!'

But nothing happened. Time had suddenly slowed down. There was nothing but silence from the street and from the empty house beneath him. He looked at his watch again – 6.40 – then 6.45. Any minute now. But still the minutes ticked away and nothing happened.

It was nearly seven when he heard the noise that he had secretly been dreading all along – the faint hum of a car approaching down the street. Then he saw it – the Mercedes was gliding slowly underneath his window and in to the villa where it stopped. The gates were opened and he saw Marie descend and go inside the house.

The nightmare started then, with Biggles sitting petrified beside the window. He glanced at his watch again. It was now five past seven, and for one mad moment he considered rushing down and out into the street to warn them – anything to save Marie. But luckily for him there was no time for that, and suddenly all hell broke loose. There was the roar of engines overhead and then a deadly *whoosh*. A split second later the whole attic seemed to rock as the bombs struck home, and the attic window shattered. Biggles was blown back by the explosion and when he stumbled to his feet and stared out from the window he saw at once how beautifully his plan had worked – and how efficiently Squadron 666 had carried out his orders. Von Stalhein's villa was little more now than a pile of rubble.

Biggles was still staring, mesmerised by the horror of it all, when the old housekeeper entered. She was smiling – the first time she ever had since Biggles came, and she was carrying a tray with a glass and a bottle of good brandy.

'You've done your work, monsieur,' she said quietly. 'A drink to celebrate before you go?'

Biggles had little memory of what happened then – or how he finally got back to England. Two of the original Resistance men from Fontainebleau came to the house later that night and found him very drunk and in a sort of numb despair. Somehow they smuggled him away. They were both understanding men who thought they realised the strain of his ordeal, and they looked after him for several days, grateful that the Germans could not blame the French for what had happened. No hostages were shot, and Algy collected him without a hitch in the Lysander, from the field near Fontainbleau, a few nights later.

'What's up, old lad?' said Algy when he saw him. 'You look as if you've seen a ghost.'

'I have,' said Biggles, wearily. 'For Pete's sake, let's get back to England.'

'But didn't the whole business go off perfectly? It seemed to be bang-on.'

'It was, old boy. The God-forsaken plan went off like clockwork.'

'Then what's the matter, Biggles? What on earth went wrong?'

'Later, Algy! We'll talk about it later. Just let's get back.'

Raymond had known that Biggles was being fetched from France and it was something of an honour that he was actually at Tangmere to welcome him when he arrived.

'Congratulations, James,' he said. 'You had us worried for a while with the time you took to send the message through, but your fellows did a lovely job. Bombs absolutely spot on, James. A great tribute to the way you've trained 'em, eh Algy? No other squadron in the R.A.F. could possibly have done it.'

'Any news, sir, about the people in the villa?' asked Biggles flatly. 'None of the chaps at Fontainebleau appeared to know for sure . . .'

'You mean von Stalhein, James? Well, that's the devil of it all.

We can't be absolutely certain even now. The Huns have
blanketed the whole affair with top security, but one of our agents
has reported that someone was taken from the house alive.'

'For God's sake, who?' asked Biggles quickly.

Raymond shrugged his shoulders. 'We just don't know.
Someone was admitted to the German hospital at Passy. It could
have been von Stalhein, but even if it was, from the sound of
things he won't be around to trouble us for quite some while. But
let's just hope that it was someone else. Now, get some sleep, old
boy. You look as though you need it.'

The next few days were naturally a time of hideous anxiety for
Biggles. He rang Raymond's office endlessly but there was no
further news from France and soon the Air Commodore was
becoming just a little sick of Biggles' calls.

'Now take it easy, James. I promise that I'll let you know the
instant that there's something definite.'

Algy was getting worried now by what was happening to
Biggles. Throughout the long years of their friendship he had
never known him in such a state. This puzzled him, for he
couldn't understand why he should be so worried if von Stalhein
were alive or dead. Finally he asked him – and it was then that
Biggles told him the whole story.

'So you see, dear old chap,' concluded Biggles bitterly, 'I've
just got to know what's happened to Marie. I can't go on like this.
It's torture. If she's dead, so be it, but I've got to know.'

'But you can't blame yourself,' said Algy logically. 'Fortunes of
war, old thing. She knew what she was up to, living with von
Stalhein.'

'Oh, I know,' said Biggles. 'I've been over it and over it and
I've no illusions. But it was a dirty business all the same – not the
sort of warfare you and I believe in, Algy. And I tell you one thing
that's for sure. Whatever Raymond says or does in future, I'm not
getting mixed up in that sort of thing again. You and I are fliers,
Algy. Not bloody murderers.'

Two days later, news came through from Raymond.

'Sorry, James. Bit of a disappointment for you, I'm afraid. It
was von Stalhein who escaped. The blighter's just been taken
back to hospital in Berlin. No fault of yours, of course, and I'm
seeing that you're recommended for a decoration just the same.'

'I'd rather that you didn't, sir,' said Biggles coldly.

'Why not, James? Good Heavens man ...'

'I'd just rather you didn't, sir,' repeated Biggles, and slammed the telephone down.

The death of Marie Janis was a turning-point in Biggles' life and it explains much of what subsequently happened, not only to him, but to Squadron 666 as well, for he was firm in his refusal to become involved again in Raymond's cloak-and-dagger world. On the surface, relations between him and the Air Commodore were much as they had always been – mutual respect and slightly wary friendship on both sides.

But that autumn, there was a stormy interview at Whitehall when Biggles flatly refused to take part in another of Raymond's plots against von Stalhein – who by then was totally recovered and was the brain behind German Intelligence in Berlin. Algy, as usual, patched things up between the two men by telling Raymond the true facts about the death of Marie Janis, and it was really as a result of this that Squadron 666 resumed its role as an active service squadron stationed out of Britain. They fought in North Africa in 1942 (described by Captain Johns in *Biggles Sweeps the Desert*), and at the end of 1944 saw service in the Far East (a period which has been chronicled by Johns in *Biggles in the Orient*).

It was not until the war in Europe drew towards its close that 666 was back in England, covered with battle honours and with Biggles finally promoted Wing-Commander. It was a splendid squadron, fighting together as 'a band of brothers', and its members played a most distinguished part in the Normandy invasions and the subsequent attacks on Nazi Germany.

But Biggles always bore the scars of Marie's death, and for the remainder of his life she and she alone would be the woman he loved, and had lost; nobody could ever take her place.

10

Biggles and the Mafia

'Of course I'm glad it's over!' exclaimed Biggles sharply. 'Only a homicidal maniac could possibly want the war to continue, but atom bombs, and those poor devils in Hiroshima blasted to kingdom come . . . I know the Japs had asked for it, but what a way to go!'

'Still,' said Algy, 'they've surrendered now, and that'll save an awful lot of lives in the long run.'

'Oh, I know, I know,' said Biggles. 'But, good grief Algy, we can remember how it all began! It seems like only yesterday that I was chucking Mills bombs over the side of a stringbag onto the Hun cavalry on the Western Front, and now it's come to this – one bomber flying in at 20,000 feet, a single bomb that floats down on a parachute, and 30,000 simple citizens go up in a blinding flash. If that's what fighting in the air has come to, I'm glad I'm out of it.'

It was three days after the Japanese surrender, and Biggles and Algy had given themselves a day off from their duties with their Squadron, and driven across from Tangmere to have lunch at English's celebrated oyster bar in Brighton. They had called in to visit Algy's parents on the way. Both were now very old, but as spry and tiresome as ever. Lady Priscilla was in charge of the local branch of the Women's Voluntary Services, and his Lordship had several brand-new bees buzzing within his antiquated bonnet – including a plan for growing soya beans on the home farm at Lewes, and a campaign against the use of chemical insecticides, which he insisted were endangering the wild flowers of his beloved Sussex Downs. Nothing else seemed to worry him – not even the news that his sister, Biggles' mother, was now bedridden in a nursing home in Hove – and after an hour of insecticides and soya beans, the two chums were grateful to escape to Brighton.

Perhaps it was the sight of what he called 'those two old fogeys' – as much as the thought of Hiroshima – that had put Biggles in the dumps, and certainly the lunch itself did little to improve his humour. He still had tender memories of English's from before the war, but war had changed things drastically. Oysters were creatures of the past; instead, they were served a dried-egg omelette, followed by a fish called snoek which tasted, in Algy's memorable phrase, 'like seaboot fried in engine oil'.

But, as Algy knew quite well, the true cause of his cousin's discontent was his feeling that an era in the air was over. Ever since the ending of the war in Europe the Squadron had been starting to run down, and Biggles knew that he would soon be facing what the other ranks called 'Civvy Street'.

'But you can't give up flying, just like that!' said Algy, as he bravely tackled a synthetic-cream meringue. 'Flying's in your blood. Good grief, man, you'd go off your head without a crate to fly.'

Biggles looked up sharply. Age had not dealt unkindly with those boyish features, and at forty-six he still looked ten years younger – this in spite of the fatigue and tension lines around his eyes.

'But what on earth *can* I fly, old boy? Be reasonable. It's not like after the last war when we set up Biggles and Co. together. We were so much younger then, mere boys when you come to think of it, and dear old Smyth could keep the aircraft going with fuse wire and a pair of pliers. Remember Brooklands in those days, and how easy it all was? Now you need a form to brush your teeth, and as for Brooklands, well it's finished. No, old chap, it's very kind of you to be concerned, but I have no illusions. I'm too old, Algy, and there's nothing more pathetic than an old pilot trying to keep up with the boys.'

'Nonsense, Biggles!' Algy interjected. 'You have what all the young whipper-snappers lack entirely – a lifetime of experience.'

'Exactly Algy, and often it feels like a lifetime too. No, I'm retiring, dear old boy. As long as you have no objections, I think that I'll withdraw my bit of capital from the account of Biggles and Co. and find myself a little place to settle down. Dorset or Somerset perhaps. I rather like the country, and I've been thinking lately that I wouldn't mind a crack at writing. Old Bill Johns seems to do all right at the writing game – particularly with my exploits – so I honestly don't see why I shouldn't have a go myself. There's still an awful lot of good material.'

'But Biggles, that's ridiculous,' said Algy. 'Writing's a dog's life, and the majority of writers are as poor as church mice. If you're interested in books, for God's sake be a publisher at least.'

'Well, I don't know, Algy. Possibly you're right. You know, I'm going to miss the Squadron terribly when we're de-mobilised.'

'And how d'you think I feel, old bean?' said Algy solemnly. 'I'm not such a moody sort of cuss as you, but my future's pretty bleak as well, unless I feel like growing soya beans. I had thought of setting up a little air charter firm but, stone the crows, the costs are astronomical.'

'What's astronomical?' chimed in a familiar voice behind them. 'The cost of Gordon's gin, or Biggles' thirst?'

The chums spun round, and there behind them, a dapper figures in a houndstooth check, stood Air Commodore Raymond.

'Caught you both, eh?' he beamed. 'Playing hookie from the Squadron? It'll never do, you know. Dreadful example for the other officers.'

'Well, I suppose I could say the same for you, sir,' replied Biggles, brightening at once. 'But since the war's over, Algy and I were treating ourselves to what one might term a celebration lunch.'

'Splendid!' said Raymond breezily. 'That makes three of us. I'm celebrating too, but not just the ending of the war. The Home Secretary's offered me a fascinating job, and to tell the truth I'm feeling just a little bucked.'

'Congratulations, sir!' said Biggles. 'You must tell us all about it, or is it too hush-hush for the likes of us?'

'Good heavens, no,' said Raymond with a grin, 'but first we must have a bottle of something suitable to celebrate.'

'You'll have a job, sir,' replied Algy wryly. 'Nothing in the bar except wartime gin and pale ale.'

'Oh, I don't know,' said Raymond stroking his moustache, 'I'm something of an habitué here, don't you know, and Fred the barman's an old friend of mine. Fred!' he cried, signalling to a burly character behind the bar. 'Could you come here a minute, please?'

Fred lumbered up and frowned lugubriously.

'Sir?' he groaned.

'Fred, you must cheer up,' said Raymond. 'Happy days are here again, and my two friends and I require a bottle of champagne. What would you recommend? Veuve Clicquot, Bollinger, Dom Perignon? Price no object.'

'You're joking, sir, of course' replied the gloomy barman.

'Well, possibly, but do the best you can, there's a good fellow.'

The barman muttered something and made off, but soon returned bearing, incredibly, a bottle of quite passable champagne.

'That's a good omen, sir,' said Biggles, sipping the first champagne that he had had for several years. 'Now what exactly is this job that all the excitement is about?'

'Something completely new,' the Air Commodore replied. 'At least in theory, although in fact it's not a great deal different from the sort of work that you two characters were doing for me long before the war. You see, the government are worried by the possibilities of air crime in the future. As you probably both know, there's already been a lot of smuggling by aircrews from abroad. Only a month or so ago, a transport pilot based in Germany had the nerve to bring in a complete Mercedes car by air. Just goes to show what can be done. But most of the crime's concerned with smaller stuff that's much more difficult to spot – gold bullion, diamonds, currency. It's quite an industry.'

'One hears about these things,' said Algy drily. 'I can't say that I approve, but on the other hand one can't exactly blame the fellows. They've been fighting while the chaps at home have all been doing very nicely thank you.'

'That's not the point,' said Raymond sharply. 'And what's really worrying isn't what's happening now, but what's going to happen if the trend continues. Already, the airlines are starting up their peacetime routes, and very soon there'll be a crime explosion in the air, unless we do something positive about it.'

'I take it that's where you come in, sir,' interjected Biggles. Raymond nodded.

'Right as usual, James. Yes, the Home Secretary has asked me to take charge of a small department at New Scotland Yard, dealing exclusively with airborne crime. Officially, of course, I'll be responsible to the Commissioner of Police, but in fact I'll be very much my own master. Luckily, I think I know the ropes, but I'll be building up the whole confounded shooting-match from scratch. Hell of a task, but quite exciting in its way.'

'I'll say,' said Algy. 'I rather envy you.'

'Do you indeed?' replied Raymond dividing the remainder of the bottle into the empty glasses. 'Then perhaps you can give me some advice. My biggest problem's simply personnel. Devil's own job to pick the right chaps for this sort of show, and everything depends on that. But your ordinary police detective's not much good and, frankly, the money's not sufficient to attract ambitious youngsters from the services.'

'I shouldn't have thought the money was too big a problem,' said Biggles thoughtfully, 'but what sort of fellows do you really want?'

'Well,' replied Raymond with a smile, 'without trying to flatter you too much, I'd say characters not unlike your own good selves – experienced fliers, no obvious criminal record, house-trained, reasonably healthy and able to hold their liquor like gentlemen. If there are any fellows in your Squadron you can recommend, for Lord's sake let me know.'

'We will, sir,' answered Biggles. 'But I'd say you'll have your work cut out trying to find anyone like us. Algy and I are quite unique. Aren't we Algy?'

'I like to think so, but we'll do our best.'

'Excellent!' said Raymond, beckoning for the bill. 'We'll be in touch then. You can get me at the Yard. Same old number as before.'

The flat in Mount Street hadn't changed perceptibly during the years of war – except to become a little shabbier. Some of the windows had been broken in the bombing, and the sitting room ceiling still bore the scars of an incendiary bomb that nearly set the place alight, but otherwise it all remained as familiar and chaotic as ever. Biggles and Algy had kept it on throughout the war, although they rarely saw it while they were serving with the R.A.F. The indomitable Mrs Symes, now widowed, had moved in. Friends used it for odd nights when they were on leave in London, the rent was paid each month by banker's order, and that was that.

But for Biggles and Algy, Mount Street was home. It was where they kept their old civilian suits, their souvenirs and all the clutter of a lifetime, and now that the war was over, it was to Mount Street that they automatically returned, since their service with the R.A.F. was coming to an end. Officially they were both on 'demobilisation leave', but in effect they were both free men and were glad to be away from Tangmere and the gloomy business of disbanding their beloved Squadron.

At first, the days passed swiftly. They had old friends to see and were occupied getting the flat in order. But post-war London was a somewhat dreary place. Restaurants were bad, theatres packed, and pubs impossible. There was no petrol, so the famous Bentley stayed where it had been throughout the war – on blocks in the coach-house down at Lewes. Algy was trying to keep up a desultory romance with a W.A.A.F. called Anthea. She was another of his large, blonde amazons, and worked as a coding clerk at the Air Ministry in Whitehall, but she too had been affected by the ending of the war. Her eyes were clearly set on marriage, and Algy's were becoming shifty.

'Nice girl, Anthea,' he'd say to Biggles, 'but for some bally reason she keeps nagging me to take her down to Lewes. Wants to meet the parents. For the life of me I can't think why.'

(Finally, the problem solved itself when Anthea transferred her favours to a man called Smith who owned a garage on the Kingston by-pass.)

Within a week or two it was obvious that the cousins were getting on each other's nerves. Algy was restless. Biggles still talked about his cottage down in Dorset, but did nothing about it. Both of them drank too much, and there were several minor rows.

There had been no news from Air Commodore Raymond since they had seen him down at Brighton. Biggles had taken him at his word, and recommended half a dozen names of likely members of his Squadron, but without acknowledgement.

'Drat him!' said Biggles. 'The old devil could at least have telephoned.'

'Forget him,' counselled Algy. 'He must be furiously busy and there's no earthly reason why he should now be bothered with the likes of us.'

But Algy was wrong, and the very next morning an official-looking letter turned up on the breakfast table inviting them both to dinner two days later at the Blazers' Club.

'Ah, James, Algy, quite like old times, what!' exclaimed the Air Commodore as he met his guests in the pillared entrance hall of his exclusive London club. But he was being over-optimistic, for the Blazers' Club, like most of London, had patently seen better days. The walls were dingy and unpainted, and old Tatham, the legendary head-porter (once described by the Prince of Wales himself as 'the discreetest man in London') had died, so it was said, of drink. Raymond, too, was looking distinctly the worse for wear – quite different from the ebullient individual the chums had seen in Brighton just a month before.

'And a great treat to be back here, sir,' said Biggles brightly. 'Both of us have been looking forward to it since we received your invitation, haven't we Algy?'

He nodded 'How's the new job going, sir? We've often thought about you.'

'That's decent of you, Algy,' the Air Commodore replied, with a somewhat weary smile. 'I feel in need of all the sympathy that I can get.'

'Difficult?' asked Biggles.

'Diabolical!' replied Raymond with a fleeting frown. 'Still, I mustn't burden you two with my troubles. Come and have a drink.'

Two pink gins and twenty minutes later, the friends were seated in the famous Adam dining-room, their taste buds quivering in keen anticipation of the treat in store.

'Well now, let's see,' said Raymond as he screwed his monocle in place with a well-remembered gesture, and turned his attention to the menu.

'Rather good, tonight! We even have a choice. Rissoles or shepherd's pie. Frankly, I think I would advise against the rissoles. Never quite sure what goes into them. There are rumours...'

'Quite,' said Biggles, doing his level best to hide the disappointment in his heart. 'I always have been one for shepherd's pie, ever since I was a boy. Good old nursery food. Can't beat it!'

'Absolutely,' echoed Algy sadly. 'Shepherd's pie for me sir, if you please.'

'Capital,' said Raymond. 'And with any luck the wine waiter might be able to produce something suitable to go with it.'

'The Moroccan red, Air Commodore?' inquired the Club *sommelier* respectfully.

'I think so, Warburton. And please make sure that it's at room temperature.'

'Of course, Air Commodore,' replied the old retainer.

The shepherd's pie fulfilled their worst forebodings – 'I think they must have put the poor old shepherd *and* his blinking dog into it,' said Algy afterwards – and the Club Moroccan, even when beautifully decanted, looked and tasted like red ink. It hardly helped the conversation, and the first half of the meal passed in dismal silence, interspersed with ill-directed shafts of Algy's so-called wit. Finally, Biggles could bear the atmosphere no longer.

'What's up, sir?' he asked as gently as he could. 'What exactly has gone wrong with this new job of yours? It sounded absolutely corking when you told us all about it down in Brighton.'

Raymond pushed the grey remains of the shepherd's pie away and shook his head.

'Afraid I spoke too soon, James my boy. A weakness I suppose I've always had. No, it's turning out to be an absolute fiasco, and it's really my own fault.'

'Why on earth?' said Biggles, with quite genuine amazement.

'I can only suppose I'm losing my grip, James, or perhaps I'm just too old a dog to learn the new tricks that the job requires. Truth is, there's an awful lot of jealousy at Scotland Yard – I'm telling you all this in strictest confidence, of course.'

'Of course,' said Biggles. 'But who's being jealous?'

'Most of the senior officers. Quite incredible, you know, that grown men could behave like so many silly spinsters, but it appears that there is considerable resentment at the way I was appointed over their heads. Never had to deal with this sort of thing before and I'm not very good at it. Also, politics comes into it. The airlines are anxious to have their own security organisation and have done their best to keep me out. Can't find the personnel I need, and the long and short of it is that the whole confounded shooting match looks like becoming a disaster.'

'But what about the actual crime wave in the air that you were telling us about the other day? Somebody must be tackling it,' said Algy.

'Ah-ha! You'd think so, wouldn't you dear boy. But not so,' replied Raymond bitterly. 'Tell you the truth, that's what really worries me. I'm not particularly concerned about my own career. I've got my yacht, and it would quite suit me to retire for a bit and cruise around the Med. Might even write my memoirs. But the fact is, Algy, that the actual situation's far, far worse than I imagined. Already with the ending of the war, several really big-time international crooks have moved into the airlines, and there's one area in particular that worries me.'

'What's that?' asked Biggles quickly.

'Dangerous drugs. Chiefly heroin but also morphine and cocaine. There are fortunes to be made by smuggling them from the East through Britain to America, and I know that already quite a large part of the traffic goes by air. That's what I want to stop.'

'Why don't you have a go then, sir?' asked Biggles.

'That's what I want to do, of course,' the Air Commodore replied, 'but I've got no one to rely on. It takes far longer than you'd imagine to train up the sort of organisation we require, and amateurs would do more harm than good. No, what I need are two or three professionals who can really carry through a complicated case, but it's dashed difficult to find them.'

There was a silence, and Biggles looked inquiringly at Algy, who nodded back at him.

'I think I know just the chaps you're looking for,' said Biggles thoughtfully.

'You do, James? Capital! Who are they then?' the Air Commodore replied.

'A pair called Bigglesworth and Lacey. I think I can recommend them.'

There are conflicting versions of the beginning of the Special Air
Police, but the truth is that this world-famous organisation really
began effective life that night in the dining room of the Blazers'
Club. Nothing was put down on paper and the whole
arrangement was informal to a degree. The chums accepted
what Air Commodore Raymond termed 'a temporary attach-
ment' to the force, which suited them ideally. Their work soon
proved to be a logical continuation of the sort that Biggles and
Co. had done for Raymond in the years between the wars.
Neither of the chums really needed the money, which was just as
well, since their official salaries would barely have paid the rent
in Mount Street – let alone their extras and their self-
indulgences, such as Algy's Bentley (a generous petrol allowance
proved to be one of the perks of the job), their dinners at the Ritz
(they didn't like the changes that the war had brought to the Café
Royal), and Biggles' hand-made Turkish cigarettes. On the other
hand, the Special Air Police undoubtedly did give a point and
purpose to their lives, and let them continue with that life of
'flying and adventure' they had always wanted.

All this lay in the future though, and neither of the chums had
much idea what they were in for when they descended from their
taxi on the Embankment at nine o'clock next morning, strolled
past the Duty Sergeant at New Scotland Yard, and had
themselves directed to the sixth floor abode of their new lord and
master.

Somewhat to his chagrin, the Air Commodore had not
succeeded in reclaiming his pre-war office with its splendid view
across the river. (In his absence it had been firmly nabbed by the
Scotland Yard solicitor-in-chief who was determined to hang on
to it.) But, although his surroundings were less imposing than
they used to be, Raymond himself was very much the office
martinet they remembered, and behind his desk that steely
presence was quite different from the discouraged figure they had
dined with just the night before.

'James, Algy, good to have you back on strength!' he barked as
they entered.

'Quite like old times, sir,' replied Biggles with a grin.

'Well, yes and no,' replied Raymond, with a frosty smile. 'I
think you'll find that it's a tougher world than it used to be, and
certainly the gang that we are up against in this heroin racket

seem better organised than any of the criminals we've dealt with in the past. I warn you, it will be a tough assignment.'

'But we really have a free hand, do we sir?' inquired Biggles. Raymond nodded.

'That's what we agreed last night, but I must warn you that I need results. As I told you, everybody's breathing down my neck, and that's not a situation I particularly enjoy.'

'What information do you have already, sir?' asked Biggles.

'Precious little. That's the trouble. All that we have to go on at the moment are the reports we've been receiving from the narcotics branch of the American Treasury Department, complaining that a great deal of their illicit traffic comes through Britain. Also, the Customs boys at Heathrow recently arrested a B.O.A.C. steward, boy by the name of Hinds, with half a million dollars' worth of heroin on him.'

'How was he carrying the stuff?' asked Biggles.

'Hidden inside a tube of shaving cream. Old trick of course, but something about the boy aroused the officer's suspicions and he gave him a thorough going over. Very smart of him. First real break we've had.'

'And what about this steward. Has he admitted anything?' Raymond shook his head.

'That's the devil of it all,' he said. 'I've had a go at him myself, but all that the little blighter will admit is that the stuff was given to him during a stop-over in Rome by a man he'd never seen before. He was to be paid a hundred dollars to deliver it to someone who would meet him in New York.'

'No hint of who this someone was?'

'Of course not. He would be waiting by a news stand in Times Square, but by the time we told this to the F.B.I. the gang had obviously heard their fellow was arrested, and the bird had flown.'

'That's all we've got to go on then?' said Biggles thoughtfully.

'Afraid it is, dear boy. I told you it would be a tough assignment.'

During that first day at Scotland Yard, Biggles and Algy had to spend most of the time doing what Raymond called 'getting acquainted with the ropes'. This included meeting the

Commissioner himself, learning their way around the building, and finding out what resources the Special Air Police had at its disposal. It was soon obvious that there were precious few. Biggles and Algy had been allocated a cramped little office on Raymond's floor, and had to share it with several dark green filing cabinets and a hefty secretary called Brenda. They were also introduced to various other members of the section.

'Not a particularly inspiring set of colleagues, Algy, old chap,' remarked Biggles when they were alone again. 'Most of them seem to be old-time coppers on the verge of retirement.'

'Or else nutters no one else would work with,' replied Algy grimly. 'Poor old Raymond was obviously right when he complained about the jealousies of the senior policemen. Small wonder that he's not been getting very far.'

'Exactly! And you'd hardly say that anybody has given us a particularly rapturous welcome. Still, I suppose it's understandable. New boys like us coming straight in from outside – people are naturally suspicious. All the more reason for us to make a real success of this affair, old fruit.'

'Very high quality, I'd say, so obviously produced in an up-to-date laboratory and almost certainly in Europe. You don't get heroin as good as this produced in the Far East, unless it's in Formosa and Japan, and this hasn't come from there.'

The white-coated figure in the police laboratory looked up from his microscope and showed signs of starting on a lengthy lecture on the manufacture and analysis of heroin. Normally, Biggles and Algy would have heard him out, for Biggles in particular enjoyed listening to experts on their favourite subjects. But, they were in a hurry to get down to interview the steward, Hinds, who was still being held at the Hounslow Police Station.

'I take it that you know the way this stuff's produced?' began the expert slowly.

'Pretty well,' replied Biggles, trying not to sound too know-all, but remembering the time. 'Starts off as opium, doesn't it? The opium is processed into morphine and that in turn is then converted into heroin. I suppose that this required a fair degree of skill and a good laboratory.'

The expert shook his head.

'Not at all. I've known heroin produced in the wash-room of a Chinese restaurant, but it was pretty dreadful stuff. But this is the real mackoy. Ninety-seven per cent pure, which isn't bad at all. That's why I say the processing was almost certainly done in Europe.'

'You can't be more specific?' queried Biggles.

'Afraid I can't. But I'm fairly sure the original opium base came from Turkey. A lot of it does these days, and it's better quality than the Far Eastern stuff. Anything else you need to know?'

'Not for the moment,' replied Biggles diplomatically. 'We're both in something of a rush to interview the joker who was smuggling the stuff.'

'Are you indeed? Then give the blighter hell. This little haul alone would have spelled living death for twenty thousand addicts in America. If I had my way I'd hang anyone caught smuggling heroin these days.'

'And what about the big boys behind the trafficking?' asked Biggles.

'I'd crucify them – except that slow death would be too good for them.'

Despite the analyst's grim imprecations, it was hard for Biggles not to feel a certain pity for the object of his anger. Air Steward Hinds could never have been an impressive figure of a man. Now he was pathetic, with his white face, bloodshot eyes and terrible moustache. Biggles soon realised something else about the wretched fellow. He was terrified.

Biggles and Algy interviewed him at the Police Station, and to begin with, he did little more than repeat the tale he had given Raymond. He hadn't realised what he was doing, and had no idea who was behind the traffic.

'Who was the man who gave you the tube of shaving cream in Rome?' asked Algy.

'No idea,' said Steward Hinds with an adenoidal croak. 'He was just some geyser in a club.'

'What club?'

'I can't remember.'

'Perhaps you'd better try. Whereabouts was it in Rome?'

'I dunno that either. It was just a club. I went there for a drink, with one of my mates, and this character came up and asked me if I wanted to earn myself a hundred dollars. You know the rest.'

Biggles nodded. He did not particularly enjoy the role of police interrogator.

'Who was this "mate" of yours who took you to the club? Was he another steward?'

Hinds gave a jump of pasty-faced alarm.

'I didn't say so,' he said quickly.

'Oh, I know you didn't,' replied Biggles casually. 'I assumed it. Was I right?'

'I'm not saying. I'm not saying anything. Why don't you let me be?'

'All right, we will,' said Biggles gently, 'but you realise you'll go to prison for a pretty hefty sentence? They're getting tough on traffickers, and the men behind it all go free. If you helped us, we could help you in return. It's the big boys we really want – not you.'

'Leave me alone,' groaned Hinds. 'That's all I'm asking.'

'O.K.' said Biggles breezily, 'but don't forget my offer, and thanks for all the help you've given us already.'

'I haven't told you anything,' the steward said with fresh alarm.

'Oh, yes, you have. Rather a lot, as it happens. I'm very grateful, and I'll make sure everybody knows about it.'

'For God's sake, don't do that,' whispered Hinds pathetically.

'Why not?' inquired Biggles.

'Because they'll kill me if they think I've squealed, and I haven't. It's not fair.'

'Fair or not,' said Biggles, 'that's what I intend to say. I've a few friends in Fleet Street and it won't take much to get a paragraph or two into the papers, saying how pleased Scotland Yard is with its heroin investigation and how co-operative a particular steward has been.'

'You'd not do that?' gasped Hinds.

'Wouldn't I?' replied Biggles. 'If you really want me to keep quiet, you'd better trust me, and start talking pretty quickly.'

'So the bluff worked, did it James? I never realised that you were so unscrupulous. You'll make a good policeman yet. Congratulations!'

Air Commodore Raymond bared his somewhat battered teeth into the semblance of a grin and winked at Algy.

'I had to give my word that not a hint of what we've learned will be betrayed to anyone,' replied Biggles somewhat stiffly.

'Of course, of course,' said Raymond quickly. 'But why d'you think the blasted man's so scared? Who's he afraid of and why, when he'll soon be safe inside one of His Majesty's prisons?'

'Good question, sir,' said Biggles, 'and I've a hunch that the answer is an important key to this whole business. Even when he broke down in the end, Hinds wouldn't tell. But there's no question but that he was totally convinced that if these people find out he's betrayed them, he will die.'

'Never heard such nonsense in my life,' said Raymond jocularly. 'You make it sound like something from the Mafia.'

Biggles nodded silently. 'It's possible. We just don't know, and Hinds didn't dare say, who these people were. I'm not even sure he knows himself, but whoever they are they've put the fear of God into him.'

'But good grief, man,' exclaimed Raymond, 'this is England.'

'And we're dealing with a full-scale international racket.'

'That's true,' said Raymond thoughtfully. 'And what else did you learn from Hinds?'

'Oh, quite a lot really, sir. It seems he did know the name of the bar all the time. It's called the Jockey Club and it's on the Via Veneto in Rome. Several other stewards are in the racket. He wouldn't tell me who they were, but apparently they've been visiting the Club for quite some time and picking up the drugs for delivery later in New York. It's all carefully worked out and on delivery they're paid immediately through an account in Switzerland.'

'And did he tell you anything about this contact that he had in Rome?'

Biggles shook his head.

'Not a great deal, I'm afraid. They would arrive there at a certain time, and when they left, the drugs would be waiting for them in a hold-all in the cloakroom. They'd get delivery instructions over the telephone back at their hotel.'

'So they would never see a soul?'

'Nobody, except for a man he called "the Barber" who was sometimes at the Club and who seemed to be a sort of strong-arm man for racketeers. Hinds disliked him, and described him in some detail. He's bald, extremely fat, and the second finger of his left hand is missing.'

'Well done,' said Raymond, brightening considerably. 'You've made a start. All we need now is proof so that we can smash this racket once and for all.'

'And that's what I intend to get, sir,' replied Biggles, thrusting out his chin.

Late next afternoon one of the few aircraft on the strength of the Special Air Police – a single-engined Proctor monoplane which had seen better days – landed at Rome Airport with Biggles and Algy at the controls. It had been an uneventful flight, and both the chums had found the Proctor rather a boring little aircraft after the fighters they were used to from the war. All the same, it was wonderful to be in the air again after so many bleak months without an aeroplane to fly, and the flight across the Alps had been magnificent. The prospect of Rome excited them as well – if only as a change from a wet London spring – and both chums were in the best of spirits.

No sooner had they taxied the little aircraft off the runway than they were being given a true Roman welcome by an old friend, Brigadiere Grattapalli of the Italian Carabinieri, the official Roman representative of Interpol.

"*Ciao* Biggles, Algy!' boomed the Brigadiere, an impressive man with a silver-braided uniform and a magnificent handlebar moustache. He put his arms round Biggles and gave him an effusive hug, which Biggles found a shade embarrassing.

'It's good to have you both in Rome at last! I can return a little of that hospitality you gave me in London. Now, Biggles, listen carefully. I know a little trattoria off the Corso where you get the finest pasta in the whole of Rome. Not even my old mother makes it better. Then we can have asparagus, spring lamb, a bottle or two of good Barolo and perhaps some strawberries and a little cheese to follow. What do you say, old friend?'

Biggles nodded just a trifle warily.

'Marvellous, Luigi. But we're not here on a gastronomic trip. We've work to do.'

'Work?' laughed the cheerful Brigadiere. 'What is that old English saying? All work and no food makes Jack a small boy. Tomorrow we will work. Tonight we eat.'

He had a big official car, and Biggles and Algy made their entrance into Rome in style, – at ninety miles an hour, with siren screaming. Biggles had had the sense to book a good hotel – at the top of the fashionable Spanish Steps, with a fine view of Rome below its windows. As he explained to Algy, 'It's most important to give a good impression to Italians. They call it *figura*, and they rather judge a fellow by the sort of *figura* that he makes.' Certainly it appeared to work with Brigadiere Grattapalli, who seemed impressed and rather grateful when Biggles asked him in to have a drink with them.

'Listen, Luigi,' Biggles said, when the door had closed behind them and they were sipping their Campari sodas with the whole of Rome stretched at their feet. 'I'm afraid this dinner of yours must wait. Tonight there's business to attend to and we need your help.'

'Of course, Biggles my old friend,' replied the Brigadiere with sadness in his voice. 'My wife keeps telling me I eat too much. What can I do for you? All the men at my command are yours.'

'Extremely kind of you,' said Biggles quickly. 'Now first, I want a man arrested.'

'Is that all, my friend?' the Brigadiere replied with an enormous grin. 'You mean we're giving up our dinner just because of that? Who is this *cretino* who is so important?'

'A British airline steward by the name of Burt, Charles Burt. His plane will be landing at the airport in forty minutes' time. He will be staying here one night, and tomorrow morning flying back to London, then on to the United States. He is said to look rather like me, and I would like him brought here straight away, then guarded safely for the night and put back on his plane tomorrow morning.'

'No trouble,' said the Brigadiere, 'but what has he done, this Charles Burt of yours?'

'Nothing,' said Biggles, 'but it's because of what I know he will do if he's left free in Rome tonight that I want him safely under

264 BIGGLES—THE AUTHORISED BIOGRAPHY

lock and key. You see, Luigi, I intend to take his place, and from
then on my life will be entirely in your hands.'

By the standards of the Via Veneto, the Jockey Club appeared
distinctly dull when Biggles entered it just before eleven o'clock
that evening. Outside, there was a neon sign with a horse's head
in bright mauve lights, but the actual bar was down a flight of
steps, and rather dimly lit. Not surprisingly, Biggles felt distinctly
ill at ease in his airline steward's uniform as he picked himself a
table and beckoned to the barman for a drink. Burt was a thinner
man than Biggles, and the trousers pinched uncomfortably
around the waist, but apart from this he made a reasonable-
looking British airline steward, and in the dim light of the Jockey
Club, no one would notice the deception.

The bar was fairly full, and Biggles had to wait some time for
his Scotch and soda. He sipped it slowly and looked carefully
around him. He was the only person there in uniform and most of
the customers appeared to be tourists or good-time girls.
Somebody played a Frank Sinatra record on the juke-box – a
singer Biggles particularly disliked – and he was just about to
drown his irritation in another drink, when a voice said, 'Mr
Burt?'

Biggles looked up to see a short bald man of extraordinary
girth grinning at him from the entrance to the bar. Biggles
nodded and the fat man ambled over.

'Can I join you for a drink?' he asked.

'Please,' said Biggles affably.

As the fat man lowered himself into his seat, Biggles' eyes were
drawn to his hands. They were large and very white, and the left
hand was without its second finger.

'I must introduce myself,' the fat man said. 'I am known as
"the Barber".'

'And so you see,' concluded Biggles an hour and several whiskies
later, 'I'm just not risking it. My old pal Hinds told me it would
be all right, and that I'd get $100 for my trouble, but he's in
prison. It's not good enough.'

The Barber smiled like a humorous blancmange and shook his head.

'You are too nervous, Mr Burt. There is no danger. Your friend Hinds was a fool. He took unnecessary risks, but even so he will be well looked after. We are a powerful organisation, Mr Burt.'

'That cuts no ice with me, and $100 is ridiculous. You've heard the rumours?'

'What rumours?' asked the Barber softly.

'That the new British Special Air Police are on to this. They've got two men in Rome at the moment. I even know their names.'

'Who are they, Mr Burt?'

'Now, not so fast,' said Biggles quietly. 'I need money. A lot of money. Far more than $100. And you can tell the people that you work for that if I don't get it, I am going to this Special Air Police and giving them everything I know.'

'That would not be wise, Mr Burt,' said the fat man with a gentle smile.

'Wise or not,' replied Biggles, 'I need money, and I know enough about the people that you work for to know that you can pay me properly. A thousand dollars for the names of the men from the Special Air Police, or you're in for trouble.'

The fat man shook his head and sighed.

'Somehow, I don't think that we're the ones who are in for trouble, Mr Burt,' he said.

Biggles was certain he was being followed as he left the Club, and made a point of keeping to the brightly lit main thoroughfares as he began walking back to his hotel. He was aware of the danger he was in. Indeed, he had purposely created it, but he was counting on the gang's anxiety to find out all about the Special Air Police to stop them killing him – for the time being, at any rate.

All the same, he could not be sure. Perhaps the Barber, or his bosses, would decide to annihilate him without more ado. Perhaps a shot from a passing car, or a blow on the back of the head – anything. It was not the situation for a squeamish individual.

But Biggles had been in tougher scrapes than this before, and if there was one thing he was used to it was the art of taking a calculated risk with his life. He gave no sign of fear, but strolled from the Via Veneto down the hill towards the Piazza Barberini. Late though it was, the street was fairly crowded, and he had almost reached the main piazza when a car screeched up behind him, somebody leapt out, and something hard was thrust against his ribs.

'Into the car before we plug you, mister,' said an Italian voice with a strong Brooklyn accent. Biggles made no effort to resist. Someone already in the car grapped his arms, then the door slammed, and the car roared off into the Roman night.

A hood was thrown over his face, but he judged that the journey lasted half-an-hour or so, and just before the car stopped, there was a drumming noise as if they were driving over cobble stones.

'Get out,' barked the same voice when the car had skidded to a halt. The hood was still held firmly round his head. Someone kicked him, and he nearly fell. Then, with men each side of him and his arms twisted painfully behind his back, he was dragged into a house and up some stairs. He heard a door slam heavily behind him, then a thin voice with a harsh Italian accent said, 'Remove his hood!'

Biggles blinked, both with surprise and at the unaccustomed light, for he was standing in an enormous ballroom. Chandeliers sparkled from the ceiling and were reflected in the gilt and the mirrors on the walls. Straight in front of him stretched a long table, with perhaps a dozen men seated around it. The man who had ordered the removal of his hood seemed to be presiding, and it was he who now began the questioning.

'What do you know about the agents from the British Air Police who are now in Rome?'

Biggles bit his tongue and shook his head.

'Come now, Mr Burt, if that's your real name, don't play the fool with us. I give you just one chance to speak.'

Once again Biggles shook his head.

'Very well. Aldo – hurt him, just a little.'

Biggles tensed, and then as someone wrenched his arms behind his back, pain seemed to sear his body like an electric shock.

But he knew that at all costs he must spin things out, until Algy and the Brigadiere arrived. It had been carefully worked out that they would shadow him – then follow his abductors to their destination. Right now, they should be closing in on the house.

'Why should I tell you anything?' he said defiantly, gritting his teeth and staring his interrogator in the eye. He was a grey-faced skeleton of a man with closely cropped white hair and a nervous tic that distorted the left-hand corner of his mouth.'

'Aldo! Again please, but a little harder!'

This time the pain was more extreme and an involuntary groan burst from Biggles' lips.

'All right,' he said, 'I'll talk, but tell your thug to let me be. And I'd like a chair to sit on please, for this is going to take time.'

The skeleton allowed himself a ghostly smile.

'Such British arrogance – I find it rather pleasing! Aldo, a chair for the gentleman. And now sir, let us hear please what you have to tell us – but quickly. My friends and I have business to attend to and we can't stay here all night.'

'For God's sake, Brigadiere,' shouted Algy, as the army-green Alfa Romeo hurtled past the Colosseum in the rain, 'we can't have lost them just like that.'

'Patience, Signor Lacey! Patience!' the Brigadiere replied. 'They must have a racing driver in that car of theirs to have given us the slip like that, but never fear! Our other cars will pick them up, now that they have the car's description.'

'They'd better,' answered Algy grimly. 'While we're looking for them, they could be doing anything to Biggles.'

'Somehow I think that Signor Biggles can look after himself quite well. Ah, this sounds like something now.'

As he spoke, the high-pitched squawk of the police radio filled the car, and the two armed carabinieri in the seats behind them muttered something Algy failed to catch.

'The car's been sighted heading down the Via Appia Antica, and two of our squad cars are following.'

He switched the radio to transmit and gabbled an order in Italian.

'There,' he said. 'I've told them to see where the car goes, but not to close in till we arrive. We haven't lost much time, Signor.

Biggles will be all right and we can catch the whole gang as he intended. We must get moving!'

Saying this, he put his foot down hard and the powerful car sped like a bullet through the deserted streets of the ancient city. Another message came across the radio.

'We're in luck, Signor Lacey,' said the Brigadiere. 'They've taken Biggles to a big house in the country just beyond the airport, and we've already got the place surrounded. Also, we know who owns the house.'

'Who's that?' asked Algy.

'A Neapolitan called Don Gesualdo. He's very rich and quite notorious. As a young man he was in America with the Chicago Mafia, and for years he was one of Lucky Luciano's top men. Just before the war, the Americans deported him back to Italy, and while we've known that he was running a lot of the black market here in Rome, we've not been able to pin anything on him. I'm not surprised he's mixed up in narcotics. It all makes sense – and thanks to your friend Biggles, we can catch him and his gang red-handed.'

He shouted something in Italian to the men behind him, and Algy heard the deadly click of sub-machine-guns being cocked. Then came the racket as the car hit the cobbles, and a few minutes later they screeched up beside a long white wall. The Brigadiere leapt out, and raced towards the big steel gates that led to the house. There was a small microphone beside them in the wall, and he bellowed, 'Open up! Carabinieri here!' There was no reply, but all the lights suddenly went out in the house beyond. He beckoned to one of the carabinieri and pointed at the gate. The man fired a short burst at the lock, and the big gates suddenly swung open.

By now, a dozen or so more Carabinieri had joined them, and at a cry from the Brigadiere they stormed the house. As they did so, gunfire rattled from an upper window. One of the carabinieri fell, but some of them were firing back, and the rest rushed on, Algy with them.

It didn't take them long to clear the house. Someone found the mains switch and the lights went on. They found the ballroom with the tables and the chairs in place, and soon Algy saw a dozen or so grim-faced gangsters with their hands above their heads being herded out into the courtyard. But, to his horror, there was no sign of Biggles.

'Where is he? Where's Biggles?' he called to the Brigadiere.

'No sign of him anywhere,' the Brigadiere replied, with the beginnings of alarm in his voice. 'We can't find Don Gesualdo either.'

There was a pause, then someone shouted in Italian from the far end of the house, and a spotlight from one of the police-cars jabbed the darkness. Three figures had emerged and stood there silhouetted in the light. One was fat, another very thin. Both of them held guns, and they were shielding themselves with a familiar stocky figure – Biggles.

'Give yourselves up! You can't escape!' shouted the Brigadiere.

'If you come any nearer,' croaked the thin man in his high-pitched voice, 'we shall be obliged to shoot the Englishman.'

'Don't be a fool, Don Gesualdo,' shouted the Brigadiere. 'You can't get away.'

'Oh yes we can,' came the reply. 'I require one of your cars, and we're taking the Englishman with us hostage. Any nonsense from you and he dies.'

Silence followed, and Algy could see the obvious emotion on the Brigadiere's face as he struggled to decide exactly what to do. It was a hideous decision for a man to have to take, and for a moment Algy thought he would refuse. But finally, he nodded.

'All right, Don Gesualdo,' he replied, 'but not a hair on the head of the Englishman must be harmed.'

'That's up to you and your policemen,' the Neapolitan calmly answered. The next minute the two gangsters had dragged Biggles into one of the police cars, and were roaring off the way they had come along the cobbled road. The carabinieri followed them at a discreet distance, with Algy and the Brigadiere in the leading car.

'Where d'you think they're heading for?' shouted Algy.

'It looks as if they're making back for Rome,' the Brigadiere answered, then a moment later added, '*Dio mio*, no, they're not. They're heading for the airport, Signor Lacey.'

The sky had cleared, and from an altitude of 6,000 feet, Algy had no great difficulty keeping the tail light of the plane he was following in sight. It was an underpowered Piper Cub and even the old Proctor had the edge on it for speed.

No sooner had the gangsters and their hostage reached the airport than they had commandeered the plane, apparently with Don Gesualdo at the controls. From a distance, Algy and the Brigadiere had watched as the Barber had ordered Biggles aboard at gunpoint, and the little plane had taken off and headed south. Luckily the Proctor was nearby and had been refuelled and overhauled on arrival, so that within minutes of the gangsters' take-off, Algy, the Brigadiere and two heavily-armed Carabinieri were in pursuit.

Few pilots could have managed Algy's task of following another plane at night without arousing the suspicions of the pilot, but Algy's memories of stalking night-flying Fokkers on the Western Front thirty years before stood him in good stead. He held his height advantage, worked out the pilot's blind spot behind his tail, throttled back, and kept his distance from the tiny light that danced ahead.

The compass showed that they were flying south-south-east on a course that took them down the coast as far as Naples. For a while, he thought that he had lost the Cub, and all but panicked, imagining that it had crashed or landed somewhere. But, when he climbed, he saw the little plane a long way off, sticking to its course.

By now the dawn was coming up, and soon he could see the rim of the ascending sun gleaming across the waters of the Straits of Messina that divide the toe of Italy from Sicily.

'So that's where they're making for!' said Algy.

'But naturally,' replied the Brigadiere. 'Don Gesualdo is an important man in the Mafia, a *capo mafioso*, and the Mafia have their real strength in Sicily. I would imagine that he has some secret stronghold there, and knows that once he reaches it he's safe.'

'And Biggles?' Algy asked.

The Brigadiere shook his head. 'Once he's served his purpose as a hostage, I'd not give a great deal for his chances.'

As the Brigadiere spoke these fateful words, Algy realised the time had come for him to act decisively if he wished to see his chum alive again.

Away on the left horizon he could see the smouldering tip of

Etna, Sicily's volcano, and the land beneath was mountainous. He looked at his petrol gauge, and was disturbed to see that they had barely twenty minutes' flying time remaining. The small town of Adrano passed beneath them, then Paterno, and from his map Algy could see that they were flying thirty or so miles inland from the city of Catania. Then the mountains were behind them, a stream appeared below, and Algy realised the Cub was going down to land.

He could see what looked like a ruined castle set in a dusty plain. There seemed to be some sort of runway and as the Cub came in to land he could see a lorry already racing up to meet it. He increased the Proctor's speed, and changed course so that he now approached the air-strip from the sun. The altimeter read five thousand feet. Below him, he could see the Cub had taxied to a halt, and ant-like figures were scurrying towards it. 'Hold tight,' he shouted to the Brigadiere above the screaming of the Proctor's engine, 'we're going down.'

It was a terrifying power-dive, the sort that Biggles had himself made something of a personal speciality. The throttle was wide open and the aircraft was hurtling downwards like a bomb. The noise was frightful, and from the corner of his eye, Algy saw the Brigadiere cross himself with fear, and one of the men behind him started shouting to the Virgin Mary.

Everything depended now on absolute precision as the ground came rushing up to meet them. Algy knew the Proctor wasn't built for treatment such as this, but it was a risk he had to take. By now, he could see a small group gathered round the aircraft on the landing strip and sighted the plane straight at them. They were already looking skywards with alarm, but the sun was in their eyes and dazzled them. Then one man lost his nerve and ran. Another followed, and in that last split-second of the dive, Algy could see them scattering in all directions.

Then, and only then, with the Proctor a few hundred feet above the other aircraft, did he wrench back on the joy-stick, and it seemed as if the plane missed the ground by inches. It was a virtuoso piece of old-style aerobatics, the sort of stunt that brought the crowds to their feet at air displays before the war, but Algy was stunting now for something more than thrills. As the Proctor had gone zooming off he spotted a familiar figure on the ground, as Biggles hared away from the other members of the gang. But clearly he still needed help, to stop the gang regrouping.

Algy had never acted faster in his life. Round came the Proctor in a terrifying bank and once again he swept down on the terror-stricken men below, all but hitting them with his undercarriage. Then came a loop-the-loop and then another dive, at the end of which he flattened out, banked gently, and brought the aircraft into the neatest landing of his life, barely twenty yards from where Biggles stood.

'Quick!' shouted Algy, opening the cockpit door, but Biggles needed no encouragement – especially as the gangsters had now recovered their nerve and were already firing at the plane. A bullet struck the engine cowling and went whining off. Another hit the windscreen.

'Good to see you, dear old chap!' panted Biggles as he heaved himself aboard. 'Nicest little exercise in dive-bombing I've seen in years.'

'Never knew that you could run so fast, old thing,' replied Algy with a grin. 'And now I think perhaps we'd better make ourselves scarce, unless we want to face your friends' machine-guns.'

As Algy spoke, the rattle of a Browning gun sounded above the racket of the engine, and a neat line of holes appeared in the Proctor's wing.

'With any luck we've just sufficient petrol to get us over to Catania. And from then on it's up to you, Brigadiere.'

'After the last ten minutes, it will be a holiday to deal with the whole Sicilian Mafia,' answered the ashen-faced policeman.

They never did find Don Gesualdo. The canny old *capo mafioso* simply disappeared in that island which was always famous for its disappearing tricks. But all the other members of the gang were caught – except for the Barber, who was killed in the gunfight when the castle in the plain was raided. It was there, too, that the Carabinieri found the up-to-date laboratory where the heroin had been produced.

Biggles and Algy had their dinner with the Brigadiere in the little restaurant off the Corso – it was the best food they had eaten since before the war – and the next day they flew back to

England. The smuggling of heroin on British planes was over, for a while at least, and the Special Air Police had finally achieved its first resounding victory.

11

The Missing Missile

The triumphant conclusion of the heroin affair by Biggles and Algy was an historic achievement in its way. Not only did it keep the British airways free from narcotics smuggling for several years to come, but it also gave the Special Air Police what it desperately needed – a genuine success.

The chief beneficiary, of course, was the man at the top – Air Commodore Raymond. The Press began to sit up and take notice of the new department at the Yard, particularly after the Home Secretary himself had praised it in the House of Commons. The budget doubled almost overnight, and most important of all for the Air Commodore, his status at the Yard improved immeasurably. He could ignore the jealousy of senior detectives. Respect for him increased among the lower orders and finally, a few months later, when the Yard's solicitor-in-chief conveniently expired, the Air Commodore regained his old room with its view across the river.

One would have thought that all this would have made him grateful to the chums – and probably he was, deep down. But Raymond was a strange and contradictory man. In adversity no one was a better ally, but when things started to go well he was inclined to grow suspicious, a tendency that had increased with age. Biggles' theory was that he hated owing anything – particularly gratitude – to anyone. Perhaps he was also worried that a successful subordinate like Biggles might one day prove a

threat. This was ridiculous, of course. Apart from the genuine
respect that Biggles had always felt towards the older man, the
last thing he wanted was a desk job with its never-ending load of
tiresome responsibilities. Like Algy, Biggles remained what he
had always been – a man of action, and a dedicated flier. He had
no interest in power, wealth or titles. He despised politics and
politicians more than ever and was honestly delighted that a man
like Raymond should be once again enjoying the success and
influence he patently deserved.'

But at the same time, Biggles would have been less than human
had he not felt slightly miffed at the way that he and Algy were
beginning to be treated by their boss. No further invitations to the
Blazers' Club had followed the big Old Bailey case which marked
the end of the narcotics network. (Six airline stewards were sent
down with hefty sentences, and the Special Air Police were
warmly commended by the judge.) And whilst Biggles was
reasonably satisfied to be offered the rank of detective inspector
in the force, he was incensed to hear that all that Algy would
receive was the position of detective sergeant.

'It's all right, dear old boy,' Algy had remarked when the news
arrived at Mount Street in a cool official letter from the Police
Establishments Department. 'Sergeant suits me rather well, and
what does it matter what a fellow's called these days? Pass me the
marmalade, there's a good fellow.'

But Biggles could not imitate his cousin's nonchalance.

'That's gratitude for you!' he fumed. 'And after all these years
and all we've done for him. *He* doesn't risk his bally neck. He
simply sits on his backside and orders us around. And then he
offers you the rank of sergeant! It's an insult, Algy, and I'm going
to tell him so.'

'Now, now, calm down,' said the pacific Algy. 'I rather like to
be back among the other ranks after all these years, and Mrs
Symes will certainly be most impressed. Her husband was a
police sergeant, you know. But seriously, Biggles, what does any
of this matter? Raymond's a tricky character – always has been.
But the main point is that if we stick with him, we'll get the sort of
work that we enjoy, and frankly Biggles, what's the alternative?'

'Oh, I know all that,' said Biggles, 'but I hate meanness in a
man.'

'Forget it. But I do suggest we concentrate on getting a few of our former chums to join us. That would improve the atmosphere no end. There's Ginger Hebblethwaite for instance.'

'But Ginger's in New Zealand running that bally sheep-farm he inherited.'

'Wrong again, old scout. He's back. He rang last night when you were out. Apparently he couldn't stand the place. Got bored to tears, and so he's sold the farm and is back here with his tail between his legs looking for something he can do. He sends you his regards.'

'I should jolly well think he does,' roared Biggles, all thought of his annoyance with the Air Commodore instantly forgotten. 'Where is the wretched fellow?'

'Staying at the Cumberland Hotel.'

'The devil he is! You should have asked him round. His room's still here.'

Algy grinned and nodded cheerfully.

'Just what I thought myself. I've ordered him to report here this morning. That's probably him at the front door now.'

'Great suffering catfish!' expostulated Biggles as his former protegé appeared. 'I'd given you up to the Antipodes for good. How wonderful to see you!'

'And wonderful to be back, I can tell you Biggles! What's been happening in my absence?'

'Oh, all sorts of things. You'd be surprised! But before we start getting down to that, we must get a few facts straight. Firstly, you're coming back here to the flat to live.'

'If you say so Biggles,' replied Ginger with a grin.

'I do say so, and so does Algy. Secondly, have you got a job?'

Ginger shook his head.

'Well, you have now, you lucky lad. You're joining an outfit called the Special Air Police. Your country needs you, Ginger. And for that matter, so do we.'

As luck would have it, Ginger's arrival at New Scotland Yard coincided with a period of furious activity, most of which has now been faithfully recorded by Captain Johns. As commercial travel in the air advanced, air crime kept pace with it – sabotage, smuggling, mail-bag thefts, and kidnapping by air – the list was endless, and wherever a British aircraft was involved, the Special Air Police became involved as well. This rather suited Biggles, who enjoyed nothing more than disappearing to the far side of the globe at a moment's notice, and the full range of his investigations was phenomenal.

One moment he and Algy and the ebullient Ginger would be off to Central Africa investigating the suspicious loss of a private monoplane with a wanted criminal aboard. A few weeks later, they were in Canada investigating a horrendous series of disasters caused by bombs planted in the luggage holds of domestic aircraft. They collaborated ceaselessly with their French opposite number, Marcel Brissac of the French Sûreté, and sometimes found themselves in Rome, where they were always glad to work with the cheerful Brigadiere Grattapalli of the Carabinieri. Early in 1949 they were in the Antarctic, successfully salvaging a lost cargo of bullion from a wreck, a mission Captain W. E. Johns describes in *Biggles in the Antarctic*. Later that same year they helped foil one of the earliest attempts at hijacking a commercial aircraft, when Biggles flew to Addis Ababa and overpowered a demented Ethiopian who was threatening to blow up a British aircraft on the runway.

It was shortly after this that another of Biggles' favourite cronies from the past joined the Special Air Police. This was the deceptively lethargic, monocle-wearing, former racing driver, Lord Bertie Lissie. At first, the Air Commodore had jibbed at the idea of having a member of the House of Lords on the payroll as an ordinary Air Constable.

'Really James,' he complained to Biggles, 'the man's a member of my club. How can I possibly expect him to obey my orders? And besides, a chap like Lissie as a humble member of the Force – it's quite ridiculous!'

But Biggles patiently explained that Bertie never used his title, and that his appearance as a sort of stage-door-Johnnie was deceptive.

'The man's a splendid flier,' he explained, 'and a thoroughly good egg. Besides, he was a member of the Squadron in the war, and I can't speak higher of a man than that.'

'All right then, James,' replied the Air Commodore with somewhat weary resignation. 'You win, as usual, but people are beginning to complain that the Special Air Police is simply Biggles' Private Army.'

'Well, what's wrong with that, sir?' countered Biggles with a grin. 'It seems an excellent idea to me. If only I could persuade old Nobby Smyth to join us, it would be just like old times again.'

The Air Commodore groaned.

'Please James, spare me that. But since you mention it, what has happened to your old mechanic?'

'He's become very rich,' said Biggles. 'Started his own aircraft component business down at Farnborough, and he's become a regular tycoon – Rolls-Royce, house in the South of France, the lot, so I think you're pretty safe.'

'Well, thank the Lord for that!' the Air Commodore replied.

During these years of expansion of the Special Air Police, there was one vital area of activity which by necessity has had to remain secret until now – the special assignments Biggles and his friends performed for the British Secret Service. For, although Air Commodore Raymond was officially on the staff of the police, he still maintained his contacts with the spy world he had known in the past. And sometimes, when the need arose for the special skills that Biggles and his friends possessed, they would find themselves seconded to some hush-hush operation which had nothing much in common with the routine work of the Special Air Police. Biggles always would object to being called a spy – 'sounds like some seedy fellow in a dirty mackintosh', he used to say – but the fact was that he still enjoyed the Secret Service world, and nothing gave him greater pleasure than the undercover tasks that sometimes came his way. Many of these are still affected by the Official Secrets Act and so will have to wait for their historian. Others are of marginal interest to the actual story of Biggles' life, but there is one affair which can finally be revealed and which is of such importance to the life of Biggles that it requires treating in some detail – the conclusion of his involvement with his oldest enemy of all, Hauptmann Erich von Stalhein.

Captain Johns himself described the beginning of this strange episode in a book which he entitled *Biggles Buries a Hatchet*. It was an appropriate title for the story of the curious events which ended with Biggles and a task force from the Special Air Police rescuing his old enemy from a Soviet prison camp on the island of Sakhalin, off the mainland of Siberia.

The story behind von Stalhein's imprisonment is strange enough. With the ending of the war, the wily Prussian had thrown in his lot with the Secret Service of the Peoples' Federal Republic of East Germany, and for several years had worked against the West. This was not entirely surprising, for although an old-style Prussian aristocrat, von Stalhein was a citizen of East Germany by birth, and the undercover world of spies and sabotage remained his natural habitat. He played a vital part in building up the East German Secret Service – but then his star began to wane. He was clearly not a dedicated communist, and several somewhat costly failures in the early sixties sealed his doom with his new political masters. (Biggles himself had played his part in his enemy's eclipse when he foiled von Stalhein's attempt to recover an important cache of secret documents which a former Nazi Intelligence Officer called Wolff had hidden in Jamaica. It was shortly after this that von Stalhein was arrested, tried by a people's court in Lubeck and finally consigned to the grim work-camp at Sakhalin.)

Quixotically enough, one of von Stalhein's final acts before arrest had been to get a warning through to Biggles of an attempt by the Russian K.G.B. to assassinate him. Why he did this is anybody's guess. Perhaps some lingering sense of honour made the Prussian feel that murder in cold blood was indefensible. Perhaps he was getting back at the people who arrested him. Whatever lay behind it, von Stalhein's warning certainly saved Biggles' life. One good turn deserved another, and Biggles, Algy, Ginger and Bertie Lissie undertook the sea-plane flight to the island of Sakhalin which resulted in the spectacular release of von Stalhein himself.

But although it seems a slightly touching story – as indeed in many ways it was – there was far more to this 'burying of the hatchet' with von Stalhein than was revealed at the time. Whilst Biggles and his chums went off to rescue von Stalhein for reasons of gratitude and, as Biggles put it, 'really for old time's sake', Raymond was quite immune to all such sentimental motives. His cold, calculating brain had worked out in advance that the Hauptmann would be quite a prize – and a much-needed feather in the cap for British Intelligence in its competition with the American C.I.A., and once von Stalhein was in British hands, Raymond was determined to exploit him to the full.

Biggles, who now had few illusions about his boss, had guessed as much from the beginning, and did his best to save von Stalhein from the excesses of the faceless men in the British Secret Service. Indeed, he had quite a set-to with the Air Commodore on the subject just a few days after his return from the hell-hole of Sakhalin. Von Stalhein was still recovering from his ordeal in the carefully guarded mansion outside Brighton, which the Secret Service used to house its most valuable guests, and when Biggles asked to see him, he was greeted with a blank refusal.

'Sorry, James old chap! Quite out of the question I'm afraid,' the Air Commodore replied.

'But why, sir?' Biggles asked with some asperity. 'I've known von Stalhein almost all my life, and now we've rescued him I'd like a chance to see that he's all right.'

'Oh, he's all right – you can set your mind at rest on that score, James.'

'But ordinary good manners would demand that I should visit him. Besides, sir, I know von Stalhein well enough to know that if he's going to spill the beans to anyone, he's far more likely to do so to me than to some cold-blooded interrogator from British Military Intelligence.'

'James,' sighed Raymond wearily, 'do me a favour. Just stop being sentimental. You know as well as I do that von Stalhein is the biggest prize we've had for years. The professionals are dealing with him, and can't have chaps like you around to muck things up. So just forget von Stalhein. You don't owe him anything – after all, you saved the wretched fellow's life.'

'That's not the point, sir, He's a human being, and an officer and a gentleman, whatever else he may have been – which is more than I can say for these damned "professionals" of yours. I'm appealing to you, sir, to let me visit him.'

'Quite out of the question, James,' the Air Commodore replied, slapping the desk with his stainless steel ruler. 'And now, if you'll excuse me, I have work to do.'

'It's a really dirty business,' Biggles fumed that night when all the chums were gathered in the flat.' 'And when I tried to reason with him he dismissed me like the confounded office-boy. I tell you, Algy, it's the last bally straw. I'm resigning.'

'Oh, calm down Biggles,' answered Algy, sipping a lethargic Scotch and soda, 'what's the use of that? It'll make no difference. Von Stalhein knew what he was in for when he came back with us. The Secret Service boys have got to do their job, and he'll be O.K. in the end. When they've finished with him, they'll get the plastic surgeons to give him a nice new face and find him a job somewhere under a new name – which is more than the other side would have done for us. You can save your indignation for someone other than the Hauptmann Erich. Don't you agree, Bertie?'

Bertie Lissie nodded.

'Quite,' he drawled. 'Frankly, can't see what all the fuss is about. Always thought von Stalhein was a pain in the bally neck.'

'Of course, he was,' retorted Biggles. 'He was the most determined enemy we ever had, but that's precisely why I feel responsible for him. If you can't see that, Bertie, then I'm sorry for you. What do you think, Ginger?'

Ginger Hebblethwaite shrugged his shoulders.

'As far as von Stalhein goes,' he said, 'I think that I agree with Bertie. He'll be all right, and if he isn't I don't think I'll lose much sleep. But honestly, Biggles, what does worry me is Raymond's attitude to us, and I suspect that that's what really worries you as well.'

'What d'you mean, old boy?' asked Biggles.

'Well,' replied Ginger thoughtfully, 'it seems to me that Raymond has been taking us too much for granted. In the old days he was fairly human, but he's becoming impossible now, and since the department's been successful – largely thanks to us – he's been treating all of us like blinking sheep. I don't like it – and I sympathise with Biggles.'

'Thanks Ginger,' replied Biggles sombrely. 'You can see it if the others don't – although I do mean what I said about von Stalhein. No, Algy, I've had enough of Raymond and his confounded job. If you chaps can take it, then good luck to you. Perhaps I'm just a bit old-fashioned, but I don't like the way that things are going, and I've no intention of being treated like a blinking doormat at my time of life.'

'You mean you're serious about resigning?' Algy said, aghast.

'Absolutely, dear old boy. Never been more serious in my life.'

Biggles' resignation from the Special Air Police was carefully hushed up, although the papers did their best to make a story of it. There were several angry scenes when journalists tried to nobble the Air Commodore at his flat in Duke Street, St James's, to question him about it, and there was speculation in one Sunday newspaper that the Special Air Police was undergoing what it called 'internal difficulties'. There were even rumours that Algy Lacey, Ginger Hebblethwaite and Bertie Lissie were about to leave as well in sympathy with their old friend. But these rumours came to nothing, and Biggles insisted that the whole argument was purely between himself and Raymond.

'No point at all in dragging you into it, old scout,' said Biggles stoically to Algy. 'It's not your battle, and besides, the Special Air Police would utterly collapse if all of you pulled out, and that would never do.'

'But Biggles,' Algy said with genuine concern, 'what are you going to do? You need looking after, and without your chums to keep an eye on you, you're simply bound to end up in some frightful pickle.'

Biggles smiled and patted Algy's arm.

'There, there, my dear old chap,' he said. 'It's decent of you to speak like that, and I do appreciate it, but I'll be all right, and it's not as if we'll not be seeing one another. I'll still be living in the flat – if you'll put up with me – and I'm probably too old for the temptations of this wicked world. Besides, I've got a job already, and I'm rather looking forward to it.'

'You've got *what?*' exclaimed Algy incredulously.

'A job. Rather a good one as it happens, and with somebody you know.'

'I don't know anybody in his right mind who'd offer you a job, old scout,' said Algy smiling with relief. 'Who is it?'

'Our old pal Nobby Smyth. He rang me up the moment he heard that I was leaving Scotland Yard. They always say that when you're up against it you discover who your real friends are.'

'Well, good for Nobby,' answered Algy. 'Always did say he was one of the best. What sort of job?'

'Oh, he requires what he calls a sales executive. Blowed if I know exactly what it means, but I gather I'll be a sort of salesman for his firm. Bags of foreign travel, fat expense account, nineteen-year-old secretary and a company car – the usual racket. I'm rather looking forward to it all.'

'That's absolutely capital! You can become a prosperous fat businessman at last. It'll rather suit you, Biggles.'

'Suit me be damned!' growled Biggles. 'Still, it's better than the dole, and as Nobby says, I've got a lot of contacts in the airline business round the world. You never know, one day I could even be touting you for business.'

'You might at that. By the way, one thing I meant to ask you. How did old Raymond take it when you handed in your resignation? You never told me.'

'Not much to tell you, dear old chap,' replied Biggles with a frown. 'The blighter wouldn't see me. Said we had nothing to discuss. Rum way of behaving when you think of it, but if that's the way he feels...'

Algy's doubts nothwithstanding, Biggles was surprisingly successful as a businessman, and much as he pretended to despise his new-found trade, he actually enjoyed himself. One week he would be off to Bangkok discussing aero-engines with an old acquaintance who was now the chief executive of Thai Airlines. The next he would be in South America selling fuel tanks to Argentinians, and from there he would double back to Washington to look up several contacts with the Pentagon. Old fliers form a sort of international trade union, and everywhere that Biggles went he found friends who would go out of their way to help him and provide fresh business.

At the same time, his relations with his new boss could hardly have been better. Business was booming, and although it was several years yet before Nobby Smyth received his inevitable knighthood, he was already quite a power in the land. It was a situation that could easily have been difficult – particularly with somebody as touchy as Biggles – but fortunately Nobby Smyth possessed considerable respect for his old C.O. He also realised his value to the firm, and Biggles was allowed to be very much his own master, with his own small office in the Smyth Organisation

H.Q. in Park Lane, and all the other business perks that he expected – including the effective use of the company's De Havilland Dove whenever he felt like flying.

The only drawback to this whole new way of life was that he inevitably started to lose contact with his chums in Mount Street. He saw them frequently of course, and often treated them to lunch. His kit remained in his old den at the flat, and when he was in London he used it as his home. But, although no one would admit it, the fact was that Biggles was in a very different world now from the others. They had the excitements of their work, he had his business to attend to and, naturally, their paths diverged. It was hard to tell how much this worried Biggles. Sometimes it seemed as if he really missed the thrills and camaraderie of days gone by.

'Lucky blighter,' he would say to Algy as he donned his dark blue suit and grabbed his briefcase for an early-morning business conference. 'It's all right for you, off playing cops and robbers. *I've* got to earn my living by the sweat of my blinking brow.'

But as time went by, he seemed less and less interested in the work of the Special Air Police – so much so that sometimes, when Algy started telling him about his latest exploits, Biggles would have to hide a yawn. Algy noticed this of course, and became upset, but there seemed nothing anyone could do to set things right, and he resigned himself to the gloomy thought that their old partnership was over. The final disappointment came when Algy mentioned summer holidays. For as long as either could remember, Biggles and Algy had always taken them together, and Algy not unnaturally assumed that this would be happening again. His three weeks' leave was due at the end of June, and he mentioned it to Biggles.

'Sorry, old scout, you'll have to count me out this year,' he answered somewhat shiftily.

'Count you out, Biggles? Why? Doesn't Nobby give wage-slaves like you a summer holiday? I'll have to have a word with him!'

'No, don't do that old boy,' said Biggles quickly. 'Fact is that Norah's invited me down to Cannes for a sort of house party affair, you know.'

'Norah!' expostulated Algy. 'Who the hell's Norah?'

'Norah Smyth, old boy. Nobby's wife. You must remember

her. It's rather expected of a chap to go when his employer and
his wife invite him specially. Confounded bore, of course. You
simply must excuse me.'

So that year Algy went on holiday to Trinidad with Bertie Lissie,
while Ginger held the fort at Scotland Yard with several of the
new, less colourful members of the Force. And Biggles was at
Cannes, living the so-called 'good life' to the hilt. In fact, it rather
suited him. The Smyths were extremely rich by now and
entertained extensively. Not all their guests were Biggles' cup of
tea, but most of them were mixed up in the world of aeronautics
so he was not exactly bored. His old pal, Wilkinson, last seen
before the war reorganising the Bolivian Air Force, and now a big
wheel in a South American airline, was staying at the Eden Roc
with his fourth and very nubile wife, and Marcel Brissac of the
Sûreté was camping *en famille* near Cannes. Biggles wined and
dined, mixed business gossip with reminiscences of the past, and
generally enjoyed himself. He even gambled once or twice at
Monte Carlo, recalling as he did so those far-off days before the
war when he and Algy had been young and carefree, spending
the profits they had made from Biggles and Co. in the gilded
precincts of the *salles privées*. He missed Algy now, and one night
when he and Nobby Smyth had spent a happy evening on their
own, dining together at the *Chapon Fin*, and losing a small fortune
at roulette, he became slightly maudlin on the subject of his
ancient crony.

'Dashed pity that it had to break up as it did, Nobby old thing,'
he said gloomily. 'Of course I couldn't be more grateful to you
and Norah for everything you've done, but you must know how I
feel'.

Nobby nodded sympathetically. He was a rather dapper figure
now in his midnight blue tuxedo, and Biggles found it hard to
picture him as the young mechanic in the greasy overalls he had
originally known at Maranique.

'Truth is, you know Nobby, I miss the past – flying, risking
one's neck, facing an honest enemy, even being broke. It was fun,
wasn't it? Whereas now . . . Confound it, Nobby, I'm getting old.'

'Nonsense Biggles,' answered Nobby loyally. 'You're the best
sales executive we've got, and I've a surprise for you. I've been

talking things over with Norah and the Board. We'd like to offer
you a full directorship.'

'A what?' expostulated Biggles.

'You heard me. We'd like you on the Board of the Smyth
Organisation What do you say about it, Biggles? We'd be very
honoured.'

'Poppycock, my dear old chap!' replied Biggles gruffly.
'You're being very kind, but I couldn't possibly accept.'

'But why not? You must excuse me speaking to you like this,
but the past is over. Algy and Ginger have their lives to lead – and
so do you. Why not allow yourself to make the best of it?'

Biggles nodded.

'Well, we'll see,' he said. 'Any objection if I take a day or two to
think things over?'

'None at all. And now perhaps we should be getting back to
Norah. Oh, incidentally Biggles, perhaps we shouldn't tell her
quite how much we lost tonight. Women like Norah worry about
such things.'

But when the two men returned to the apartment on the
Grande Corniche, they found that the motherly Norah Smyth
had other matters on her mind.

'Biggles,' she said excitedly, 'so there you are! Someone's been
ringing you all evening from London. Seemed in quite a state.
He's trying you again at midnight.'

'Stone the crows, Norah!' answered Biggles wearily. 'Can't
they ever let a fellow be? Who on earth was it?'

'He refused to leave a name, but I think I recognised the
voice.'

'Really Norah? That's extremely clever of you. Who was it?'

'Your old friend, Air Commodore Raymond.'

'Ever thought of joining the old Club, James?' said Air
Commodore Raymond. 'Now you've become so high and mighty
you might well consider it.'

'Join the Blazers' Club, sir? But I'm hardly in that league.
Dash it all, it's the most exclusive club in London.'

'Come, come James! You mustn't underrate yourself, and
since I've become chairman of the membership committee I

think it can be arranged without much difficulty. It could be useful to you now you know, my boy.'

It was the following evening, and Biggles was already kicking himself for allowing Raymond to talk him into breaking off his holiday to fly back to London at a moment's notice. His old boss had always known how to twist his arm – and on the telephone had made it sound a matter of life and death. Biggles had done his best to sound extremely cool. (Indeed, until that moment he had always sworn he'd never speak to the Air Commodore again.) But once the rasping voice began to talk of 'a matter of some urgency I must discuss with you', Biggles really had no chance. The Smyths had been most understanding when he had said apologetically, 'Well, I suppose I'd better see what the old devil wants'. Nobby had insisted that he took the Dove, and even drove him into Nice next morning in his own Rolls Royce.

But, now that Biggles found himself tackling a tornedos in the all too familiar surroundings of the Adam dining-room, he wondered what the fuss was all about. One thing he knew for sure, the Air Commodore hadn't summoned him from the Riviera simply to propose him for the Blazers' Club. But, as usual, Raymond had to take his time, and it was not until the port was circulating that he allowed himself to speak his mind.

'Quite like old times, eh what?' he said, polishing his monocle on his napkin. 'We miss you, James, you know.'

'That's kind of you, sir', Biggles answered coolly.

'And when one thinks of the successful coups we've planned here in this very club. That record breaking flight you made to Singapore, the von Sternberg business – you know, James, it takes you back.'

'Quite,' said Biggles, wondering what was coming next.

'But something has cropped up, something that could make everything we've done before pale into insignificance.'

'Really?' said Biggles, trying to disguise his natural interest, but knowing Raymond's habit of hyperbole.

'I've finished with the Force, sir,' he replied. 'Ginger and Algy and young Bertie Lissie are extremely competent, and this new job of mine is most demanding.'

'Balderdash, James, and you know it!' thundered Raymond. 'Chaps like us never leave the Service. You have a duty, James, a patriotic duty, and I'm appealing to it now.'

'To do what, sir?'

'To help us. You're the only one who can.'

'I like to think I'll always do my duty,' Biggles answered stiffly. 'But tell me how.'

'Well James, it's difficult. You see, I realise I owe you an apology over the von Stalhein business. You were quite right and I was wrong. All through his debriefing last year he was asking to see you. I, as you know, refused. Since then he's been living in America. The C.I.A. officially requested a chance to interrogate him too, and we agreed. He's been at their place in Vermont. Just a few days ago I heard from them. They're in a devil of a state.'

'That makes a change,' said Biggles grinning cynically.

'No, but seriously, they are. And all because of our old friend, von Stalhein. You probably don't know, but von Stalhein's proved a mine of information to the West – not only over the usual names of agents and spy networks that one expects from a defector, but also for specific information on the East's offensive hardware. He's an incredible chap, von Stalhein – sharp as they come and memory like an I.B.M. computer.'

Biggles nodded.

'You don't have to tell me anything about von Stalhein, sir. I've never underestimated him. Why has he put the wind up our friends in Washington?'

'Because of what he's been telling them about the Russian missile system – and in particular about their new top secret effort known as the Budnik.'

'Go on,' said Biggles.

'He didn't mention it to us, but the Americans kept on at him and from what I hear, the Budnik is the weapon to end all weapons. It's compact – about twelve feet long – but it has nuclear capability and flies above the speed of sound. More to the point, it's ninety per cent accurate up to three thousand miles, and proof against all known methods of detection and defence, including radar. So, you can understand why the Pentagon's in such a tizz.'

'Absolutely,' Biggles answered. 'It presumably puts the Russians streets ahead of anything the West possesses and upsets the apple-cart between the super-powers. Very tricky.'

'And to make it trickier still,' said Raymond, 'the East is stolidly denying its existence in the current round of disarma-

THE MISSING MISSILE 289

ment talks in Prague. You can see the Budnik's what our allies
call "a hot potato".'

'Of course,' said Biggles nodding shrewdly, 'but why are you
telling me this? I can't believe you brought me back from France
simply to lecture me on Cold War strategy.'

'Ah, sharp as ever, James!' the Air Commodore exclaimed,
lighting a Fiorita from the eighteenth-century candelabra in the
middle of the table. 'No, dear boy, there's a method in my
madness, for it seems that you, and you alone, have suddenly
become a key figure in this whole schemozzle. According to von
Stalhein, our good friends the Russians did quite a lot of early
testing of the Budnik near a place called Sukhumi on the Black
Sea, and eighteen months ago one of them went adrift – some sort
of design fault. But instead of heading for the Caucasus, it
doubled back and landed somewhere in Turkish Anatolia.
Naturally, they tried to get the damned thing back but it was
difficult. To start with, Turkish Anatolia's an enormous place
with a lot of virtual desert, and no one seemed to know where the
Budnik landed. Secondly, the Russians had to be extremely
careful with the Turkish government. They're not the best of
friends, and if a gang of Russians had gone scouring the country
looking for a top-secret missile of this sort, there'd have been hell
to pay. So, the Russians turned for help to their old friends, the
East Germans, and between them they cooked up a so-called
archaeological expedition to Eastern Turkey. Von Stalhein was
in charge of it.'

'And did they find what they were looking for?' asked Biggles.

'Officially not,' replied the Air Commodore. 'Remember that
by then von Stalhein knew the skids were under him, and that he
had his private doubts about his Russian masters. No, after two
months scouring the country, he and his expedition returned to
Germany and he reported there was no sign of the missing missile.
Not long after this, he was arrested, and you know the rest.'

'What's all the fuss about then?' Biggles asked impatiently.

'Well,' replied Raymond, pouring himself another glass of
vintage port, 'according to an excitable gentleman who came to
see me yesterday from the C.I.A., von Stalhein is now saying that
in fact he did find the Budnik – or at any rate, knows where it is.
He claims that it's intact and lying in a shallow mountain lake a
hundred or so miles to the south of Lake Van. He wouldn't tell

290 BIGGLES—THE AUTHORISED BIOGRAPHY

the Russians, but the Americans are clamouring for him to help
them find it. He's apparently agreed on one condition.'

'And what's that, sir?' asked Biggles tersely.

'That you go with him. Since you rescued him, you're the one
Westerner he trusts.'

'Biggles, by all that's good and holy, how wonderful to see your
ugly mug again!' ejaculated Algy as he saw his old pal sitting in
the briefing room at Scotland Yard. 'I thought you were still on
your business jamboree in the south of France! What are you
doing here? We were dragged back from Trinidad for some
confounded new assignment the old boy's cooked up. It wouldn't
be anything to do with you, by any chance?'

'Afraid it is, old thing. At least, indirectly. It looks as if you're
going to have to put up with me again on a temporary basis for a
week or two. Sorry and all that, but the boss-man will explain
when he arrives. I think you'll find we're off to Turkey – along
with Ginger and the admirable Bertie. Raymond and I have
been completing the arrangements. It could be rather interesting
– oh, and this time we'll have an extra member of the team.'

'Not Nobby Smyth? That would be terrific!'

'No, Algy, no such luck. He's far too busy rolling in the shekels
like the sensible fellow he is. No, the old firm's got a new recruit.'

'Cripes, Biggles!' Algy groaned. 'Not another of Raymond's
wonder-boys, still wet behind the ears? You could have spared
us that!'

'No Algy, this one's all right. Tough as they come and you
know him rather well. Hauptmann Erich von Stalhein.
Apparently he felt that since he couldn't beat us, he'd better join
us.'

Algy was still recovering from shock when the Air Commodore
arrived – along with Ginger Hebblethwaite and Bertie Lissie –
and the morning passed in detailed planning of the operation.

'No need for me to emphasise the desperate importance of this
enterprise,' said Raymond. 'You could say that the future
security of the West depends on your success. James here has very
decently agreed to take command.'

He looked around and gave his cold reptilian smile.

'I take it, gentlemen, that that will meet with your approval?'

Three heads nodded their assent in unison.

'Excellent! James seems to think the ideal aircraft for the operation would be a four-engined R.A.F. Hercules. It's slower than a comparable jet but it has all the space and lifting power you'll need and it's adaptable and rugged, and can land almost anywhere. Bertie and Ginger, you've been trained for under-water operations and will be using standard Naval breathing gear. We've been discussing the retrieval of the missile from the lake-bed with the experts in the Royal Marine Commando, and they seem to think that it will present no great problem. They have their apparatus – lifting tackle, inflatable dinghies and so forth – and one of their best men, Major William Armstrong, will be travelling with you and taking charge of that side of things.'

'Is he O.K., sir? Algy queried.

'I wouldn't suggest him if he weren't,' said Raymond with distinct acerbity. 'Bit of a rough diamond, like all Marine Commandos, but you can take it from me, my boy – Bill Armstrong knows his onions. Now, there's one further matter of considerable importance. I've been in contact with the Turkish government, and Turkey, as you know, is officially one of our N.A.T.O. allies. But – and it's a big "but" I'm afraid – the last thing that they want is trouble with their Russian neighbours. So, very wisely in the circumstances, the Turks have said that they don't want to know about you. The Hercules will have civilian markings and it's up to you to be efficient and discreet. The last thing we can possibly afford is a diplomatic incident, and if anything goes wrong – and pray the Lord it won't – the Foreign Office will disown you, and so, I'm afraid gentlemen, will I. Is that understood?'

'Fair enough,' said Algy, somewhat unenthusiastically. 'But there's one more important question – von Stalhein. I appreciate the need for working with him, but are we certain we can trust him? Just suppose he were a double agent after all? It's not impossible.'

Raymond nodded.

'Nice point, Algy, and the answer is we can't be absolutely certain. We've checked and double-checked his story – so has the C.I.A. – and we're sure as dammit that he's genuine, but we've all been in this racket long enough to know that no one can be absolutely trusted.'

'But surely, sir,' said Biggles staunchly, 'with someone like von Stalhein, whom we rescued from a Russian gaol ourselves, that's inconceivable? Besides, we've checked his story about the Budnik and we know the Russians lost one exactly when he said.'

'Agreed,' said Raymond, 'but since Algy asked the question, I have given you the proper answer. Trust nobody!'

'Where do we meet him, sir and when?' asked Ginger.

'In three days' time in Istanbul. That should give you time to finish all your preparations, and you can fly to Turkey on Friday morning. The Americans will be delivering him there late that same afternoon. He will be staying that night at the Park Hotel under the name of Ingrams. You're at the Istanbul Hilton. That way, you'll have a chance to meet him properly, finalise your plans, and have a good night's sleep and make an early start next morning. Any further questions?'

Algy shook his head.

'You seem to have thought of everything, sir.'

'I do my best,' replied the Air Commodore, with a modest smile.

'Well, what d'you think of her, old scout?' bawled Algy over the racket of the thundering engines.

Biggles raised a gnarled thumb.

'Not a bad old ship,' he shouted back. 'She's certainly no bally Concorde, but she's solid, I'll say that for her.'

As he spoke, the last of the great grey pinnacles of the Alps had disappeared behind them in the glare of a perfect north Italian morning, and the chequerboard of Lombardy stretched green and succulent to the horizon. Ginger, Bertie and the heavy-featured Major Armstrong were sitting in the crew seats and behind them, in the big plane's cavern of a cargo-hold, were stacked the packing-cases with the battery of equipment they required – rubber dinghies, two long wheel-based Land Rovers, underwater apparatus, lifting gear and a small armoury of weapons – 'just in case', as Biggles put it when he had supervised the loading earlier that morning.

Everyone was in the best of spirits, for jaunts like this were now becoming rare, and it was wonderful to be united as the chums had been in days gone by. Biggles was particularly euphoric, and however much he might pretend to be a businessman, there was no mistaking the expectant gleam in his hazel eyes at the prospect of a spot of action. He was still wonderfully preserved, and as Algy glanced towards that chiselled profile framed in the battered wartime flying helmet, he found it difficult to credit all the years that they had been together. The face was just a little fuller than when he had first caught sight of it at Maranique so many years before – only its enemies had changed: Once there were Halberstadts and Fokker triplanes. Now, that same face was questing missiles that could fly above the speed of sound. But there was something reassuring in the rock-like indestructibility of his oldest friend, his voice, his sayings, even his outbursts of ill-humour. No, he told himself, they don't make chaps like Biggles any more.

Algy was interrupted from his reverie by the first gleam of the Adriatic under the starboard wing-tip. It was considered far too risky to fly over Yugoslavia and Bulgaria – there was no point in offering the opposition even the faintest chance of tracking them – so they continued down that narrow sea, skirted Albania, then went grinding on across the mountains of northern Greece. Algy was navigating and he got all the old airman's satisfaction when Biggles brought the lumbering aircraft in to a perfect landing at Istanbul slap on schedule, late in the afternoon. Thanks to some neat liaison with the British Embassy, the Hercules was taken charge of by a troupe of swarthy gentlemen in white mechanics' overalls, and twenty minutes later a discreet saloon was dropping the four friends by the outlandish gridiron of the Istanbul Hilton with its view across the Bosphorus.

'Everything gone like clockwork, eh, old scout?' said Biggles as he stretched himself and stepped out on his balcony to take in the stupendous view. 'Always a bad sign if my experience is anything to go by. Still, let's make the most of it. Ring for room service, Algy, there's a good fellow. What're you all drinking, Ginger, Bertie? How about a bottle of good champagne to start this whole affair in style?'

None of the chums took much persuading, and the bellboy was soon speeding on his way to execute their bidding. Two minutes later he was back with a glistening bottle on a silver tray.

'Mr Bigglesworth?' he said inquiringly.

Biggles nodded.

'A package for you, sir – left at reception a few minutes ago.' He handed Biggles a neatly tied brown parcel addressed in a florid European hand. 'Anything else that you require, sir?'

Biggles shook his head and tipped the bellboy handsomely. 'I'll deal with the champagne myself,' he said, then added, as he turned to Algy, 'Who the devil can be sending me a present? No one's supposed to know I'm here.'

'Perhaps it's a little keepsake from old Raymond,' Algy replied. 'You never know quite how the old thing will behave these days.'

'More likely to have been left by von Stalhein for services rendered,' chuckled Ginger. 'Here, let's have a look.'

But Biggles was already tugging at the wrapping.

'Deuced difficult to open,' he exclaimed. 'Why will people use this blasted sellotape?'

In fact it was the sellotape that saved his life, for suddenly he froze, and then a moment later dashed across the room and hurled the parcel over the balcony.

'What the devil are you up to, Biggles?' asked an appalled Algy, who thought that his old chum had suddenly gone mad.

The answer to his question came from the street below – a quick explosion followed by the sickening noise of falling glass – and when the chums peered down, they saw a cloud of thick black smoke rising from the pavement.

'Crikey, Biggles!' Algy said, aghast. 'Thank God your reactions are as good as ever. That would have blasted us to kingdom come.'

Biggles nodded grimly. 'There was something ticking inside it, and half-a-pound of fulminate of mercury by the smell of it. Nice little visiting card to welcome us to Istanbul.'

'But who the heck d'you think left it?' Bertie asked.

'Somebody who knows exactly why we're here and disapproves of what we're up to, my dear Watson,' replied Biggles, breaking the tension with a somewhat artificial smile. 'We were about to have a drink. I think we need it,' he added, pouring the foaming liquid with a rocklike hand.

'Mr Ingrams,' said Biggles, thrusting out his hand. 'It's good to meet you after all this time. I trust you're well.'

'Ah, Mr Bigglesworth. The pleasure is entirely mine.'

The one harsh voice was softened by an unmistakable New England burr, and neatly brushed back grey hair had replaced the aggressive Prussian haircut Biggles knew so well. The duelling scars had disappeared, the nose was different and the gold-rimmed spectacles completely changed the aspect of those flinty eyes. Grey-suited, faintly hesitant, he could easily have been a prosperous American on holiday. Only the ramrod back and something familiar about the chin told Biggles that this was certainly von Stalhein.

One of the oddities about the Park Hotel – a heavily Germanic building in the centre of the city – is that it has its foyer on the ninth floor, and its restaurant on the first, so when introductions were completed, the party solemnly descended in the lift and entered the all but empty restaurant together. It was an awkward gathering to start with – despite the abundant Black Sea caviar Biggles had ordered in an attempt to liven the proceedings, for apart from the strangeness of working with a former enemy, the little expedition's recent brush with death had made them nervy, and no one felt like small-talk.

'Not good, not good at all,' von Stalhein said, shaking his head as Biggles told him of the bomb attack. 'You were all lucky to escape, but we must assume from this that the Russians know exactly why we're here. The Turks had no idea, I take it, who left the parcel at the Hilton?'

'None at all,' said Biggles. 'That's the devil of it, and the police are taking it quite seriously. This sort of trouble with the authorities is just what we didn't want.'

Von Stalhein sucked his teeth – a mannerism Biggles remembered of old.

'You've no idea, of course, how this leak occurred?' he asked finally.

Biggles shook his head. 'Far too many people knew about this project from the start. Our people, the Americans...' He raised his hands resignedly.

'And me' said von Stalhein softly. 'Come now, gentlemen, we're in this together, and we must be frank with one another. If I were in your place I'd be suspicious and there's not much I can do to reassure you.'

'I'd believe your word as an officer and a gentleman,' said Biggles stiffly.

'Ah, but would you in your heart of hearts? And even if you did, what about the others?'

'Well, what the devil do we do?' replied Biggles angrily. 'Call the whole thing off because the Russians have found out about us, and we don't trust each other? That's ridiculous.'

'But it could be the wisest course,' said von Stalhein slowly. 'Whatever happens, we are going to be up against a most determined enemy. Perhaps the odds against us are too great. You must decide.'

A long silence followed his remarks, broken in the end by Bertie Lissie.

'Never heard such blinking nonsense in all my life,' he drawled. 'If this confounded missile thing is as important as everyone says, how can we possibly back out? Von Stalhein here says that he knows exactly where it is, and we're equipped to bring it back. For God's sake, let's get on with it and cut the cackle!'

Biggles nodded.

'My own thoughts in a nutshell, dear old chap,' he said calmly. 'It's not as if we haven't faced a spot of danger on and off in days gone by. Agreed, Ginger, Algy, Bill?'

The others nodded as one.

'Excellent. Then that's decided gentlemen!' He faced von Stalhein. 'That's our decision, and we'll trust you until you give us cause to do otherwise. Should that happen, you can expect no mercy from us. Fair enough?'

'Perfectly,' replied von Stalhein, with something of the old Prussian glitter in his eyes.

'One thing we can do,' continued Biggles, 'is to win at least a certain element of surprise. We'd planned to fly at dawn. It mightn't be a bad idea to act as if that's still the plan, but meet here at eleven and depart at midnight. Oh, and one further thing, von Stalhein – as I'm sure you know, people who work with me call me Biggles – that goes for you as well.'

Von Stalhein gave one of his rare, slow smiles and finally replied, 'O.K., Biggles. And my name's Erich.'

It was raining heavily and a bitter wind was blowing from the Golden Horn, but take-off went without a hitch. Algy was navigating and had checked his course in detail with von Stalhein, while Biggles secured last minute clearance from the Turks – despite objections from a desperately anxious security officer from the British Embassy.

'Confounded diplomats are all the same,' growled Biggles as he eased the lumbering aircraft off the runway and the chums saw the rainswept lights of Istanbul recede below them.

'How long d'you think we'll take?' he bawled to Algy.

'Six hours at least,' came the reply. 'We should arrive just after dawn. According to Erich there's a landing place that we can use about ten miles from the lake, but there's a track of sorts that'll be all right for the jeeps. Once we arrive it shouldn't take too long. This time tomorrow night we could be on our way back to England, home and beauty.'

'Touch wood quickly,' Biggles answered with a grin. 'Now, the rest of you had better get some sleep,' he shouted. 'It looks as if we'll have a busy day ahead of us.'

Biggles was in his element at last, but as the great plane thundered eastwards at a height of 20,000 feet, more than one anxious pair of eyes was following its course on radar screens along the way.

'Sorry, Bertie,' Biggles said, 'but it seems that you're the odd man out. Somebody must stay behind to guard the plane, and Algy and Ginger both have work to do with their underwater gear when we reach the lake.'

'Suits me, Biggles,' replied the peer, stretching a lengthy leg and yawning. 'Never have been one for water. That's why I joined the R.A.F. you know. I'll be O.K.'

'Good man!' said Biggles, patting him affectionately on the shoulder. 'Are we ready, Bill? Let's go!'

It was barely six o'clock, but an enormous orange-coloured sun was already glaring like a bloodshot eye across the plain and lifting the shadows from the distant mountains. The flight had passed without an incident and, half an hour before, Biggles had brought the aptly-named Hercules in for a perfect touch-down on the boulder-strewn plain. The chaps had breakfasted on steaming coffee from the galley, and everything was ready. No sooner had the aircraft rumbled to a halt, than the rear door on the fuselage swung open, ramps went down, and the first of the laden Land Rovers rolled out with Armstrong at the wheel. Algy followed in the second. For the journey, Biggles and von Stalhein travelled with Bill Armstrong, and Ginger in the second vehicle with Algy.

It proved a bumpy, often scary, journey, for the track was barely fit for mules and at times the Land Rovers were slithering and grinding round hairpin bends with nothing but the sheerest drop beneath them. Several times the passengers got out to push and Biggles was grateful to have von Stalhein there to lead the way.

'Not far now, Biggles,' he would say imperturbably, as he put his shoulder to the rear of the Land Rover and helped to heave it back onto the track, its wheels spinning on the shaley surface of the mountainside. Puffing away beside him, Biggles could do little but admire the older man's resilience.

But finally the track began to level out, and soon they were travelling across a sort of rocky up and covered with patchy scrub and boulders. They had to ford a stream and finally reached a headland, and the water of the lake lay blue and very clear below them.

'This is the place,' von Stalhein said with brief excitement in his cold grey voice.

'And where's the missile lying?' Biggles asked him quickly.

'Just over there, beneath the cliff in about twenty feet of water. Come, I'll show you!'

Von Stalhein jumped down from the cab and, sure-footed as a mountain goat, went bounding off towards the cliff, with the remainder of the expedition straggling behind him. When they finally caught up with him he was standing on the cliff-edge, pointing down towards the surface of the lake. Biggles was the first to join him.

'It's all right, Biggles,' he said softly. 'It's still there. Can you see it? Just beyond those dark grey rocks.'

Biggles strained his eyes, but to start with could see nothing but the shimmering of sunlight on the rock-strewn lake-bed. Then, he spotted it – a long, grey, fish-like object half buried in the mud. This was the missile that could hold the West to ransom.

'Can you see it, Bill?' shouted Biggles excitedly. 'Will it be difficult to salvage?'

'Ought to be straightforward,' said the expert sagely. 'Of course, you can't say for sure until you get down to it. We'll bring the dinghies round and have a closer look.'

The hard work really started then. The sun was blazing down as they brought the Land Rover round to a shingly beach a mile or so away and started to unload. They had compressed air to inflate the dinghies but the lifting gear was heavy, and once more Biggles was amazed by von Stalhein's toughness as he helped Bill Armstrong manhandle it in place. Then Ginger, Algy and Bill Armstong donned their rubber frogman's gear and soon the two grey boats were churning up the placid waters of the lake.

Once they were above the missile, Armstrong went overboard to inspect it, and Biggles could see him clearly in the limpid water, like a large black frog with only the line of bubbles from his breathing mask to show that he was human. Soon he was surfacing and clinging to the dinghy's side to report to Biggles.

'No real problems as far as I can see,' he gasped. 'We should be able to fix a cable round her nose and tail fin, then winch her up and beach her.'

'Good man,' said Biggles with a grin. 'In you go Algy, Ginger – and for Pete's sake get a move on. We've a lot to do and I'd like to be on our way back home this afternoon.'

'Right you are, Biggles,' shouted Ginger as he fixed his nose-clip, and with a hefty kick submerged and followed Algy to the bottom of the lake. Biggles watched fascinated as the three black-suited frogmen started the slow business of fixing the nylon cable round the Budnik.

'Ever done this sort of thing before, Biggles?' asked von Stalhein as they waited in the gently rocking dinghy.

'Never, thank God,' said Biggles fervently. 'The air's my element. Anything in the water – or under it – gives me the creeps. What about you?'

'Oh, I don't mind too much,' von Stalhein answered, in that strange, formal way he had of speaking. 'During the last war, you know, I took a special course with German U-boats and they used to tell me drowning was a very easy death. Does the idea of dying worry you then, Biggles?'

'Not any more,' said Biggles with a faint smile. 'As long as it's fairly quick.' He glanced across the glittering surface of the lake, to where the heat-haze made the far-off mountains shimmer in the heat. 'Funny conversation to be having in such a peaceful spot,' he added. 'Wonder how they're getting on down there?'

As if in answer came a tug from the sea-line that connected one of the dinghies with the bottom of the lake, and when Biggles peered through the water he could see Armstrong signalling that the cables were secure and it was time to pull away.

The dinghies were connected with a specially devised platform on which the small hand-winch was bolted. Biggles took one handle, von Stalhein the other, and when they heaved they felt the sudden lift as the tail of the Budnik escaped the mud and floated free. Then the nose came up, and slowly, turn by turn, the long black shape was lifted until it hung between the dinghies like a captive whale. Armstrong passed a final cable round it to secure it, then raised his hand to Biggles – who could see the smile of satisfaction on his face beneath the frogman's mask. The next moment he was heaving himself aboard – followed swiftly by Ginger and Algy.

'Fine piece of work. Well done!' exclaimed Biggles, as he started the first of the outboard motors. 'All that we've got to do now is deliver this piece of scrap-iron back to Raymond and our duty's done.'

The other outboard started and the ungainly vessel turned in a wide arc and headed back towards the vehicles.

'Couldn't have been easier,' chortled Ginger. 'And you know, Biggles, I thoroughly enjoy this underwater business. You ought to have a go yourself. You know you'd . . .'

Suddenly his voice cut short, and the smile froze on his lips.

'D'you hear what I hear?' shouted Algy.

Biggles nodded imperturbably.

'Thought it was too good to be true,' he muttered. 'Chopper, by the sound of it, eh Ginger?'

Ginger throttled down the outboard motors and now they could all hear the steadily increasing thwack-thwack-thwack of an approaching helicopter

'Could be a Turkish government machine,' said Algy hopefully. 'They use them to patrol the border further north.'

'And it could be my Aunty Fanny,' answered Biggles rudely, as the outline of a big twin-engined Russian military helicopter came over the nearby range of mountains. For a while it hovered like a cautious dragon-fly over the far end of the lake. Then slowly it began to edge towards them.

'I'd give everything I've got for a Lewis gun, old chap,' said Algy.

'Wouldn't do much good, I fear,' replied Biggles. 'We're at the blighter's mercy and he knows it. Give him a lovely smile and hope to goodness he's impressed.'

By now the din was deafening and the helicopter hovered less than twenty feet above them. For a moment Biggles wondered if it would open fire, knowing full well that in a moment it could blast them all to kingdom come. At such close quarters it was like being sniffed at by a hungry beast of prey – but finally the beast lost interest, dipped its tail, and roared away. As it did so, Biggles could clearly see the impassive faces of the pilot and co-pilot staring down at him. Two minutes later the helicopter had vanished over the mountain whence it came, and peace and stillness were restored to the lake.

'Phew!' said Algy, 'and what d'you think that was in aid of?'

'Blowed if I know,' said Biggles, 'but they've made it pretty clear that they know exactly what we're up to and can pick us up whenever they feel inclined.'

'So what do we do?' asked Armstrong.

'Not much we can do, dear old chap,' Biggles answered with a wistful grin. 'We can't stay in the middle of this blasted lake, and we've only one way back – the way we came. I guess we'll have to take it.'

'What about the missile?' Ginger asked.

'That comes too, of course,' said Biggles quickly. 'That was what we came to get, and while there's life, there's hope.'

'You think the Russians must have tracked us here by radar?' said Biggles to von Stalhein. 'They obviously knew what we were up to from the start, and after the failure of their bomb attempt in Istanbul, decided to risk sending that helicopter in to catch us with our pants down.'

'Pants down, Biggles? I don't understand,' replied von Stalhein.

'Colloquial English phrase, old boy. Means when we're particularly vulnerable. Dashed awkward situation to be in.'

Biggles and von Stalhein were in the leading Land Rover with Algy and Ginger, bumping and slithering their way back down the mountain track. Behind them came the second vehicle, driven by the unflappable Bill Armstrong, whose only passenger was now the Budnik, all twelve feet of it, secured on a specially constructed cradle so that its snout protruded over the front of the bonnet, and its tail hung from the rear. Thanks to Bill Armstrong's preparations, the winching of the Budnik on to the Land Rover had gone like clockwork. The dinghies and the other pieces of equipment had been left behind, the sun was high in the clearest of blue skies, and but for that single visit of the Russian helicopter, everybody would have been elated. Instead, they made their journey now clutching their weapons and imagining that any minute could be their last.

But nothing happened. The long trail down the mountainside was still as deserted as when they came, and by early afternoon they could see the dusty plain below. Shortly after this, Biggles shouted, 'Well, the old Hercules is where we left her. You never know, miracles could still have happened.'

'They could, old boy,' said Ginger realistically, 'but in this case something makes me doubt it.'

But the closer they approached the Hercules, the more it seemed that Biggles could be right. The great aircraft was exactly as they left it – the ramps still down, the rear door open, the big propellors glinting in the sun. As he approached the aircraft, Biggles accelerated with excitement at the thought that there was still a chance to get away, and put his thumb down on the horn. But there was no reply.

'Funny,' said Biggles, as he circled the aircraft and still saw no sign of life. 'Perhaps old Bertie's gone to sleep. Can't say I blame him.'

He drew up by the ramps and, clutching his revolver, entered the big cargo section of the Hercules with Ginger just behind him.

'Bertie,' he shouted. 'Where the devil are you?'

Still no reply, and Biggles scrambled forward to kick open the small door that led into the cockpit section of the plane. The door swung inwards, and at that instant Biggles saw two figures sitting on the crew seats facing him. They wore olive-coloured uniforms and held sub-machine-guns in their hands.

'Mr Bigglesworth,' said a third figure standing behind them. 'I think you should drop your gun. Someone might get hurt.'

As these words were spoken, several other Russians, who had been carefully concealed in the cargo-hold, revealed themselves, so that in one sudden moment Biggles' group was expertly surrounded. Out of the corner of his eye, Biggles could see that Algy was just about to make a fight of it. His gun was poised, and had he fired there would have been dreadful carnage, but Biggles quickly shouted, 'Drop it Algy! There's no point old boy.' Algy did as he was told.

'Very wise, Mr Bigglesworth,' said the character who seemed to be in charge, a short, somewhat chunky figure in a nondescript grey suit. With his enormous shoulders, heavy brows and boxer's jaw, he could have been an all-in-wrestler or dance-hall bouncer, but he was very much in command, and spoke near-perfect English.

'Where's our friend, Bertie Lissie?' Biggles muttered.

'Quite safe and sound I can assure you. He put up something of a fight, and we had to deal with him, but I think that there's no lasting damage. He's in the forward cargo locker. You can see him in a minute, but first, if you'll excuse us, we have work to do.'

An order was barked out in Russian, and Biggles and his friends were swiftly searched.

'Excellent!' exclaimed the Russian when they were totally disarmed. 'I should introduce myself. My name is Leovitch of the Soviet K.G.B. I feel that I should thank you gentlemen for the expert work you did in salvaging my country's property from that lake. My helicopter pilot radioed a most flattering report of the operation. He should be back here any moment now, and then we can be on our way.'

'Where are you taking us?' asked Biggles tersely.

'We're not taking you anywhere, Mr Bigglesworth. You're taking us, in this splendid aeroplane of yours, together with the Budnik. Have you heard of the city of Batumi? It's on the Russian Black Sea coast about three hundred miles to the north of here. There is a military airport and my countrymen will be glad to see you all at last. We have several scores to settle with your so-called Special Air Police.'

'I would advise you not to try anything of the sort, Mr Leovitch, or whatever you call yourself,' barked Biggles. 'We are in neutral territory, and kidnapping's a serious international offence. We will demand to see the official British representative in your country.'

The Russian cut him short.

'Really, Mr Bigglesworth, don't make me laugh! This is the twentieth century and your silly little country counts for very little.'

Biggles flushed at this, and made as if to strike the grinning Russian.

'How dare you, sir!' he shouted.

But one of the Russians already had Biggles' arm in an agonising lock behind his back and another thrust the muzzle of his automatic in his ribs.

'Now, now. Calm down, Mr Bigglesworth,' purred Leovitch. 'There really is no time for this sort of nonsense, and you can discuss it with your interrogators in Moscow.' He followed this with a quick order in Russian, and the members of the little expedition were herded to the front of the aircraft, their hands above their heads.

As von Stalhein passed the K.G.B. man, Biggles heard the Russian shout the word 'traitor' at him, and there was a hideous thud as a gun butt caught the Prussian on the head. But von Stalhein scarcely seemed to notice, and managed to smile ruefully at Biggles.

'Charming people, don't you think?' he said quietly in English.

Seconds later the Land Rover with the Budnik came bumping up the ramps with one of the Russians at the wheel. The rear door closed, and Leovitch turned to Biggles.

'Now, Mr Bigglesworth,' he said in his oiliest manner. 'Into the cockpit with you please – and you too, Mr Lacey. It's time we took off for Batumi. Our mission's nearly over.'

'What if I refuse?' growled Biggles.

'Then I shall be obliged to shoot you both. It will be regrettable, of course, and your sacrifice will prove quite useless, for I can easily radio the helicopter for a Russian pilot. It will delay us by an hour or so, that's all.'

'What d'you think, Algy?' Biggles asked his friend.

'Don't seem to have much choice, old scout, and that's a fact,' replied Algy realistically. 'It's pretty sickening it has to end like this, but all the same...'

'Good!' snapped the Russian. 'Then we can prepare at once for take-off. If you are sensible, I'll do my best to see that your co-operation is mentioned at your trial in Moscow. We Russians are not as heartless as your Western statesmen paint us.'

'I should save your breath, Leovitch, muttered Biggles.

The memory of that flight was one that haunted Biggles for the remainder of his life. It was bad enough to have to fly an aircraft with the cold muzzle of an automatic thrust against his neck, but worse was the sense of dreadful failure in his heart. Biggles was not a loser – and he was all too well aware of the dire consequences of his failure to bring back the Budnik to the West.

His course lay almost due north and he circled the take-off area to gain height before facing the first range of mountains. Heavily laden as she was, the Hercules climbed slowly in the thin mountain air, so that the highest peaks seemed perilously close as they thundered on above them.

Leovitch was sitting in the navigator's seat where he could check the course, and suddenly he gave a cry of horrified alarm.

'Increase height,' he ordered. 'We nearly hit that crag below us. Can't you see, you idiot?'

'Did we?' said Biggles nonchalantly. 'I didn't notice.'

Another peak loomed ahead.

'Look out, for God's sake!' yelled the Russian.

Biggles screwed up his eyes, and pretended to peer around him in surprise. Only when it seemed as if the Hercules must surely crash head on against the granite face of rock, did he touch the throttle, flip the great aircraft's wings slightly to one side, and pass the mountain peak with feet to spare.

'Maniac!' screamed the Russian. 'Increase height, I order you!'

But Biggles shook his head and shrugged his shoulders sadly.

'Impossible,' he said, and pointed through the cockpit window at one of the starboard engines. It had stopped. He held three fingers up towards the Russian to emphasise his point.

'Only three engines left,' he whispered. 'There's not much chance, but I'll do my best.'

Algy said later that the next half hour was the finest piece of virtuoso flying he had ever witnessed in his life. The Hercules was crossing range upon range of mountains, but Biggles flew that underpowered transport plane like a stunt machine as he took it down the valleys and went zooming up between the mountain passes, dodging inevitable death by inches. Sometimes the aircraft seemed to stall and then recover in the nick of time. Once, its wing-tip brushed against a fir-tree on a jagged mountain-side. The horror seemed to mount and Biggles threw up his hands.

'More height,' begged the Russian now 'Can't you do anything? You'll kill us all.'

His voice was weak with fear, but once more Biggles shook his head.

'I think we're getting trouble with another engine,' he said hopelessly. 'We'll never make it to Batumi, will we Algy?'

'Not a hope in hell,' his chum replied.

Another mountain range, higher than the last, was looming up ahead.

'What can we do?' the Russian moaned.

'Not much choice, old chap,' said Biggles sombrely. 'Either we crash or we change course. From the map you'll see we're twenty miles or so from a place called Ezerum and there's an airport there. Which is it to be, Leovitch?'

There was a moment's pause in which the Russian's fear did battle with his sense of duty. It was his fear that won.

'Change course,' he whispered finally and, just in time, Biggles pulled the huge machine round in a spectacular turn and headed west for Ezerum.

Even there it seemed that trouble wasn't over. It was a small airport, and as the Hercules came in to land, the out-of-action starboard engine suddenly revived.

'Look out, old chap, we'll overshoot!' yelled Algy. 'Take her up again.'

'Too late, old boy,' Biggles shouted back, and there was a sickening thud as the undercarriage hit a drainage ditch on the perimeter of the field and shattered. A hideous racket followed as the aircraft slithered to a halt on its fuselage, and the wing-tip caught a marker beacon.

'Well,' said Biggles with a look of quiet satisfaction on his face, 'I certainly made a bish of that one. Sorry, Leovitch old chap, but at least we're all alive.'

It was several weeks before the diplomats and politicians sorted out the upset caused by the crash-landing of a British aircraft, with a British crew, a defecting Prussian and a dozen or so heavily armed Soviet troops aboard, at the Turkish town of Ezerum. Ambassadors were summoned, and protest notes exchanged before the affair blew over and the Turks released their unwelcome foreign visitors and sent them packing.

Not that any of this diplomatic shindig really mattered, and Biggles never did discover quite what bargaining went on behind the scenes to make sure that the Budnik found its way from Turkey back to London and then on to the United States – not to mention von Stalhein, who was safely returned to his new life in America.

All that he really knew for sure, was that when he and the chums returned to London several pounds lighter after their fortnight in a Turkish gaol, the Air Commodore insisted on dining them all in style at the Blazers' Club. Indeed, that cantankerous old gentleman had never seemed more grateful or more charming to them in his life.

'When are you coming back to join us, Biggles?' he inquired as the evening ended.

'Give me time to think, sir,' Biggles answered with a grin. 'I've only just got out of prison.'

Postscript

There is not a great deal to be added about the final years of Biggles' life. He never did rejoin the Special Air Police – despite Raymond's urgent invitations after the Budnik business – and never really made his peace with the old spy-master. Occasionally, they would dine together at the Blazers' Club and reminisce about the past, but Raymond no longer had much influence in the Secret Service world, and the sort of independent operations he and Biggles had delighted in were over. Besides, Raymond was a sick man by the late sixties, and no one was particularly surprised when he expired from a massive heart attack while playing golf at Hunterscombe.

'Not a bad way to go,' said Biggles at the time, and he certainly didn't seem to be particularly upset at the departure of this key figure in his past. The break with Raymond and the Special Air Police also inevitably meant that Biggles saw less and less of his oldest friends. He continued working for Sir Robert Smyth until his retirement, when he came to live in Camberley – but Algy, Bertie and Ginger carried on in the Special Air Police until the whole outfit was disbanded shortly after Raymond's death. The chums still kept in touch, of course, and Biggles would often go to stay at Lewes, particularly after Algy succeeded to the Lacey title when his old father died in 1968. Like Biggles, Algy never married, and although he has determinedly kept up his interests in flying—he has spoken several times on air defence in the House of Lords – he seems to have inherited his father's interest in botany, and, late in life, is now engaged in editing the old man's unpublished papers. The Lacey title will of course die with him. Since his retirement, Ginger Hebblethwaite has returned to Yorkshire – he has a little farm near Sheffield, and appears extraordinarily contented with his lot.

Lord Bertie Lissie was less fortunate. The disbanding of the Special Air Police seemed to deprive him of a purpose in life and aggravated the drink problem he had always suffered from. His death in a car crash on the Brighton Road a few months later was not completely unexpected by his friends, but it upset Biggles badly at the time.

One of the strangest friendships that developed during these final years of Biggles' life was with von Stalhein. Soon after the Budnik business, the Prussian was granted American citizenship and settled outside Washington, where he worked as an adviser to an international security firm. As such, he frequently came to London, and he and Biggles often met and corresponded.

There was an important bond between the two men now, in the person of von Stalhein's daughter, Irmgard. It was only after the Budnik business that Biggles learned of her existence. She was born out of wedlock in Berlin in 1940, with Marie Janis as her mother, and had been with von Stalhein's family near Lubeck when Marie was killed. She had remained with them after the German defeat and Russian occupation, and when von Stalhein finally defected to the West, she had been compelled to stay on in East Germany.

It was largely thanks to Biggles' efforts – and pressure from the British Foreign Office – that she was finally allowed to leave East Germany, and Biggles met her. He told me all about it later. She had flown into Heathrow and was due to go on that afternoon to Washington to be reunited with her father.

'I thought I'd better see the girl, for old time's sake, and so I'd arranged to meet her at the airport and give her lunch. I'd no idea what she was like, or anything much about her. I was inquisitive as much as anything, but you know, I recognised her instantly. It was just as if her mother was walking through Immigration. And she knew me too. "Hullo," she said, "you must be Biggles." Just like that. Funny business, when you think who she was.'

Funny or not, this rediscovery of Marie Janis in her daughter became the most important fact in Biggles' life. From now on, his life possessed a real interest, for, as he admitted, he came to regard her almost as a daughter of his own. She was twenty-eight, recently divorced, and very pretty. She settled with her father for a while, then moved on to New York and worked in publishing, and all this time, she and Biggles corresponded. He saw her several times – in London and America – and the last journey that he made before he died was to Vermont to attend her wedding.

I remember his return quite vividly. He had been depressed, I thought, before he went. His back had been troubling him again, and he was probably worrying about the man Irmgard was marrying, (an older man in her publishing house with grown children. He was Jewish, and von Stalhein disapproved of him). But when he came back to Ferndene Cottage, Biggles was obviously delighted at how things had gone. He liked the bridgroom, and had managed to persuade von Stalhein to do the same. He and von Stalhein had spent several days together after the wedding, and Biggles had a lot of photographs – of von Stalhein's house, of Irmgard and her husband, and of von Stalhein too, looking like a well-fed, prosperous elderly American. Only a certain something about the mouth betrayed his origins.

But Biggles was clearly tired by the visit, and I was surprised to hear that he was going to the Battle of Britain anniversary celebrations, being held that year at Tangmere. He'd never gone before, but several of the former members of 666 were turning up, and he was invited as a guest of honour. As part of the celebrations, a rich American called Maberley had brought over a beautifully restored Mark VI Spitfire from Texas. It was a rarity, of course, a true collector's piece, and, judging from the photographs I saw, perfect in every detail.

Apparently, one of the young R.A.F. pilots had been scheduled to fly the Spitfire at the head of the fly-past of the latest British jets, and just before take-off, Biggles was standing next to Algy on the tarmac, examining the machines. No one will ever know what got into him – or how he managed it. Presumably the sheer temptation of that wonderful old aircraft standing there, ready for take-off, was too much for him. A momentary old man's impulse, a brief resurgence of his youth – or had he somehow planned this all along? I wonder.

He took everybody by surprise, including Algy. The pilots were just about to board their planes, when he darted forward, shouting, 'Scramble, chaps!' And before anyone could stop him, Biggles had swung himself with practised ease into the Spitfire's cockpit, slammed back the canopy, and started up the engine. It happened very quickly, and from that point there was nothing much anyone could do to stop him. The Controller did his best, of course (he was entirely exonerated at the subsequent inquiry), but Biggles totally ignored the poor man's frantic messages over the radio. All he replied was 'O.K. 666. Prepare to intercept the enemy. Large formations of Heinkels and a pack of Messerschmitts coming in from northern France. Fourteen thousand feet. Do your best, chaps!'

Then the radio went dead, and the Spitfire slowly taxied past the crowds, none of whom realised what was going on. He made a perfect take-off, with the jets following him as planned. From the ground the fly-past seemed immaculate, with Biggles' solitary Spitfire in the lead. Then the crowd saw the Spitfire turn, sweep back across the airport, flipping its wings in a salute, then climb towards the sun, and the coast of France. And that was the last that anybody saw of Biggles.

It was a little hard on Mr. Maberley, of course, after coming all that way from Texas, though presumably his Spitfire was insured, and they gave him back the bits of wreckage which some fishermen at Dover brought ashore a few days later. Of Biggles there was mercifully no trace, and the verdict at his inquest was quite simple – accidental death. His will left everything to the daughter of his old love, Marie Janis.

'Johnnie' Johnson

WING LEADER

The pilots came from all walks of life – engineers, farmers, bank-clerks – to find themselves either hunters or hunted, fighters or bombers.

World War II's top Allied fighter ace, 'Johnnie' Johnson, was one of the hunters. His name is a legend. **Wing Leader** is the story behind that legend.

Gone is the chivalry of the First World War 'dog-fight'. The Luftwaffe asked for no mercy and got none in return. 'Johnnie' Johnson's aim was simple – to flush, stalk and kill the enemy in the shortest possible time.

Wing Leader is about skill, determination – and guts. It ranks with the finest stories to come out of the war.

General Editor:
Shelford Bidwell

WORLD WAR 3

Within five years the events in this book could be a horrifying reality. World War 3 – total devastation – may have already begun . . .

With more and more countries in possession of nuclear weapons the prospect of worldwide conflict is terrifying.

The facts are ominous. The Soviet bloc has built up a massive superiority in conventional weapons – while cuts in Western defence spending constantly increase NATO'S reliance on the nuclear deterrent.

One day the deterrent might not be enough.

World War 3 looks at the rivals and their weapons. It describes the way in which the third – and maybe the last – world war could develop. As tensions mount in North West Europe, nuclear attack ceases to be merely a possibility . . . All too soon it could be history.

John Dunning

TRULY MURDEROUS

Truly Murderous is a terrifying collection of modern murder cases, brilliantly reconstructed by John Dunning. As Colin Wilson says in his introduction, 'Dunning has the journalist's eye for the gruesome, for human oddity, and for sheer dramatic tension ... nearly every story could be turned into a film or TV drama.'

Anyone fascinated by the patterns of murder and the nature of the ultimate in crime will find this powerful documentary of twentieth-century murder truly unforgettable.

NON-FICTION

GENERAL

☐ Guide to the Channel Islands — J. Anderson & E. Swinglehurst — 90p
☐ The Complete Traveller — Joan Bakewell — £1.95
☐ Time Out London Shopping Guide — Lindsey Bareham — £1.50
☐ World War 3 — Edited by Shelford Bidwell — £1.25
☐ The Black Angels — Rupert Butler — £1.35
☐ Hand of Steel — Rupert Butler — £1.35
☐ A Walk Around the Lakes — Hunter Davies — £1.50
☐ Truly Murderous — John Dunning — 95p
☐ In Praise of Younger Men — Sandy Fawkes — 85p
☐ Hitler's Secret Life — Glenn B. Infield — £1.50
☐ Wing Leader — Johnnie Johnson — £1.25
☐ Me, to Name but a Few — Spike Mullins — £1.00
☐ Our Future: Dr. Magnus Pyke Predicts — 95p
☐ The Devil's Bedside Book — Leonard Rossiter — 85p
☐ Barbara Windsor's Book of Boobs — Barbara Windsor — £1.50

BIOGRAPHY/AUTOBIOGRAPHY

☐ Go-Boy — Roger Caron — £1.25
☐ The Queen Mother Herself — Helen Cathcart — £1.25
☐ George Stephenson — Hunter Davies — £1.50
☐ The Queen's Children — Donald Edgar — £1.25
☐ Prince Regent — Harry Edgington — 95p
☐ All of Me — Rose Neighbour — £1.00
☐ Tell Me Who I Am Before I Die — C. Peters with T. Schwarz — £1.00
☐ Boney M — J. Shearlaw and D. Brown — 90p
☐ Kiss — John Swenson — 90p

HEALTH/SELF-HELP/POCKET HEALTH GUIDES

☐ Pulling Your Own Strings — Dr. Wayne W. Dyer — 95p
☐ The Pick of Woman's Own Diets — Jo Foley — 95p
☐ Woman X Two — Mary Kenny — 90p
☐ Cystitis: A Complete Self-help Guide — Angela Kilmartin — £1.00
☐ The Stress Factor — Donald Norfolk — 90p
☐ Fat is a Feminist Issue — Susie Orbach — 85p
☐ Related to Sex — Claire Rayner — £1.25
☐ The Working Woman's Body Book — L. Rowen with B. Winkler — 95p
☐ Woman's Own Birth Control — Dr. Michael Smith — £1.25
☐ Allergies — Robert Eagle — 65p
☐ Arthritis and Rheumatism — Dr. Luke Fernandes — 65p
☐ Back Pain — Dr. Paul Dudley — 65p
☐ Pre-Menstrual Tension — June Clark — 65p
☐ Migraine — Dr. Finlay Campbell — 65p
☐ Skin Troubles — Deanna Wilson — 65p

REFERENCE

☐ What's Wrong with your Pet? — Hugo Kerr — 95p
☐ You *Can* Train Your Cat — Jo and Paul Loeb — £1.50
☐ Caring for Cats and Kittens — John Montgomery — 95p
☐ The Oscar Movies from A–Z — Roy Pickard — £1.25
☐ Questions of Law — Bill Thomas — 95p
☐ The Hamlyn Book of Amazing Information — 80p
☐ The Hamlyn Family Medical Dictionary — £2.50

GAMES & PASTIMES

☐ The Hamlyn Book of Brainteasers and Mindbenders — Ben Hamilton — 85p
☐ The Hamlyn Book of Crosswords Books 1, 2, 3, and 4 — 60p
☐ The Hamlyn Book of Crosswords 5 — 70p
☐ The Hamlyn Book of Wordways 1 — 75p
☐ The Hamlyn Family Quiz Book — 85p

FICTION

GENERAL

☐ Stand on It	Stroker Ace	95p
☐ Chains	Justin Adams	£1.25
☐ The Master Mechanic	I. G. Broat	£1.50
☐ Wyndward Passion	Norman Daniels	£1.35
☐ Abingdon's	Michael French	£1.25
☐ The Moviola Man	Bill and Colleen Mahan	£1.25
☐ Running Scared	Gregory Mcdonald	85p
☐ Gossip	Marc Olden	£1.25
☐ The Sounds of Silence	Judith Richards	£1.00
☐ Summer Lightning	Judith Richards	£1.00
☐ The Hamptons	Charles Rigdon	£1.35
☐ The Affair of Nina B.	Simmel	95p
☐ The Berlin Connection	Simmel	£1.50
☐ The Cain Conspiracy	Simmel	£1.20
☐ Double Agent—Triple Cross	Simmel	£1.35
☐ Celestial Navigation	Anne Tyler	£1.00
☐ Earthly Possessions	Anne Tyler	95p
☐ Searching for Caleb	Anne Tyler	£1.00

WESTERN BLADE SERIES

☐ No. 1	The Indian Incident	Matt Chisholm	75p
☐ No. 2	The Tucson Conspiracy	Matt Chisholm	75p
☐ No. 3	The Laredo Assignment	Matt Chisholm	75p
☐ No. 4	The Pecos Manhunt	Matt Chisholm	75p
☐ No. 5	The Colorado Virgins	Matt Chisholm	85p
☐ No. 6	The Mexican Proposition	Matt Chisholm	75p
☐ No. 7	The Arizona Climax	Matt Chisholm	85p
☐ No. 8	The Nevada Mustang	Matt Chisholm	85p

WAR

☐ Jenny's War	Jack Stoneley	£1.25
☐ The Killing-Ground	Elleston Trevor	£1.10

NAVAL HISTORICAL

☐ The Sea of the Dragon	R. T. Aundrews	95p
☐ Ty-Shan Bay	R. T. Aundrews	95p
☐ HMS Bounty	John Maxwell	£1.00
☐ The Baltic Convoy	Showell Styles	95p
☐ Mr. Fitton's Commission	Showell Styles	85p

FILM/TV TIE-IN

☐ American Gigolo	Timothy Harris	95p
☐ Meteor	E. H. North and F. Coen	95p
☐ Driver	Clyde B. Phillips	80p

SCIENCE FICTION

☐ The Mind Thing	Fredric Brown	90p
☐ Strangers	Gardner Dozois	95p
☐ Project Barrier	Daniel F. Galouye	80p
☐ Beyond the Barrier	Damon Knight	80p
☐ Clash by Night	Henry Kuttner	95p
☐ Fury	Henry Kuttner	80p
☐ Mutant	Henry Kuttner	90p
☐ Drinking Sapphire Wine	Tanith Lee	£1.25
☐ Journey	Marta Randall	£1.00
☐ The Lion Game	James H. Schmitz	70p
☐ The Seed of Earth	Robert Silverberg	80p
☐ The Silent Invaders	Robert Silverberg	80p
☐ City of the Sun	Brian M. Stableford	85p
☐ Critical Threshold	Brian M. Stableford	75p
☐ The Florians	Brian M. Stableford	80p
☐ Wildeblood's Empire	Brian M. Stableford	80p
☐ A Touch of Strange	Theodore Sturgeon	85p

NON-FICTION

GENERAL COOKERY

☐ The Best of Dial-a-Recipe	Audrey Ellis	80p
☐ Hints for Modern Cooks	Audrey Ellis	£1.00
☐ Comprehensive Guide to Deep Freezing		50p
☐ Cooking For Your Freezer		80p
☐ Home Made Country Wines		50p
☐ Salads the Year Round	Joy Larkcom	£1.25

KITCHEN LIBRARY SERIES

☐ Know Your Onions	Kate Hastrop	95p
☐ Home Preserving and Bottling	Gladys Mann	80p
☐ Home Baked Breads and Cakes	Mary Norwak	75p
☐ Easy Icing	Marguerite Patten	85p
☐ Wine Making At Home	Francis Pinnegar	80p
☐ Mixer and Blender Cookbook	Myra Street	80p
☐ Pasta Cookbook	Myra Street	75p
☐ The Hamlyn Pressure Cookbook	Jane Todd	85p

GARDENING/HOBBIES

☐ Restoring Old Junk	Michèle Brown	75p
☐ A Vegetable Plot for Two—or More	D. B. Clay Jones	£1.00
☐ The Sunday Telegraph Patio Gardening Book	Robert Pearson	80p
☐ 'Jock' Davidson's House Plant Book		£1.25

NAME ....

ADDRESS..

....

Write to Hamlyn Paperbacks Cash Sales, PO Box 11, Falmouth, Cornwall TR10 9EN.

Please indicate order and enclose remittance to the value of the cover price plus:

U.K.: 30p for the first book, 15p for the second book and 12p for each additional book ordered to a maximum charge of £1.29.

B.F.P.O. & EIRE: 30p for the first book, 15p for the second book plus 12p per copy for the next 7 books, thereafter 6p per book.

OVERSEAS: 50p for the first book plus 15p per copy for each additional book.

Whilst every effort is made to keep prices low it is sometimes necessary to increase cover prices and also postage and packing rates at short notice. Hamlyn Paperbacks reserve the right to show new retail prices on covers which may differ from those previously advertised in the text or elsewhere.